Practical Wisdom and Resilience Overcoming Downside Risk

Kazuyo Hanai · Rangarirai Gavin Muchetu ·
Laban Kithinji Kinyua · Yoichi Mine
Editors

Practical Wisdom and Resilience Overcoming Downside Risk

Grassroots Voices in Africa Under COVID-19

Springer

Editors
Kazuyo Hanai
Institute for Future Initiatives
The University of Tokyo
Bunkyo, Tokyo, Japan

Laban Kithinji Kinyua
African Studies Center
Tokyo University of Foreign Studies
Fuchu, Tokyo, Japan

Rangarirai Gavin Muchetu
College of Intercultural Communication
Rikkyo University
Toshima, Tokyo, Japan

Yoichi Mine
Graduate School of International Relations
Ritsumeikan University
Kyoto, Japan

JICA (Japan International Cooperation Agency)
Chiyoda, Tokyo, Japan

ISBN 978-981-96-4454-4 ISBN 978-981-96-4455-1 (eBook)
https://doi.org/10.1007/978-981-96-4455-1

This Springer imprint is published by the registered company Springer Nature Singapore Pte Ltd.
The registered company address is: 152 Beach Road, #21-01/04 Gateway East, Singapore 189721, Singapore

Acknowledgments

This book is the result of the research project "Exploration of Practical Wisdom and Resilience Overcoming Downside Risk: Collecting Grassroots Voices in Africa under COVID-19" conducted over three years from December 2021 to November 2024. The core members of this research project consist of the board members of the Japan Society for Afrasian Studies (JSAS). We established this academic association in 2018, mainly with African researchers in Japan and Japanese researchers of African studies, as a platform for research connecting Asia and Africa.

In 2021, under the COVID-19 pandemic, we launched this research project with a grant from the Hitachi Fund Support for Research Related to Infectious Diseases. We then conducted field surveys in collaboration with local research institutions in seven African countries.

The authors express their deepest gratitude to the Hitachi Foundation for the grant and to the reviewers who adopted this research project and provided valuable advice at the Annual Report Meetings and on other occasions. We are grateful to Prof. Atsuo Kishimoto (Osaka University), Mr. Masaki Inaba (Africa Japan Forum), and Prof. Ayako Takemi (The University of Tokyo) for their expert advice as advisors to this project. We extend our gratitude to the support of the Institute for Future Initiatives at the University of Tokyo, especially Ms. Yuka Ishikawa and Ms. Ayumi Hirosawa, staff members of the SDGs Collaborative Research Unit, and Dr. Kei Kurushima and Dr. Wang Muyun for their support in promoting this project.

It is thanks to everyone's support that our research team was able to collect the grassroots voices in Africa. We are proud that while our research was based in Japan, it was conducted at the initiative of African researchers in collaboration with local institutions.

Kauyo Hanai

Contents

Editors and Contributors

About the Editors

Kazuyo Hanai Project Assistant Professor at the Institute for Future Initiatives, The University of Tokyo, Japan and Representative Director of NPO RITA-Congo. She holds a Ph.D. in International Cooperation Studies from The University of Tokyo. She researches the role of resources in the conflicts in Africa and the responsibility of global society. In particular, her research focuses on the relations between the conflict minerals issue in the Democratic Republic of Congo and the responsibility of Japanese consumer society. Her main publication is *Justice of Resource Issue: Responsibility of Consumers on Conflict Minerals Issue in DR Congo* (Toshindo, 2016, in Japanese). She has served as a president of JSAS since 2023 and the principal investigator for the JSAS Hitachi project.

Rangarirai Gavin Muchetu Assistant Professor at the College of Intercultural Communication at Rikkyo University, Tokyo, Japan. He obtained his Ph.D. from Doshisha University, where he studied Japanese agriculture, drawing lessons for Zimbabwean policymakers. Thus, his research focuses on agrarian issues, particularly the interplay between state policy and the socio-economic relations of rural dwellers. His recent publications include *After Radical Land Reforms: Restructuring Agricultural Cooperatives in Zimbabwe and Japan (2021, Langa RPCIG)* and "South-South Cooperation in Agriculture: Impacts of Brazil's More Food International Program on Post-Land Reform Social Organizations in Zimbabwe" (2022, *Agrarian South: Journal of Political Economy*).

Laban Kithinji Kinyua Research Fellow at the Institute of Asian, African, and Middle Eastern Studies at Sophia University, Tokyo, Japan. Dr. Kinyua holds a Ph.D. in Global Studies, with a research focus on decentralization, rural livelihoods, and African youth engagement with digital platforms. His recent work investigates how digital spaces facilitate political participation and resource mobilization among rural communities. Recent publications include "Digital Spaces and Democratization in Rural Africa: Participation, Mobilization, and Laying Claim to Resources" in the *Journal of African Studies* (2023) and "Decoding Political Discourse on Digital Platforms in Africa: Rumor Networks Among Rural Populace in Kenya's 2022 Elections" in *ASC-TUFS Working Papers* (2023).

Yoichi Mine Visiting Professor at the Graduate School of International Relations, Ritsumeikan University, and Executive Director, JICA (Japan International Cooperation Agency) Ogata Sadako Research Institute for Peace and Development. His research interests include human security, international development, and African area study. He is the author of *Connecting Africa and Asia: Afrasia As a Benign Community* (Routledge, 2022) and has edited six books in English, including *Migration and Agency: Afro-Asian Encounters* (Palgrave, 2018) and *Preventing Violent Conflict in Africa: Inequalities, Perceptions and Institutions* (Palgrave, 2013). The English version of his book, *Oral History of Japan's Development Cooperation* (The University of Tokyo Press, 2023) will be published by Springer in 2025.

Contributors

Walter Chambati College of Graduate Studies, University of South Africa, Pretoria, South Africa

Scarlett Cornelissen Department of Political Science, Stellenbosch University, Stellenbosch, South Africa;
Stellenbosch University Japan Centre, Stellenbosch, South Africa

Kazuyo Hanai Institute for Future Initiatives, The University of Tokyo, Bunkyo, Tokyo, Japan

Tomohiro Hosoi Global Initiative Center, Gunma University, Maebashi, Gunma, Japan

Akemi Ishikawa Division of Agri-Business, UNIDO HQs in Vienna, Vienna, Austria

Laban Kithinji Kinyua African Studies Center, Tokyo University of Foreign Studies, Fuchu, Tokyo, Japan

Jean-Claude Maswana Graduate School of Economics, Ritsumeikan University, Kyoto, Japan

Yoichi Mine Graduate School of International Relations, Ritsumeikan University, Kyoto, Japan;
JICA (Japan International Cooperation Agency), Chiyoda, Tokyo, Japan

Odomaro Mubangizi The Proposed Hekima University, Nairobi, Kenya

Rangarirai Gavin Muchetu College of Intercultural Communication, Rikkyo University, Toshima, Tokyo, Japan

Denis Musinguzi School of Arts and Social Sciences, Uganda Martyrs University Nkozi, Mpigi, Uganda

Nakabuye Juliet Musoke School of Arts and Social Sciences, Uganda Martyrs University Nkozi, Mpigi, Uganda

Maureen Obare The Proposed Hekima University, Nairobi, Kenya

Wakiko Ohira Center for Global Education and Discovery, Sophia University, Chiyoda, Tokyo, Japan

Christian Samen Otchia Graduate School of International Development, Nagoya University, Nagoya, Aichi, Japan

Chizuko Sato Institute of Global Studies, Tokyo University of Foreign Studies, Fuchu, Tokyo, Japan

Vick Lukwago Ssali Department of English Language and Cultures, Aichi Gakuin University, Nisshin, Aichi, Japan

Chapter 1
Introduction

Kazuyo Hanai, Rangarirai Gavin Muchetu, Laban Kithinji Kinyua, and Yoichi Mine

This book is based on collected grassroots voices in sub-Saharan Africa and explores how local people perceived and coped with the impact of the COVID-19 pandemic and government prevention policies on their daily lives. We draw lessons from COVID-19 experience not only from policymakers' perspectives but also from those of ordinary people and thereby contribute to discussions in the international community as it prepares for the next pandemic.

In particular, this book examines governments' potential politicization of COVID-19 prevention measures and people's reactions to the pandemic and its preventive measures. There was criticism in several countries that politicians used government prevention measures to garner votes and favor the governing party in elections. Such biased policies undermine people's trust in government and can harm preventive measures and vaccine dissemination. On the other hand, our survey revealed that people's perceptions of the government and its policies are complex and multifaceted, often depending on the passage of time and the outcome of the policy. Moreover, ordinary people, in pursuit of survival, improvised creative activities to keep them afloat while maneuvering the containment measures. While rapid implementation of such measures is vital in preventing pandemics, they should be carefully considered from the perspective of protecting vulnerable populations and guaranteeing human rights.

K. Hanai (✉)
Institute for Future Initiatives, The University of Tokyo, Bunkyo, Tokyo, Japan
e-mail: hanai@g.ecc.u-tokyo.ac.jp

R. G. Muchetu
College of Intercultural Communication, Rikkyo University, Toshima, Tokyo, Japan

L. K. Kinyua
African Studies Center, Tokyo University of Foreign Studies, Fuchu, Tokyo, Japan

Y. Mine
Graduate School of International Relations, Ritsumeikan University, Kyoto, Japan

JICA (Japan International Cooperation Agency), Chiyoda, Tokyo, Japan

K. Hanai et al. (eds.), *Practical Wisdom and Resilience Overcoming Downside Risk*,
https://doi.org/10.1007/978-981-96-4455-1_1

At the same time, it is also important to understand the sources of people's resilience in times of hardship and to empower them with public assistance during normal times. This book reveals how COVID-19 itself and governments' containment policies have impacted people's perceptions, behavior, and lives in sub-Saharan Africa at the grassroots level. It adds a new perspective to the discussions on improving pandemic policies by governments and international organizations.

1 COVID-19 in Sub-Saharan Africa

Approximately 12.2 million COVID-19 cases and over 256,000 deaths were reported in Africa as of 2 January 2023 (Africa CDC 2023).[1] According to the Johns Hopkins Coronavirus Resource Center, the highest number of infections was about 4 million in South Africa and about 1.2 million in Morocco and Tunisia (JHU 2023). These figures are not substantial compared to the 100 million people infected in the United States and the 30 million in France and Germany. However, this was a later realization. When the then-unknown virus, COVID-19, appeared in China in December 2019 and began spreading worldwide in early 2020, African governments, international organizations, and experts were concerned that the virus could cause severe damage if it landed on the African continent. This was because the sub-Saharan African countries, battling various decades-long socio-economic challenges, did not have the necessary systems (for instance, PCR testing, isolation, and contact tracing infrastructure) to handle such a health shock. In addition, because of the "practice of sanitation and hygiene, access to water, poor road networks, population density, urban slums, social-cultural, living conditions, and other contextual factors," the infection was expected to spread at an uncontrolled rapid rate (WHO 2020a, p. 11). Furthermore, it was unlikely that many African nations could develop vaccine production facilities with sufficient rapidity. Thus, Africa was expected to struggle to produce the vaccine or acquire it from the supply chains of developed countries.

For this reason, governments implemented strict measures from a very early stage. In East Africa, the first infected person was confirmed in Kenya on March 13, followed by Rwanda on March 14 and Tanzania on March 16, prompting governments to implement containment policies for fear of the spread of infection. By May 2020, 26 sub-Saharan African countries had issued a State of Emergency, 34 countries had implemented lockdowns, and 46 countries had closed their borders (UN 2020). Rather than reacting to the spread of infection as an after effect, governments adopted strict preventive measures in advance. The cumulative cases of COVID-19 are shown in Fig. 1 (The appendix to this chapter details the situation by country.)

[1] Medical authorities and research institutions stopped collecting data in 2023.

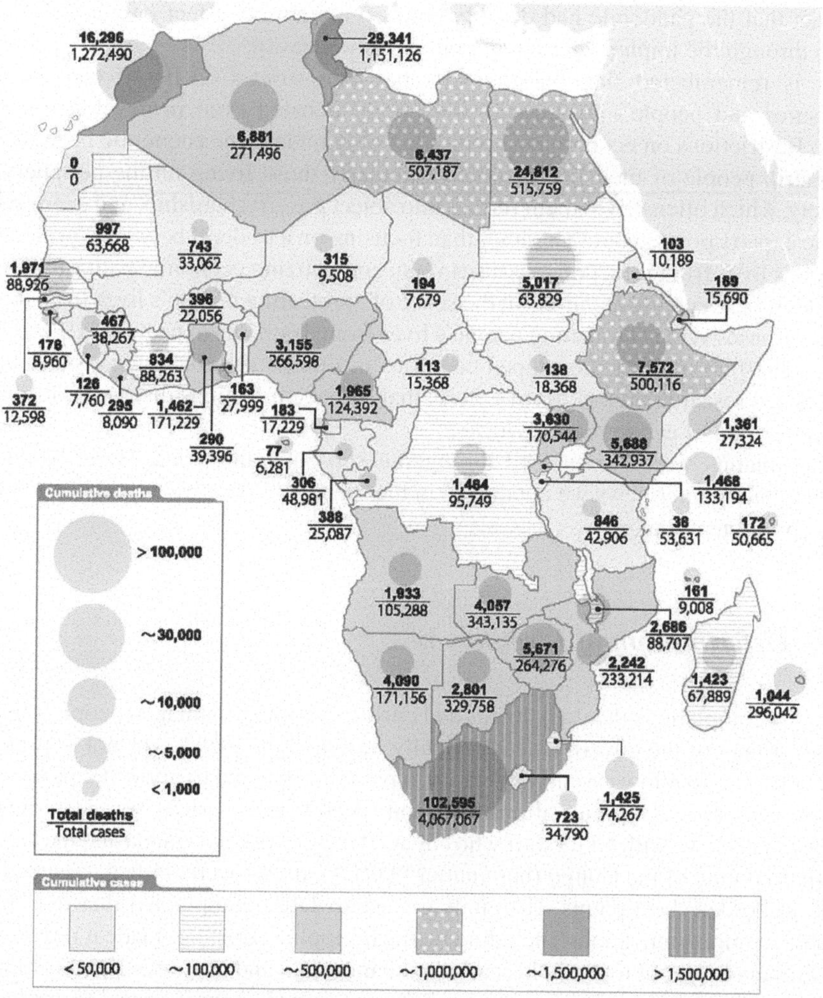

Fig. 1 Cumulative confirmed covid-19 cases and deaths in Africa, as of march 2023 (*Source* Made by authors based on data from JHU [2023])

2 Notable Issues Related to the COVID-19 Pandemic

It is difficult to give a clear answer as to whether the low number of cases in Africa compared to other regions is attributable to the success of these containment policies, the high youth population rate in Africa, or the fact that the actual number of cases is not known due to the low number of tests. Particularly, it is difficult to conclude that the hardline containment policies have successfully controlled the pandemic in Africa and saved people's lives. This is not only because of the seriousness of the impact that the pandemic had directly but also its indirect effect on people's daily lives through the implementation of containment measures.

It is remembered that the tradeoffs between strict COVID-19 containment measures and people's livelihoods were hotly debated even in developed countries. Restrictions on economic activities not only undermine economic benefits but also strip people of their livelihoods, particularly those living on the periphery of society, which often drives them further into abject poverty, hardship, and even death. Some experts pointed out that rather than focusing on a tradeoff between "protecting people's lives from infectious diseases versus prioritizing economic gain," there is a "tradeoff between life and life," in the sense of "protecting people's lives from infectious diseases versus protecting people's lives from death due to poverty" (BuzzFeed News 2020). Therefore, developed countries in Europe and the United States have conducted research on lockdown criteria that balance infectious disease control and the protection of economic activities.

Complaints were also voiced throughout sub-Saharan Africa. Here, based on several online interviews we conducted in the spring of 2020, we would like to raise three prominent issues.

2.1 Deterioration of Livelihoods

The first complaint is that lockdowns and curfews seriously damaged people's livelihoods. Many of the governments originally designed the lockdowns not to prohibit all traffic, but to allow essential workers to pass through and to allow the passage of cargo and medical supplies after inspection (WHO 2020a). However, according to online interviews with NGO staff who engaged in aid work in Uganda and the Democratic Republic of the Congo (hereinafter "DRC"), trucks were, in fact, stranded for days at border checkpoints. Hospitals in eastern DRC complained that they were unable to import any goods, including medical supplies. Curfews made it impossible for farmers to go out to the fields early in the morning, and travel restrictions limited movement within the informal economy. Farmers relied on the informal sector to sell agricultural products. Furthermore, the slogan "stay home" was also popularized in many African countries, and consequently the family would become more likely to be infected by one another if they were all confined to a house without windows. There were growing complaints about how they would earn a living if they stayed at home. For example, the DRC, one of the countries examined in our research, had a poverty rate of 72% (World Bank 2021). This means 72% of people live on less than US$1.9 per day. In these marginalized communities, "livelihood deterioration" can be directly linked to the risk of death. The appeal "hunger will kill us before the virus does" began to be heard in many places.

2.2 *Violent Crackdowns by Government Authorities*

The second complaint related to violent crackdowns by government authorities to enforce containment measures. Even when wearing masks was made mandatory, commercial masks were expensive and difficult for ordinary people to obtain. In East Africa, masks were selling for $3 a piece in the spring of 2020. As a result, police officers' enforcement of mask-wearing rules led to violence. In the DRC, a motorbike taxi driver who was not wearing a mask was shot and killed by the police in June 2020, and his fellow drivers protested violently against the police.[2] Similarly, the crackdown over curfews escalated. In Nigeria, a police officer who demanded a bribe in exchange for overlooking a bus that violated the curfew opened fire, killing a 17-year-old girl, which led to street protests (Tamai 2021). In South Africa, police violence increased from February to July 2020. In Kenya, two brothers died in the hands of the police who accused them of violating curfew guidelines, leading to widespread protests (Warah 2021).

This abuse of power and privilege undermined people's trust in the government and generated rumors that cast doubt on the COVID-19 pandemic itself. On various social networking sites, suspicions spread that COVID-19 did not really exist and that the government was creating an unknown infectious disease in order to control the population in some countries and gain electoral advantage in others. This mistrust threatened to become a major obstacle to the public's acceptance and compliance with government policies.

2.3 *Imbalance with Measures Against Other Infectious Diseases*

Third, the imbalance between the COVID-19 response and the measures taken against other infectious diseases also increased people's distrust. Africa had numerous infectious diseases long before the outbreak of COVID-19. Over 74% of the world's malaria cases are concentrated in Africa, particularly in Nigeria (27%), DRC (12%), and Uganda (5%). In the DRC, for example, an estimated 30 million people were infected and 70,738 died in 2022 (WHO 2023b). In such a situation, even during the Ebola epidemic of 2018–19, local people had serious doubts about the international community's measures against infectious diseases. The international community considered Ebola to be an extremely dangerous epidemic due to its high fatality rate. Therefore, when even a single case was confirmed, the WHO declared an outbreak and deployed medical personnel to the infected area under a strict regime. In the Ebola epidemic of 2018–20, 3481 people were reportedly infected, and 2299 died in the DRC (WHO 2020b). However, the Congolese locals felt uncomfortable that Ebola was being singled out for special treatment by the international community

[2] Armed Conflict Location and Event Dataset (ACLED), note on the event 15 June 2020.

when other infectious diseases were also killing people, so they asked, "Why only Ebola?" Moreover, when the presidential election was held in the DRC in December 2018, voting in eastern DRC was "postponed" because the Ebola-affected areas were considered too dangerous for people to gather at polling stations. These events led to 28 attacks on Ebola treatment centers in the two years of 2018 and 19. The attackers reportedly shouted, "Ebola is a lie" and warned the local female staff at the center that they should not be part of such a fraud.[3]

In the context of these other infectious diseases, COVID-19 also tended to be perceived as a case of international organizations overreacting, as the locals claimed to have never seen an actual infected person. Rumors spread that, at the very least, "COVID-19 does not exist" and that, in the worst-case scenario, "this is Western viral terrorism".[4] This mistrust kept people from going to hospital even when they got sick, increasing the risk of death and illness, not only from COVID-19 but also from malaria and other diseases. Both developed and developing countries have reported an increase in excess deaths attributable to diseases other than COVID-19, as a result of people being wary of contracting COVID-19 and delaying medical care. Of particular concern is the increase in malaria deaths during the COVID-19 pandemic. Furthermore, distrust of these governments and international organizations contributed to the success or failure of the country-level COVID-19 policy. Vaccination coverage in sub-Saharan African countries was generally low. While the rate is 47.6% in Tanzania and 40% in South Africa, Zimbabwe, and Uganda, it is only 9.2% in the DRC (Our World in Data.org 2024).

3 COVID-19 as Downside Risk

As we have discussed, the people of Africa endured significant hardships due to the COVID-19 pandemic. It must be emphasized that the pandemic was not a mere medical emergency but a crisis with a fundamentally complex nature. We refer to such situations as compounded crises, wherein challenges originating from the physical, the living, or the social system engender new sorts of crises or exacerbate one another (Tanaka 2015; JICA-ORI 2024). For instance, human activities in the social system have contributed to climate change in the physical system, which in turn elevates the risks of tropical diseases in the living system. The COVID-19 pandemic exemplifies a quintessential compounded crisis. It has not only resulted in the tragic loss of lives; the lockdowns led to widespread job losses, economic stagnation, and disruptions in food distribution, which deprived many of sustenance. Children could not attend school, intimate communication was hindered, and anxieties about the future proliferated. Such circumstances have intensified the polarization of global society and foreshadowed regional conflicts.

[3] ACLED, note on the several events during 2018–19.

[4] Online interview with NGO staff in Uganda, April 2020.

Figure 2 illustrates the changes in the Human Development Index (HDI), which is composed of three key variables: life expectancy, education, and income. Since its introduction in 1990, global human society has experienced steady progress in sustainable human development. However, the HDI significantly decreased for the first time in 2020 and 2021. In this figure, the dotted lines indicate projections based on previous growth rates of HDI; the negative impact of the COVID-19 pandemic is unmistakable (see also UNDP 2022). Human beings often fail to perceive risks objectively and often take irrational actions driven by emotions such as fear (Gardner 2008). Nonetheless, the human suffering brought by the pandemic and the ensuing upheavals in society were undeniably real. Lives were lost, educational opportunities were stripped away, and economies faltered.

The concepts of human development and human security have been deeply influenced by the theory of the economist Amartya Sen, who paid attention to "downside risks." While human development seeks "growth with equity," human security aims to ensure "downturns with security."

> Human security as an idea fruitfully supplements the expansionist perspective of human development by directly paying attention to what are sometimes called "downside risks." The insecurities that threaten human survival or the safety of daily life, or imperil the natural dignity of men and women, or expose human beings to the uncertainty of disease and pestilence, or subject vulnerable people to abrupt penury related to economic downturns demand that special attention be paid to the dangers of sudden deprivation. Human security demands protection from these dangers and the empowerment of people so that they can cope with—and when possible overcome—these hazards (Sen 2003, p. 8).

Fig. 2 Global trends in human development (1990–2022) (*Source* Made by authors based on human development data. https://hdr.undp.org/data-center)

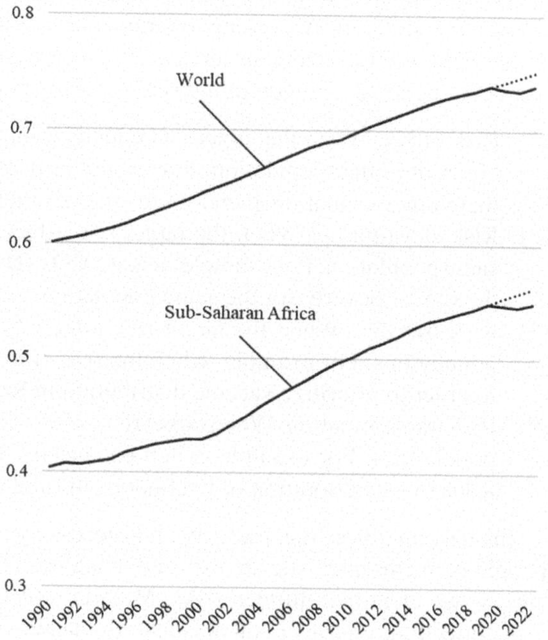

There are two types of risk: "idiosyncratic risks," such as sudden accidents, sickness, or joblessness that individuals face, and "covariant risks" that large groups of people confront simultaneously. While the former may be manageable at the household level through a combination of social security provisions and private insurance, the latter requires collective responses in the broader society and even at the international level (World Bank 2000, p. 136). While risks are generally quantifiable and can be calculated stochastically, covariant risks carry a higher degree of uncertainty. Large-scale downside risks, like the COVID-19 pandemic, are typical examples of covariant risks, which not only involve a large population but also possess a complex, multifaceted nature. Therefore, it is essential to examine the interrelationships between different risks.

3.1 *Risk Tradeoffs Posed by COVID-19 Policies*

As described in the case studies of this book, we observe that there were risk tradeoffs, not only in the COVID-19 pandemic, but also in the way the countermeasures affected people's livelihoods, exposing them to the risk of hunger, and exacerbating other infectious diseases. We would like to begin the discussion by further laying out the concepts surrounding risk tradeoffs.

In this book, risk is defined as the likelihood that something negative will happen to harm a valuable aspect of human life. When some of the most well-intentioned efforts to mitigate and target risk are found to increase other risks, the situation is called a risk tradeoff. According to Graham and Winner (1997), leading researchers in this field, the following are the types of risk tradeoffs, depending on the type of risk being targeted, countervailing risks, and the population affected:

(1) Risk offset: When the target and countervailing risks are of the same type and affect the same population. For example, if a COVID-19 containment policy, including vaccination, increases the risk of other diseases in the same population.
(2) Risk substitution: When the target risk affects different types of risks for the same population. For example, when a COVID-19 containment policy increases the risk of poverty for the same population.
(3) Risk transfer: When the target risk affects the same type of risk in different populations. For example, when the risk of infection in Region B is increased in order to prioritize vaccine distribution in Region A.
(4) Risk transformation: When target risks affect different types of risks for different populations. For example, when enhanced COVID-19 control in urban areas leads to a deterioration of livelihoods in rural areas.

In analyzing these risk tradeoffs, it is necessary to understand what risks to which people in the research site are exposed in addition to COVID-19. In our preliminary survey, we identified thirteen risks: Malaria infection, HIV/AIDS infection, Ebola virus infection, injuries in an accident, domestic violence, street violence, involvement in armed conflict, job loss, economic distress/financial problems, food shortage, natural disaster, political repression, catching the coronavirus/COVID-19, injustice, corruption or fraud. As the second chapter depicts, people in the target area do not perceive COVID-19 as high risk. Rather, economic deprivation and other problems are more severe for the people, and COVID-19 is only ranked 7–11.

What kind of risk, then, should we regard COVID-19 as? We propose the concept of "downside risk." Downside risk is originally an economic term, referring to the possibility that money or the value of something might be lost below target or expected returns. However, Amartya Sen's report on human security refers to it more generally as a danger of "sudden deprivation," which exposes vulnerable populations to multiple hardships (Sen 2003, p. 8). The COVID-19 pandemic and government policies affect not only the risk of infecting people with COVID-19 but also the risk of other diseases worsening; the risk of poverty and hunger due to deteriorating livelihoods, the risk of losing access to education due to the closure of educational institutions, the risk of domestic violence and crackdowns. Therefore, we can consider COVID-19 as a downside risk that may induce diverse risks affecting people. Because of this perspective, this book observes risk from the perspective of those exposed to risk, not only in relation to COVID-19, but also in relation to other risks.

3.2 *Dynamics of Risk Society*

Risks not only give rise to other forms of risks but also affect the lives of individuals differently. Risks "adhere to the class pattern, only inversely: wealth accumulates at the top, risks at the bottom. To that extent, risks seem to *strengthen,* not to abolish, the class society. Poverty attracts an unfortunate abundance of risks. By contrast, the wealthy (in income, power or education) can *purchase* safety and freedom from risk" (Beck 1992, p. 35, italics in original). However true this may be, many factors beyond income influence vulnerability to risks. In the case of COVID-19, age and pre-existing medical conditions greatly affected individuals' chances of survival.

To understand risks appropriately, it is crucial to grasp how they emerge and how society responds to them dynamically over time. Figure 3 illustrates fluctuations in human development across seven countries featured in the case studies of this book. As the scope expands from local to national, regional, and global levels, the trends offset each other, causing the graph to flatten. However, the reality at the national level presented in this figure reveals significant volatility of human development achievements. In addition to the pandemic, the effects of conflict and governance crises are evident. Figure 4 generalizes the dynamics shown in Figs. 2 and 3 depicting both the normative trajectory of human development and a real pathway that takes into account downside risks.

Just as in our individual lives, the development paths of communities and nations also go through continuous ups and downs. The future of human society is highly unpredictable, with "wildness" lurking on every corner (Bernstein 1996). Yet, we endeavor to foresee the scale and the nature of risks and prevent their emergence. Once

Fig. 3 Trends in human development, seven case study countries (1990–2022) (*Source* Made by authors based on human development data. https://hdr.undp.org/data-center)

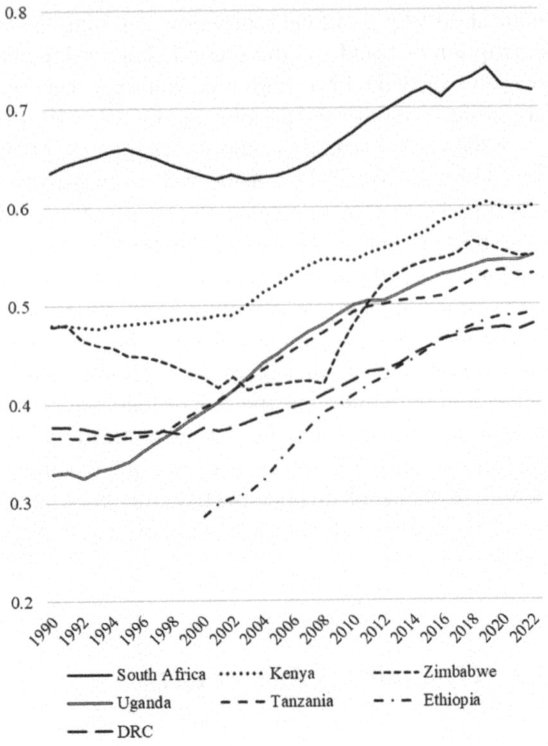

Fig. 4 Human development and security (*Source* Made by Yoichi Mine, reprint from JICA-ORI 2024, p. 9)

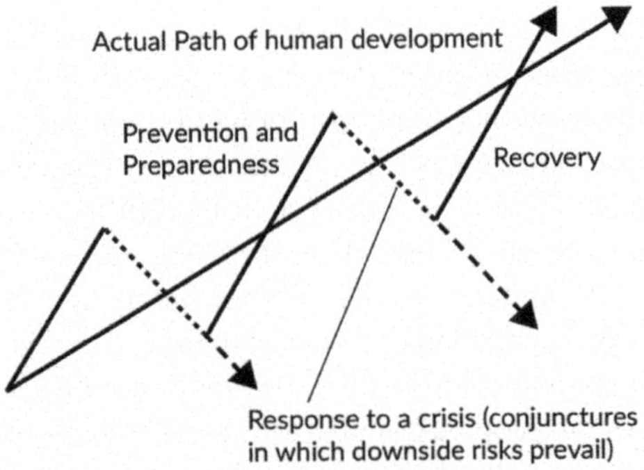

risks materialize, it is vital to ensure that people can engage in a resilient recovery process. To address downside risks effectively, we must organize mutual learning and respect practical wisdom on the ground. While the government plays a critical role in recovery phases, it can also impede bottom-up initiatives. People's empowerment is both a means and an end in itself. Although risk-avoidance mechanisms have been discussed systematically by economists like John Maynard Keynes, Frank Knight, and Kenneth Arrow, the relationship between individuals and risks is profoundly shaped by culture, subjectivity, people's mindset, and entrepreneurship. Thus, it is also helpful to approach communities, engage in their vernacular languages, and organize interdisciplinary research. "Risk entails some chance of losing something of value. If people value different outcomes, then they define 'risk' differently. As a result, defining risk is an exercise in value-focused thinking" (Fischhoff and Kadvany 2011, p. 41).

We have gone through the COVID-19 crisis. Many of us may not want to think back and reflect on it yet, but we attempt in this book an intellectual exercise looking toward the future, and for this purpose, we carefully reflect on Africa's experience during the age of COVID-19 to draw practical lessons. The pandemic's impact was anticipated to be particularly severe in Africa due to its dysfunctional healthcare systems. However, the reported cases were much lower in Africa than in the USA and Europe. This may indicate that societal resilience against diseases has been effectively embedded in African communities. On the other hand, concerning lockdowns, vaccine distribution, and information dissemination and sharing, the measures to contain the pandemic became heavily politicized in Africa. The case studies in this book closely examine these aspects, emphasizing African agency and coping strategies.

3.3 *Coping Strategies to Overcome Downside Risk*

We have always believed that people can overcome the harsh environment described above despite lacking public services and support. Therefore, we have endeavored to capture the everyday dynamics of people overcoming risk by using the wisdom of life around them. People demonstrate their resilience through the various coping strategies that they have adopted in order to recover their deteriorating livelihoods and regain educational opportunities that they have lost. The Kenya-Tanzania team called these efforts "hustling." Resilience is a psychological term that refers to the ability to overcome difficulties in a flexible manner. It is a state in which a person recovers from a state of reduced functionality due to some stress and returns to, or even exceeds, his or her original functionality. In the case of the COVID-19 pandemic, the stress people suffered was more than a one-time event. Until 2022, when COVID-19 was considered to be largely under control in Africa, the pandemic hit people over and over again, and measures were implemented repeatedly. Nevertheless, the strategies used to restore people's ability to function should also be an essential lesson from the COVID-19 pandemic.

4 Research Method and Structure

This book adopted interdisciplinary research methods in social sciences using the following four phases. First, we made six research groups led by scholars of African issues in Japan. These scholars targeted seven countries in Africa for collaboration with local research institutes: South Africa, Zimbabwe, Uganda, Kenya, Tanzania, Ethiopia, and the DRC. We then conducted field surveys collaboratively, involving researchers traveling from Japan, where our research is based, and local researchers. Second, we tailored questions specific to each field site based on a common set of research questions (see below) and conducted an online questionnaire survey covering the seven target countries. The results of this survey are presented in Chapter 2. Third, we collected grassroots voices through semi-structured interviews and focus group discussions in person and online (Chapters 3–8 describe concrete methods used for each country).

Fourth, throughout the different stages of the research period, each team brought their findings to a series of workshops and public symposiums for discussion.

The three broad research questions that each group worked to elucidate were as follows:

1) How have the COVID-19 pandemic and containment policies affected local people with diverse backgrounds?
2) How have local people recovered from the stresses imposed by the COVID-19 pandemic and containment policies?
3) What types of practical wisdom have helped people to overcome the risks?

The specific research subjects and topics varied from one country team to another. This is because the social impact of COVID-19 is different in each target country, and the subjects to be surveyed in detail are also different. Furthermore, the appropriate research methods vary depending on the research subject. For example, in Zimbabwe, where agriculture plays an important role, we focused on face-to-face interviews and focus group discussions in rural areas. On the other hand, in the DRC, where women are severely affected by both COVID-19 and the conflict, we focused our survey on women and conducted a joint commissioned survey with an international organization due to the difficulty of conducting direct field research in conflict-affected areas. The approach taken for each chapter is presented below.

Chapter 2. Common Questionnaire Survey on Risk Perceptions

Following the introductory chapter, this book is organized into thematic chapters based on analysis from seven sub-Saharan African countries. Chapter 2 offers a general analysis of a survey conducted in these countries, examining public perceptions of COVID-19 risks and how these interact with other perceived risks, showing that African countries generally have lower COVID-19 risk perception scores compared to other nations. This chapter highlights that COVID-19 risk perception is lower than other risk domains, such as economic distress and governance issues, which are prioritized. Health-related risks are generally perceived as less threatening, with malaria still receiving significant attention, while COVID-19 is viewed as less critical, especially when compared to broader societal and economic concerns. The findings in this chapter also suggest that higher COVID-19 risk perceptions are associated with health risks like HIV/AIDS and Ebola, as well as experiences of political repression and injustice. Conversely, lower COVID-19 risk perceptions are linked to street violence. The COVID-19 pandemic has notably influenced African public risk perceptions, though some countries rank COVID-19 as a lower risk factor than others.

Chapter 3. Middle Class in South Africa

Defining the middle class by income criteria and subjective social status, Chapter 3 discusses the experience and role of the South African middle class during the pandemic, noting that while researchers have investigated the impact of the COVID-19 in South Africa, the most severely affected country in the continent, they have not analyzed the experience of middle class. This chapter is anchored on four thematic categories, based on both large scale online surveys and semi-structured interviews targeted to middle-class citizens; risk perception, and COVID-19 experiences; evaluation of government policy during the pandemic; resilience and mitigation strategies; and views on the government. The chapter highlights the unique values and social positions of the middle class. The authors show that the South African middle class played a crucial role not only for themselves but for poor relatives and citizens, in overcoming the difficulties of the pandemic. This chapter therefore develops an understanding of the practical wisdom and coping strategies of middle-class South Africans during the pandemic, showing the interrelationship between people's risk perception and their evaluations of government performance.

Chapter 4. Urban and Rural in Zimbabwe

This chapter on Zimbabwe discusses the rural and urban people's personal experiences during the COVID-19 pandemic, focusing on real grassroots voices of people's fears and beliefs about COVID-19 during and immediately after the pandemic. Given the population-bloated African rural areas, the chapter looks at rural (and urban) people's perceptions and interactions with the coronavirus (biophysical) and how they affected the effectiveness of government containment measures. By comparing it with the urban experience, the chapter comprehensively explained how COVID-19 perceptions of risk, government containment measures, resilience mechanisms, and agency varied across different settings. The various resilience mechanisms people employed to survive the COVID-19 virus and their agency against the government's containment measures are explained. The chapter also identifies specific downside risks faced by agricultural communities and urbanites before scrutinizing changes in farming practices due to these risks using narratives gathered through interviews. The last part of this chapter outlines the strategies for fostering resilience in both settings, showing differing impacts and adaptation strategies between the two settings while also offering insights and lessons learned.

Chapter 5. Politics in Uganda

Chapters 5 and 6 discuss the distinct yet comparable political environments of Uganda, Kenya, and Tanzania during the pandemic. Research based on Uganda seeks to answer a critical question of how President Yoweri Museveni and the National Resistant Movement (NRM) instrumentalized the pandemic to win the 2021 elections leading to an examination of how citizens perceive government interventions and their consequences for Uganda's political future. Using this question as a foundation for argument, the chapter makes three interlocking observations: Museveni and the NRM took clear advantage of government interventions, particularly restricting public gatherings during campaigns to consolidate their political advantage. While recognizing that the central government unfairly managed the election campaigns, ordinary citizens also appraised the government's handling of the pandemic to prevent the spread of COVID-19 and to protect people's lives. Finally, the pandemic revealed a heavily centralized authority: local governments' dependency on the central government and their incapabilities. This chapter observes that, while the instrumentalization of the pandemic might have worked favorably for the ruling party, the pandemic also revealed the shortcomings of the semi-authoritarian regime. The long-term effects show that citizens grew dissatisfied with local government. Most importantly, the skewed relationship between central and local governments may challenge Museveni's regime in the future.

Chapter 6. Hustling in Kenya and Tanzania

Chapter 6 features key terms such as recovery and resilience, hustling, youth, pandemic, and politics. These terms bring out the theme that students, whose studies were disrupted by COVID-19 countermeasures, emerged stronger from the strains of the pandemic and the prevailing political climate in Kenya and Tanzania. Despite Kenya and Tanzania adopting diverging measures to curb the effects of the pandemic at the start, there were similarities in resistance by young people in these two neighboring states. This chapter employs a political ethnographic account of rural and urban students to consider the disruptions that occurred during the COVID-19 pandemic as a direct consequence or an indirect consequence of state measures to contain the spread of the pandemic. It seeks to answer the question of what ramifications the abrupt changes had on students' educational and daily lives during the pandemic and in the long term. The study identifies tangible impacts on everyday livelihoods beyond the surface-level manifestations of governmental responses and societal reactions. The students were seen to have devised coping and escape mechanisms, employing "hustling" as a strategic practice to cope with and manage the compounded precarities exacerbated by the COVID-19 pandemic. This chapter argues that hustling, especially characterized by digitalization, diversification, and social engagement, was not just a survival tactic but also an agentic effort that turned precarious circumstances into opportunities for both individual and communal advantage. This study contributes to the broader literature on work politics by offering a novel empirical exploration of how student workers transformed precarious conditions into avenues for social change and personal growth during a global crisis.

Chapter 7. Beliefs in Ethiopia

Chapter 7 focuses on vaccination, providing evidence from Ethiopia to establish misinformation as a key downside risk in COVID-19. This chapter argues that containment measures implemented early in the COVID-19 pandemic aimed to slow the spread of the virus, with vaccination emerging as the most effective strategy for curbing its impact. However, vaccine hesitancy driven by misinformation has been identified as a significant threat to vaccination. The findings indicate that both general misinformation and beliefs in conspiracies negatively and substantially affect vaccine uptake and the number of doses received. Further analysis reveals that general misinformation disproportionately affects females, while beliefs in conspiracies have a larger impact on males. Religiosity and faith appear to be important sources of resilience. These results underscore the urgent need for targeted communication strategies that leverage trusted institutions and key individuals to address and counter misinformation.

Chapter 8. Women's Resilience in DRC

Before moving on to the concluding chapter, Chapter 8 employs a mixed-methods approach, combining quantitative and qualitative data collection techniques, to delve into the experiences of conflict-affected, displaced, and violence-exposed women in the eastern DRC. This is based on the observation that the eastern DRC offers a compelling context for analyzing the psychological effects of the COVID-19 pandemic on vulnerable women. The objective of this chapter is to address critical questions such as the impact of the COVID-19 pandemic on the self-esteem and mental well-being of vulnerable women, how the socio-economic conditions of the population were affected by the pandemic, and the resulting challenges and opportunities. It also highlights the extent of psychosocial factors, such as mental health and social support networks, influenced by the prevailing crisis, and how they have adapted in response, while also articulating the level of resilience exhibited by women in the face of compounding stressors and identifying which factors contribute to their ability to cope and recover.

Chapter 9. Conclusion

The concluding chapter discusses the findings from this research, including people's perceptions of COVID-19 and government policies, the politicization of COVID-19 prevention measures, and the importance of networks and informal businesses as a foundation for resilience.

Appendix: COVID-19 Situation in Seven Target Countries

See Fig. 5.

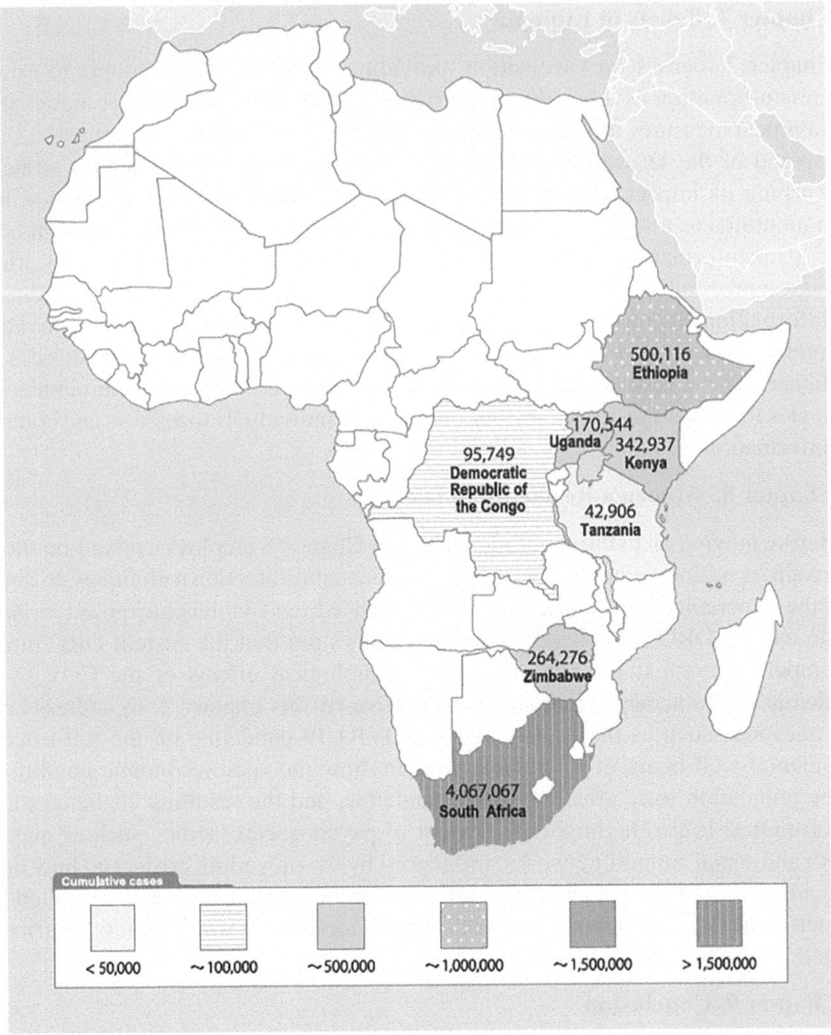

Fig. 5 Cumulative confirmed covid-19 cases in seven target countries, as of march 2023 (*Source* Made by authors based on data from JHU [2023])

South Africa

South Africa was the worst affected by COVID-19 in sub-Saharan Africa, with its first case recorded on March 5, 2020. Within 40 days, 19,000 cases and 369 deaths had been reported (Hodel and Okiror 2020; Naidu 2020). Concerns emerged regarding the country's ability to handle a larger outbreak due to limited healthcare resources like hospitals and ventilators. The pandemic's socioeconomic impact was severe, with exports falling by 61% from March to August 2020 compared to the previous year

(Kituyi et al. 2020). Within the Southern African Customs Union (SACU), exports to member countries dropped by 63.3% month-on-month in April, threatening the revenue of neighboring nations dependent on SACU transfers (StatsSA 2020).

The Department of Health launched various interventions, including governance measures, medical supply management, and public health campaigns (Pillay and Barnes 2020). Vaccination began in February 2021, reaching over 71% of the target population. In the end, 4,076,463 confirmed cases and 102,595 deaths were recorded (Worldometer 2023). The effectiveness of early response faced scrutiny, particularly as the pandemic threatened to worsen existing social issues, including mental health challenges stemming from historical health crises like HIV/AIDS (Naidu 2020).

Zimbabwe

Zimbabwe recorded its first COVID-19 case on March 20, 2020, shortly before initiating a national lockdown on March 30 to curb the spread of the virus (VeritasZim 2023).

The first lockdown was supposed to last for 21 days. However, the virus raged on; it was followed by various extensions and phases of easing, culminating in phased stages of easing/restricting movement (strict Level 4 in January 2021 due to rising cases and other subsequent localized lockdowns). Before the pandemic, about 76% of Zimbabwe's population—12.3 million people—were engaged in the informal economy, a workforce predominantly affected by lockdown measures that halted non-essential activities (AfDB-UN-WB 2019). The economic fallout was severe, with projections of a contraction of Zimbabwe's real GDP by 7.4% in 2020, following a contraction of 6.5% in 2019 (IMF 2020). This economic decline threatened to deepen poverty levels, disproportionately impacting vulnerable groups, including women, children, and persons with disabilities. Like the rest of sub-Saharan Africa, Zimbabwe has a significant youth demography, as 67% of residents are under 35. The pandemic exacerbated existing inequalities, highlighting many households' lack of access to essential services such as healthcare and education.Economic disruptions manifested in staggering inflation rates. Food prices surged by 985%, while healthcare costs skyrocketed by 1049% by April 2020 (World Bank 2020). Over time, the government gradually relaxed restrictions while emphasizing vaccinations, culminating in a significant easing of measures in 2022 and the eventual lifting of nearly all COVID-19 restrictions by August 2023. By then, about 264,276 cases and 5671 deaths had been recorded, with approximately 44% of the population receiving at least one vaccine shot (JHU 2023). The ramifications of the COVID-19 crisis extended beyond health statistics, impacting socioeconomic conditions across the nation.

Uganda

Uganda had recorded over 170,255 cases and 3630 deaths as of October 2023 (JHU). The first confirmed case was reported on March 21, 2020. President Yoweri Museveni initiated a nationwide lockdown shortly after the WHO declared the crisis a global pandemic on March 11, 2020. By May 6, the government had begun testing, with 47,620 tests yielding 100 positive cases and 55 recoveries, with no deaths (Ajari et al. 2020). The Ugandan government closed educational institutions on March 16, banned entry and exit by land and air on March 22, and encouraged government agencies and companies to work from home, yet as of March 22, there was only one confirmed case in Uganda. Additional lockdown measures included border closures, curfews, bans on large gatherings, suspension of public transport, and school closures (Mumbere 2020; Busari and Dean 2020). Other Standard Operating Procedures (SOPs) such as handwashing, mask-wearing, and social distancing were instituted and helped maintain a lower case count. Vaccine uptake was initially low but later improved to achieve an overall coverage of 63% (UNIPH 2023). Despite initial concerns over strict measures, Uganda's prompt response and effective communication positioned it among the African countries with the lowest incidence of COVID-19, showcasing a successful pandemic strategy amid healthcare challenges (Ajari et al. 2020).

Tanzania

The COVID-19 situation in Tanzania unfolded with notable controversy and divergence from global health recommendations. The first confirmed case was on March 16, 2020, at Mount Meru Hospital in Arusha (Makoni 2021). Following this, the Tanzanian government initially implemented various WHO recommendations, including school closures and prohibiting public gatherings except for religious events. However, by April 2020, the government ceased publishing COVID-19 case statistics, asserting that only 509 positive cases, 21 deaths, and 183 recoveries had been reported since the onset of the pandemic (Makoni 2021). Under President John Magufuli, skepticism regarding the accuracy of testing kits affected the credibility of reported statistics. Magufuli publicly challenged these testing protocols, resulting in significant administrative changes, including dismissing health officials who opposed more traditional remedies (Obulutsa 2020; Kew 2021). As the government refrained from updates and continued to promote home remedies over scientific consensus, the true scale of the COVID-19 crisis became obscured, leading to widespread criticism nationally and internationally. The chaotic approach to managing the pandemic highlighted the complex interplay between governance and public health, as officials favored insular political decisions over scientific guidance. Ultimately, the Tanzanian experience illustrates a unique public health response that deviated from the global pandemic management approaches (Mtani and Ngohengo 2023).

Kenya

The first case in Kenya was identified on March 13, 2020, prompting the Kenyan government to initiate emergency measures and establish the National Emergency Response Committee (NERC) to combat the spread of the virus (Ogira et al. 2022). Throughout the pandemic, trends in public perception and health-seeking behavior revealed a troubling decline in individuals' access to healthcare services. This decline was partially due to fears surrounding COVID-19, economic factors, and the stigma associated with testing (Agogo et al. 2024). Initial surveys indicated that patients with chronic diseases faced interruptions in accessing services, leading to severe health implications (Kenya National Commission on Human Rights 2020). The Kenyan government received substantial support in its fight against COVID-19, including a $50 million fund from the World Bank to enhance the response efforts (World Bank Group 2020). Furthermore, vaccination campaigns have been ongoing, with approximately 37.6% of adults fully vaccinated as of May 2023 (Orangi et al. 2024). Despite these efforts, social challenges persisted, such as stigma against COVID-19 patients, with some reporting social withdrawal (Population Council 2020). Additionally, mental health issues were prevalent, with over half of the population indicating low mental health status during the pandemic. Kenya reported over 343,196 confirmed infections and 5688 deaths by the end of COVID-19 on May 22, 2023 (Ministry of Health 2023).

Ethiopia

The first case of COVID-19 was identified in Ethiopia on March 13, 2020. The government declared a five-month state of emergency in April 2020, causing significant declines in economic activities, including an 80% drop in demand in the flower export industry and an estimated $550 million loss for Ethiopian Airlines during the initial months of the pandemic (OSSREA 2021). By August 26, 2020, Ethiopia had surpassed 45,000 confirmed cases, over 700 deaths, and more than 16,000 recoveries. Within ten months, confirmed cases had reached 134,132, with 2071 deaths, resulting in a case fatality rate (CFR) of 1.54% (JHU 2023; Abagero et al. 2022). The pandemic disproportionately affected women, with 61% of total confirmed cases being female and most infections (74%) occurring in individuals aged 15–44 years. Most cases were reported in the capital city, Addis Ababa, which accounted for 58% of infections, followed by the Oromia region with 16% (Abagero et al. 2022). It is important to note that Ethiopian Airways was among the few airlines that continued flights within Africa and beyond (often ferrying vaccines and medical personnel) because this became a potential source of new infections. To combat the COVID-19 pandemic, Ethiopia implemented various public health measures and scaled up testing capabilities, establishing around 24 diagnostic laboratories capable of conducting over 5600 tests daily (OSSREA 2021). Ethiopia reported a total of 500,116 confirmed COVID-19 cases and 7572 deaths (38% had been vaccinated by 10 March 2023), indicating a significant impact of the pandemic on the country's healthcare system (JHU 2023). The effect on education was equally severe, with over 26 million students affected by school closures (OSSREA 2021).

Democratic Republic of the Congo

The COVID-19 situation in the Democratic Republic of the Congo (DRC) has been complex and challenging since the first case was confirmed on March 10, 2020. By late September 2020, the country had recorded 10,523 cases with 271 fatalities, which only rose to 27,552 confirmed COVID-19 cases and 726 deaths by March 22, 2021 (Hategeka et al. 2021). The outbreak prompted immediate government action, including the closure of borders, suspension of flights, and shutting down schools, significantly impacting various sectors. Experts have attributed the low infection levels to experience based on previous pandemics in the country. In a 2021 survey by the World Bank, approximately 67.7% of the people expressed a willingness to accept vaccination when made available, while 32.3% raised concerns about its safety (WB 2021). However, by the end of the pandemic, there were 99,333 reported cases and 1468 deaths (WHO 2023; Africa CDC 2023), with vaccine coverage of less than 7% owing to varying reasons such as vaccine supply, religion, cost of vaccine delivery, and administration inefficiencies during the initial stages of vaccination (Kinshasa School of Public Health 2024). Economically, the pandemic's effects were profound, as over half of the population had lower incomes than before the pandemic. Although the employment rate stabilized at 56.0%, many family-operated businesses experienced significant income declines primarily due to a lack of clients (70.5%) and the travel restrictions imposed. Food insecurity was also a pressing issue, affecting 72.4% of households, where adults reported going entire days without food due to financial limitations (WB 2021).

References

Abagero et al. (2022). A Review of COVID-19 Response Challenges in Ethiopia. *International Journal of Environmental Research and Public Health, 19*(17). https://doi.org/10.3390/ijerph191711070

Africa CDC. (2023). *Coronavirus disease 2019: Latest updates on the COVID-19 crisis from Africa CDC*. Accessed on October 8, 2024. https://africacdc.org/covid-19/

African Development Bank, United Nations, & World Bank (AfDB-UN-WB). (2019). *Joint needs assessment for Zimbabwe: Identifying challenges and needs*. https://www.afdb.org/sites/default/files/2020/01/14/zimbabwe_country_portal.pdf

Agogo, G. O., Munywoki, P. K., Audi, A., Auko, J., Aol, G., Oduor, C., Kiplangat, S., Ouma, A., Komo, T., Herman-Roloff, A., Munyua, P., & Bigogo, G. (2024). The effect of COVID-19 pandemic on healthcare seeking in an urban informal settlement in Nairobi and a rural setting in western Kenya. *PLOS Global Public Health, 4*(4), e0002968. https://doi.org/10.1371/journal.pgph.0002968

Ajari, E. E., Kanyike, A. M., Ojilong, D., & Abdulbasit, I. O. (2020). COVID-19 in Uganda: Epidemiology and response. *Electronic Journal of Medical and Educational Technologies, 13*(2), em2009. https://doi.org/10.30935/ejmets/8269

Beck, U. (1992). *Risk society: Towards a new modernity* (M. Ritter, Trans.). Sage.

Bernstein, P. L. (1996). *Against the Gods: The Remarkable Story of Risk.* New York: John Wiley & Sons.

Busari, S., & Dean, S. (2020). Uganda reports its first death from Covid-19. *CNN News.* https://edition.cnn.com/2020/07/24/africa/uganda-first-covid-19-death/index.html

BuzzFeed News. (2020). Towareteirunoha "inochi to keizai" dehanaku "inochi to inochi" no mondai: Iryou jinruigakusha ga gimon wo nagekakeru shingata corona taisaku (The question is not 'life vs. economy' but 'life vs. life' Medical anthropologist raises questions about COVID-19 countermeasures) (in Japanese) https://www.buzzfeed.com/jp/naokoiwanaga/covid-19-isono-1

Fischhoff, B., & Kadvany, J. (2011). *Risk: A Very Short Introduction.* Oxford: Oxford University Press.

Gardner, D. (2008). *Risk: The Science and Politics of Fear.* London: Virgin Books.

Graham, J. D., & Wiener, J. B. (1997). *Risk vs risk: Tradeoffs in protecting health and the environment.* Harvard University Press.

Hategeka, C., Carter, S. E., Chenge, F. M., Katanga, E. N., Lurton, G., Mayaka, S. M.-N., Mwamba, D. K., Kleef, E. van, Vanlerberghe, V., & Grépin, K. A. (2021). Impact of the COVID-19 pandemic and response on the utilization of health services in public facilities during the first wave in Kinshasa, the Democratic Republic of the Congo. *BMJ Global Health, 6*(7), e005955. https://doi.org/10.1136/bmjgh-2021-005955

Hodel, K., & Okiror, S. (2020). Coronavirus in Africa: What happens next? *The Guardian.* https://www.theguardian.com/global-development/2020/apr/08/coronavirus-in-africa-what-happens-next

International Monetary Fund (IMF). (2020). *Zimbabwe: 2019 Article IV Consultation-Press Release; Staff Report; and Statement by the Executive Director for Zimbabwe.* https://www.imf.org/en/Publications/CR/Issues/2020/03/19/Zimbabwe-2019-Article-IV-Consultation-Press-Release-Staff-Report-and-Statement-by-the-49283

JICA Ogata Sadako Research Institute for Peace and Development (JICA-ORI). (2024). Overview. *Human security today no.2: Human security, politics and society under compounded crises.*

Johns Hopkins University and Medicine (JHU) Coronavirus Resource Center. (2023). *COVID-19 dashboard.* https://coronavirus.jhu.edu/map.html

Kenya National Commission on Human Rights. (2020). *Pain and Pandemic: Unmasking the state of human rights in Kenya in containment of the COVID -19 pandemic.* https://www.knchr.org/Portals/0/Final%20KNCHR%20COVID%2019%20Situational%20Report%20June%202020-%20Incorporated%20Recommendations_1.pdf (Situational Report No. 1).

Kew, J. (2021). Tanzania's U-Turn on COVID-19 gets WHO and Africa CDC support. *Bloomberg.com.* https://www.bloomberg.com/news/articles/2021-04-09/tanzania-s-u-turn-on-covid-19-gets-who-and-africa-cdc-support?embedded-checkout=true

Kinshasa School of Public Health. (2024). Low volumes, high costs: Delivering COVID-19 vaccines in the Democratic Republic of the Congo. *Immunization Economics.* https://thinkwell.global/wp-content/uploads/2024/04/DRC-C19-costing-study-report_final.pdf

Kituyi, M., et al. (2020). *Impact of the COVID-19 pandemic on trade and Development: Transitioning to a new normal.* United Nations Publications.

Makoni, M. (2021). Tanzania refuses COVID-19 vaccines. *The Lancet, 397*(10274),566. https://doi.org/10.1016/S0140-6736(21)00362-7

Ministry of Health. (2023). *The 7th COVID-19 knowledge, attitude, and practice survey report.* https://www.health.go.ke/sites/default/files/2024-02/Kenya%20National%207th%20Covid-19%20Knowledge%20-Kenya%20Report.pdf

Mtani, F. A., & Ngohengo, J. (2023). Africa at the Crossroads: An Overview of the Covid-19 Pandemic and its Drama in Tanzania. *African Journal of History and Geography, 2*(1), 1–16. https://doi.org/10.37284/ajhg.2.1.1088

Mumbere, D. (2020). Uganda coronavirus: First death registered, cases reach 1,079. *Africanews.com.* https://www.africanews.com/2020/07/23/uganda-coronavirus-hub/

Naidu, T. (2020). The COVID-19 pandemic in South Africa. *Psychological Trauma: Theory, Research, Practice, and Policy. 12*(5), 559–561. https://doi.org/10.1037/TRA0000812

Obulutsa, G. (2020). Tanzania suspends laboratory head after president questions coronavirus tests. *Reuters.* https://www.reuters.com/article/world/tanzania-suspends-laboratory-head-after-president-questions-coronavirus-tests-idUSKBN22G28O/

Ogira, D., Bharali, I., Onyango, J., Mao, W., McDade, K. K., Kokwaro, G., & Yamey, G. (2022). Identifying the impact of COVID-19 on health systems and lessons for future emergency preparedness: A stakeholder analysis in Kenya. *PLOS Global Public Health, 2*(12), e0001348. https://doi.org/10.1371/journal.pgph.0001348

Orangi, S., Mbuthia, D., Chondo, E., Ngunu, C., Kabia, E., Ojal, J., & Barasa, E. (2024). A qualitative inquiry on drivers of COVID-19 vaccine hesitancy among adults in Kenya. *PLOS Global Public Health, 4*(3), e0002986. https://doi.org/10.1371/journal.pgph.0002986

OSSREA. (2021). *COVID-19 pandemic in Ethiopia: Literature Review.* https://www.ossrea.net/images/COYOQA/Files/Ethiopian_Report.pdf

Our World In Data. org. (2024). *COVID-19 Pandemic.* https://ourworldindata.org/coronavirus

Pillay, A. L., & Barnes, B. R. (2020). Psychology and COVID-19: Impacts, themes and way forward. *South African Journal of Psychology, 50*(2), 148–153. https://doi.org/10.1177/0081246320937684

Population Council. (2020). Kenya: COVID-19 perceptions, stigma and impact—Responses from fourth round of data collection in five Nairobi informal settlements (Kibera, Huruma, Kariobangi, Dandora, and Mathare). *COVID-19 Research & Evaluations brief*. Nairobi: Population Council.

Sen, A. (2003). Development, rights, human security. *Human security now: Commission on human security, Boxes1.3,* 8–9. Commission on Human Security.

Statistics South Africa (Stats SA). (2020). https://www.statssa.gov.za/?m=2020

Tanaka, Akihiko. (2015). *Toward a theory of human security.* (JICA-RI Working Paper No. 91).

Tamai, T. (2021). Nigeria niokeru COVID-19 nokeiken-lockdown kanioiteseikisurubouryoku (Experiences with COVID-19 in Nigeria: Violence under lockdown) (in Japanese). *Africa Report, 59*, 28–41. https://doi.org/10.24765/africareport.59.0_28

UNIPH. (2023). *COVID-19 vaccine uptake and coverage, Uganda.* https://uniph.go.ug/covid-19-vaccine-uptake-and-coverage-uganda-2021-2022/

United Nations (UN). (2020). *Policy brief: Impact of COVID-19 in Africa* (updated 20 May 2020)

United Nations Development Programme (UNDP). (2022). New threats to human security in the Anthropocene: Demanding greater solidarity, 2022 *special report.*

Veritas Zim. (2023). *SI 2023–102 public health (COVID-19 prevention, containment and treatment) (National lockdown) no. 22, amendment order, 2023, no. 44.* https://www.veritaszim.net/node/6396

Warah, R. (2021). A brutal pandemic: Kenya police under fire for the death of two brothers. *ONE.org Africa.* https://www.one.org/africa/stories/ndwiga-brothers-death-police-brutality-kenya/

WHO. (2020a). *Strategic response to COVID-19 in the WHO African region: February to December 2020.* https://www.afro.who.int/publications/strategic-response-covid-19-who-african-region-february-december-2020

WHO. (2020b). *Ebola: North Kivu/Ituri, Democratic Republic of the Congo, August 2018—June 2020.* https://www.who.int/emergencies/situations/Ebola-2019-drc-

WHO. (2023a). *COVID-19 (WHO African region).* https://www.arcgis.com/apps/dashboards/0c9b3a8b68d0437a8cf28581e9c063a9

WHO. (2023b). *World Malaria Report 2023.* https://www.who.int/teams/global-malaria-programme/reports/world-malaria-report-2023

WHO. (2024). *Data.* https://data.who.int/indicators/i/CCCEBB2/217795A https://www.who.int/data/gho/data/indicators/indicator-details/GHO/hospital-beds-(per-10-000-population)
World Bank. (2000). *World Development Report 2000/2001: Attacking Poverty.* Oxford: Oxford University Press.
World Bank. (2021). *Poverty and equity brief: Democratic Republic of Congo.* https://www.worldbank.org/en/topic/poverty/publication/poverty-and-equity-briefs
World Bank Group. (2020). Kenya receives $50 million World Bank Group support to address COVID-19 pandemic. *World Bank.* https://www.worldbank.org/en/news/press-release/2020/04/02/kenya-receives-50-million-world-bank-group-support-to-address-covid-19-pandemic
Worldometer. (2023). *South Africa COVID—coronavirus statistic.* https://www.worldometers.info/coronavirus/country/south-africa/#google_vignette

Kazuyo Hanai Project Assistant Professor at the Institute for Future Initiatives, The University of Tokyo, Japan and Representative Director of NPO RITA-Congo. She holds a PhD in International Cooperation Studies from The University of Tokyo. She researches the role of resources in the conflicts in Africa and the responsibility of global society. In particular, her research focuses on the relations between the conflict minerals issue in the Democratic Republic of Congo and the responsibility of Japanese consumer society. Her main publication is Justice of Resource Issue: Responsibility of Consumers on Conflict Minerals Issue in DR Congo (Toshindo, 2016, in Japanese). She has served as president of JSAS since 2023 and the principal investigator for the JSAS Hitachi project.

Rangarirai Gavin Muchetu Assistant Professor at the College of Intercultural Communication at Rikkyo University, Tokyo, Japan. He obtained his PhD from Doshisha University, where he studied Japanese agriculture, drawing lessons for Zimbabwean policymakers. Thus, his research focuses on international agrarian issues, particularly the interplay between state policy and the socio-economic relations of rural dwellers. His recent publication include After Radical Land Reforms: Restructuring Agricultural Cooperatives in Zimbabwe and Japan (2021, Langa RPCIG) and 'South-South Cooperation in Agriculture: Impacts of Brazil's More Food International Program on Post-Land Reform Social Organizations in Zimbabwe (2022, Agrarian South: Journal of Political Economy).

Laban Kithinji Kinyua Research Fellow at the African Studies Center, Tokyo University of Foreign Studies, Tokyo, Japan. Dr. Kinyua holds a PhD in Global Studies, with a research focus on decentralization, rural livelihoods, and African youth engagement with digital platforms. His recent work investigates how digital spaces facilitate political participation and resource mobilization among rural communities. Recent publications include "Digital Spaces and Democratization in Rural Africa: Participation, Mobilization, and Laying Claim to Resources" in the Journal of African Studies (2023) and "Decoding Political Discourse on Digital Platforms in Africa: Rumor Networks Among Rural Populace in Kenya's 2022 Elections" in ASC-TUFS Working Papers (2023).

Yoichi Mine Visiting Professor at the Graduate School of International Relations, Ritsumeikan University, Japan, and Executive Director, JICA (Japan International Cooperation Agency) Ogata Sadako Research Institute for Peace and Development. His research interests include human security, international development, and African area study. He is the author of Connecting Africa and Asia: Afrasia As a Benign Community (Routledge, 2022) and has edited six books in English, including Migration and Agency: Afro-Asian Encounters (Palgrave, 2018) and Preventing Violent Conflict in Africa: Inequalities, Perceptions and Institutions (Palgrave, 2013). The English version of his book, Oral History of Japan's Development Cooperation (The University of Tokyo Press, 2023) will be published by Springer in 2025.

Chapter 2
Risk Perceptions of COVID-19 in Seven African Countries

Christian Samen Otchia and Kazuyo Hanai

Abstract This study examines risk perceptions of COVID-19 across seven African countries, utilizing data from an online survey of 840 individuals. The research reveals a complex landscape of risk perceptions in Africa, encompassing COVID-19 illness risk alongside other health, economic, governance, and social risks. Notably, COVID-19 risk perceptions in Africa appear relatively low compared to other regions, particularly in countries like Ethiopia and Zimbabwe, where economic distress, corruption, and injustice are perceived as greater threats. Regression analysis confirms multiple risks associated with the COVID-19 pandemic, including health and governance risks, while economic risks generally show no significant association with COVID-19 illness risk. These findings partially explain why individuals in African countries, especially those facing economic challenges, tend to prioritize other risks over COVID-19. The study contributes to the literature on risk perception during global health crises and offers insights into the unique context of the COVID-19 pandemic in Africa.

1 Introduction

The COVID-19 pandemic may be human history's most significant global health crisis. From December 2019 to August 2023, the world has experienced 770 million confirmed cases of COVID-19 and the loss of 6.96 million lives.[1] In Africa, the pandemic poses unique challenges. While Europe has 276 million confirmed cases

[1] Source: Johns Hopkins Coronavirus Resource Center.

Note This chapter is a reprint of a report published as Otchia, Christian S. (2023). Risk Perceptions of COVID-19 in Africa: Belief, Values, and Personality. *African Studies, 104*. 43–46.

C. S. Otchia (✉)
Graduate School of International Development, Nagoya University, Nagoya, Aichi, Japan
e-mail: otchia@gsid.nagoya-u.ac.jp

K. Hanai
Institute for Future Initiatives, The University of Tokyo, Bunkyo, Tokyo, Japan

K. Hanai et al. (eds.), *Practical Wisdom and Resilience Overcoming Downside Risk*,
https://doi.org/10.1007/978-981-96-4455-1_2

and the Western Pacific approximately 207 million cases, Africa has reported 9.5 million confirmed cases. This situates Africa in a distinctive context, marked by exceptional circumstances and considerations. The impact of the pandemic in Africa, even though substantial, is relatively lower in confirmed cases compared to other WHO regions. However, it is important to observe that Africa encounters intricate difficulties in competently handling the pandemic, including concerns such as healthcare infrastructure, resource accessibility, and varying public health responses. This report raises two linked inquiries regarding this unprecedented international health catastrophe transmission. What are the public perceptions of COVID-19 risks in Africa? And, besides COVID-19, what other risks do people perceive, and how do these risks interact with their perceptions of the risk of COVID-19 illness?

Understanding the risk perception of the COVID-19 pandemic is of particular importance in Africa. First, risk perception is a core feature of protection-motivation theory (Rogers 1975). It affects individual choices, engagement in preventive behaviors, and compliance with government recommendations. In contrast to historical contexts, in the current period, navigating the COVID-19 pandemic involves not only individual choices but also complex public health guidelines and restrictions as countries have employed varying strategies, from social distancing to complete lockdowns to prevent healthcare systems from being overwhelmed. These contemporary factors create a nuanced backdrop against which to examine the interplay between risk perception and behavior during a global health crisis. Second, since Africa faces a triple economic shock from reduced trade and investment with China, declining demand due to global lockdowns, and a continental supply shock disrupting domestic and intra-African trade, COVID-19 risks have potentially large implications, not only for public health but also for societal and economic aspects.

This study is related to a number of empirical papers measuring risk perception during COVID-19 (Dryhurst et al. 2020; Bruine de Bruin and Bennett 2020). The closest related work is Dryhurst et al. (2020), which adopts a theory-based approach to examine risk perceptions in an international context, surveying 6991 individuals across ten countries in March–April 2020. Traditionally, this literature has relied on psychological predictors such as direct personal experience with the virus, knowledge, trust, and social/cultural norms to explain risk perception (Leiserowitz 2006; van der Linden 2015; Xie et al. 2019). Our main contribution to the literature is to extend the predictors of COVID-19 illness risk by including other risk domains. Our results suggest that COVID-19 risk perceptions are small in Africa compared to other regions surveyed by Dryhurst et al. (2020). Moreover, we identify other risk domains, such as other health risks, injustice, and political repression, as important mechanisms driving risk perceptions of COVID-19 illness risk. We finally establish that most economically vulnerable people do not consider COVID-19 as a risk.

The rest of the chapter is organized as follows. Section 2 describes the research design, data, and implementation details. Section 3 presents our main results. Section 4 concludes.

2 Methods

2.1 Study Design and Implementation

Our survey is structured in four sections. The first section, which we refer to as Prior Experience, explores respondents' past encounters with COVID-19, covering symptoms, diagnoses, and vaccination history. It also delves into the perceived impact of the pandemic on respondents, their families, and friends, along with the measures taken to address these impacts. The second section, which we call Risk Perception, investigates respondents' perceptions of exposure to risks, including health-related risks, violence, economic challenges, and natural disasters. The third section—Values and Beliefs—seeks to understand respondents' religious beliefs and practices, political leanings, levels of trust in different entities, personality traits, and behaviors. The last section gathers demographic information, encompassing age, residence, education, employment, household composition, marital status, perceived economic status, and household income.

This study was implemented using Qualtrics software, and study participants were solicited through Cint. This online sampling platform provides nationally representative quota samples of many African countries stratified by age, gender, and ethnicity. Employing interlocking age and gender quotas to ensure broadly representative samples,[2] we administered the survey to 840 individuals in seven African countries. The selected countries, including The Democratic Republic of Congo (DRC), Ethiopia, Kenya, Uganda, Tanzania, South Africa, and Zimbabwe, were chosen to capture a broad spectrum of responses during various phases of the COVID-19 pandemic. Data collection occurred in February 2023, providing robust insights when risk perceptions are no longer malleable and changing. We required our study subjects to reside in Africa and be between 18 and 54. The survey took about 20 min, and participants were paid ¥461–¥704 (US$3.00–$4.81), varying between countries. Survey instruments were crafted in English and meticulously translated into native languages by bilingual experts, guaranteeing cultural, and linguistic sensitivity. Participants were granted the flexibility to complete surveys in their preferred language. Before engaging in the survey, all participants provided informed written consent.

2.2 Measures of Risk Perception

Using self-report questionnaires to create a robust measure of risk perception presents significant challenges due to reference bias. This bias looms large when individuals are tasked with gaging their COVID-19 risk perception relative to other risks or events, some familiar and some not. For example, when respondents are prompted

[2] Ethnicity was only considered for South Africa.

to equate the risk of contracting COVID-19 with routine activities like crossing the street or dining at a restaurant, their responses inevitably intertwine with preexisting notions about unrelated risks, affecting the precision of their COVID-19 risk perception. Reference bias thus emerges when each survey participant applies distinct criteria or reference points while distinguishing between various Likert scale levels. Their perception of risk is profoundly shaped by factors like recent news, personal experiences, or anecdotes from acquaintances and family. These personalized reference frames introduce significant diversity into the dataset, posing challenges in establishing a standardized and objective COVID-19 risk perception measure. Consequently, addressing reference bias is paramount in comprehensively grasping how individuals perceive and respond to COVID-19-related risks. Instead of adopting the common approach of using anchoring vignettes to correct self-reported scores, to address the reference bias and increase the scale's reliability in this study we asked respondents to evaluate the risk exposure of their friends and family. In the empirical analysis, we used these risk perceptions to correct for the reference bias in our measure of risks.

2.3 Data

Figure 1 presents descriptive statistics of COVID-19 risk perception scores across the seven sampled countries. Panel (a) shows risk perceptions vary across these countries, with scores ranging from 2.7 to 3.6 on a 7-point scale. Compared to Dryhurst et al. (2020), our findings suggest that the African countries sampled have relatively lower COVID-19 risk perception scores compared to countries like the UK, Spain, United States, Germany, Sweden, Australia, Japan, Italy, Mexico, South Korea, where risk perception was notably higher than 4.7.[3] In our sample, we find that Zimbabwe exhibited the most elevated risk perception, with a mean score of 3.60, followed by Ethiopia with 3.52. At the same time, Uganda recorded a score of 2.7, reflecting relatively lower perceived risk. In Panel (b), we plot the COVID-19 risk perception index distribution to illuminate the wide range of risk perceptions within these countries. Notably, each country has significant variations, with countries like DRC, Tanzania, and Uganda displaying density plots skewed toward the left. Taken together, Fig. 1 identified distinct groups based on both mean risk perception and dispersion. Group 1 comprises countries with low mean risk perception and variability, including DRC, Tanzania, and Uganda. Group 2 encompasses countries with moderate mean risk perception and variability, such as Kenya, Ethiopia, and Zimbabwe. South Africa is an outlier in Group 3, characterized by a relatively high mean risk perception with moderate variability.

[3] This variation may also be attributed to the timing of data collection by Dryhurst et al. (2020), which occurred during the early stages of the pandemic when risk perceptions were still fluid and evolving.

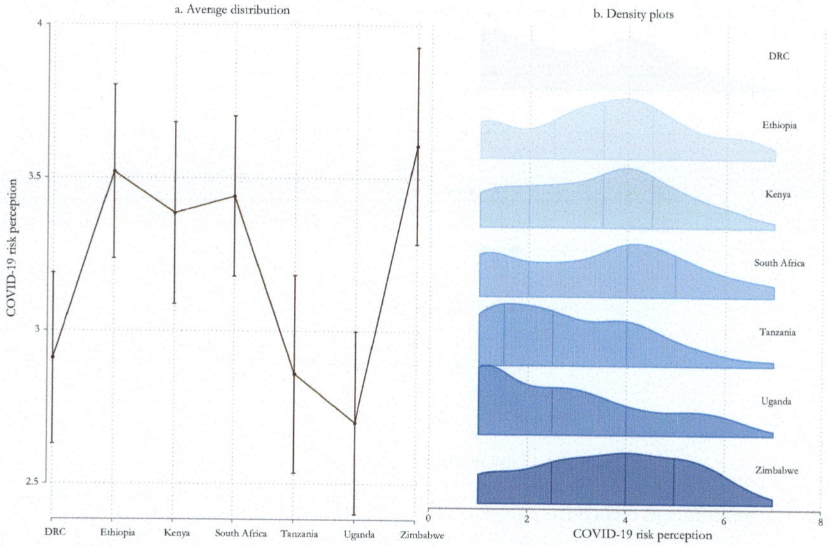

Fig. 1 Descriptive statistics of COVID-19 risk perception in selected African countries

A possible concern to consider is that people may have difficulty balancing different risk management strategies due to the coexistence of multiple risks during COVID-19. To delve deeper into this issue, we compare COVID-19 risk perception with fourteen other risk domains, as depicted in Fig. 2 One noteworthy finding is that COVID-19 risk perception is relatively lower than that of these alternative risks. In these regions, including Ethiopia, Zimbabwe, South Africa, Kenya, Tanzania, the DRC, and Uganda, COVID-19 is ranked as the 7th or lower risk factor. This indicates that individuals in these areas prioritize other risks over COVID-19.

Figure 2 further reveals the prominence of economic distress as the foremost risk in several countries. For instance, in Ethiopia, concerns regarding corruption/fraud and injustice take precedence, underscoring the significance of economic stability, and governance-related issues. Another noteworthy observation is that, except for specific cases such as Malaria in DRC (2nd), Uganda (5th), and Tanzania (6th), health-related risks generally assume a lower position in terms of perceived threat. This suggests that while certain health risks like Malaria continue to command substantial attention, the perception of COVID-19 tends to be relatively subdued, particularly when juxtaposed with broader societal and economic concerns.

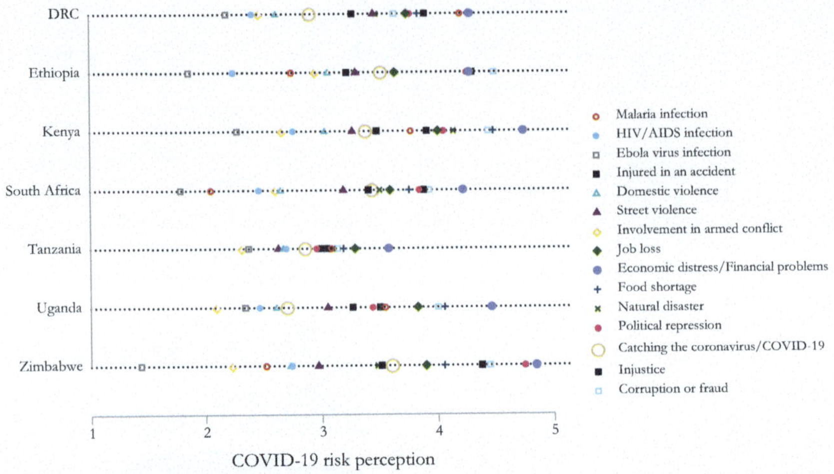

Fig. 2 The multitude of risks during the COVID-19 pandemic

3 Findings and Discussion

So far, the study has revealed that in some countries, COVID-19 is perceived as a lower risk than other risk domains, including economic distress and governance issues, which take precedence. Additionally, except for specific health risks like Malaria, COVID-19 is generally seen as less threatening than broader societal and economic concerns. In this section, we ask how these risks interplay with the perceptions of COVID-19 illness risk. The specification we estimate explains COVID-19 risk perception (dependent variable) with fourteen other risks (independent variables). We also control for other individual characteristics such as gender, age, education, political ideology, trust, personality traits, and religiosity.[4]

Table 1 presents basic results from OLS regressions for the pooled sample (column 1) and for each country (columns 2 through 8). In column 1, the analysis shows that COVID-19 risk perception is positively and significantly correlated with risk perceptions related to HIV/AIDS infection, Ebola virus infection, being injured in an accident, experiencing political repression, and facing injustice. In contrast, there is a negative but significant correlation between COVID-19 risk perception and street violence. These findings suggest that, on a broad level, individuals tend to associate higher COVID-19 risk perception with health-related risks like HIV/AIDS and Ebola, as well as with experiences related to political repression and injustice. Conversely, they tend to associate lower COVID-19 risk perception with street violence. The findings in columns 2–8 show that these correlations vary when analyzed country-by-country.

[4] This chapter does not provide the definition and descriptive statistics of the control variables due to space constraints.

Table 1 Regression results, COVID-19 risk, and other risk domains

	All	DRC	Ethiopia	Kenya	South Africa	Tanzania	Uganda	Zimbabwe
	(1)	(2)	(3)	(4)	(5)	(6)	(7)	(8)
Malaria infection	0.049	–0.104	0.257***	0.099	0.082	–0.030	0.241***	0.205**
	(0.030)	(0.094)	(0.075)	(0.099)	(0.085)	(0.094)	(0.086)	(0.101)
HIV/AIDS infection	0.109***	0.225**	–0.110	–0.014	0.009	0.201*	0.122	0.153
	(0.037)	(0.110)	(0.104)	(0.121)	(0.089)	(0.112)	(0.101)	(0.116)
Ebola virus infection	0.200***	0.272**	0.216**	0.309***	0.100	0.326***	0.435***	–0.001
	(0.035)	(0.111)	(0.094)	(0.117)	(0.085)	(0.118)	(0.103)	(0.102)
Injured in an accident	0.142***	0.072	0.437***	–0.055	0.298***	0.043	–0.019	0.106
	(0.037)	(0.114)	(0.097)	(0.111)	(0.096)	(0.117)	(0.106)	(0.098)
Domestic violence	0.059	0.065	–0.104	0.150	–0.006	0.083	–0.129	0.070
	(0.041)	(0.126)	(0.115)	(0.135)	(0.107)	(0.131)	(0.101)	(0.121)
Street violence	–0.082*	0.036	–0.103	–0.008	–0.054	–0.071	–0.029	–0.080
	(0.042)	(0.122)	(0.124)	(0.114)	(0.124)	(0.155)	(0.112)	(0.113)
Involvement in armed conflict	0.016	–0.081	0.178*	–0.173	–0.054	–0.105	0.163*	0.080
	(0.037)	(0.103)	(0.101)	(0.112)	(0.106)	(0.135)	(0.091)	(0.109)
Job loss	0.056	0.005	0.038	0.246**	0.121	–0.033	–0.067	–0.028
	(0.043)	(0.124)	(0.115)	(0.118)	(0.111)	(0.141)	(0.123)	(0.138)
Economic distress	–0.006	0.027	0.039	–0.093	0.067	0.160	–0.242	0.087
	(0.049)	(0.135)	(0.122)	(0.160)	(0.127)	(0.167)	(0.147)	(0.150)
Food shortage	–0.018	0.056	–0.181*	0.101	–0.052	–0.067	0.178	–0.068
	(0.047)	(0.142)	(0.104)	(0.140)	(0.121)	(0.156)	(0.141)	(0.142)
Natural disaster	0.061	–0.002	–0.048	–0.134	0.082	0.171	0.180*	0.182*

(continued)

Table 1 (continued)

	All	DRC	Ethiopia	Kenya	South Africa	Tanzania	Uganda	Zimbabwe
	(0.037)	(0.110)	(0.093)	(0.120)	(0.095)	(0.124)	(0.102)	(0.108)
Political repression	0.117***	0.074	0.163	0.201	0.045	0.144	–0.056	0.214*
	(0.040)	(0.099)	(0.099)	(0.127)	(0.100)	(0.128)	(0.117)	(0.122)
Injustice	0.244***	0.266**	0.055	0.234*	0.362***	0.111	0.310***	0.139
	(0.044)	(0.128)	(0.130)	(0.132)	(0.123)	(0.133)	(0.115)	(0.128)
Corruption or fraud	–0.041	–0.100	0.183	0.013	–0.147	0.011	–0.160	–0.086
	(0.040)	(0.110)	(0.134)	(0.105)	(0.108)	(0.124)	(0.102)	(0.114)
Observations	840	132	128	117	150	99	115	99
R-squared	0.466	0.469	0.588	0.538	0.533	0.602	0.603	0.527
Controls	Yes	Yes	Yes	Yes	Yes	Yes	Yes	Yes
Country dummy	Yes	Yes	Yes	Yes	Yes	Yes	Yes	Yes

Note Standard errors in parentheses *** $p < 0.01$, ** $p < 0.05$, * $p < 0.1$

The results for the DRC in column 2 indicate positive and significant correlations between COVID-19 risk perception and risk perceptions related to HIV/AIDS infection, Ebola virus infection, and injustice. Notably, the magnitudes of these correlations, particularly for HIV/AIDS infection and Ebola virus infection, appear to be relatively higher in DRC compared to the pooled regression. This difference in magnitude could be explained by several factors specific to DRC. One possible explanation is that DRC has experienced significant health challenges, including outbreaks of infectious diseases such as Ebola and a high prevalence of HIV/AIDS. Consequently, individuals in DRC may have a heightened awareness and concern about health-related risks, including COVID-19, which could lead to stronger correlations between these variables. Additionally, the level of social and political unrest and issues related to justice and governance may differ substantially in DRC compared to the pooled sample. This could also contribute to the observed differences in the magnitude of these correlations, as individuals in regions with greater instability and challenges in governance may perceive higher overall risks, including those related to COVID-19.

Column 3 shows that COVID-19 risk perception in Ethiopia is positively and significantly correlated with risk perception related to malaria infection, injury in an accident, and involvement in armed conflict but negatively correlated with food shortage. The negative correlation between COVID-19 risk perception and food shortage is intriguing. It implies that Ethiopians might perceive COVID-19 as less of a threat when food shortages are a concern. This could be because immediate survival needs to precede health concerns like COVID-19 in conditions of food scarcity.

In the context of Kenya (column 4), several influential factors impacting COVID-19 risk perception are evident. First, there is a significant positive correlation between COVID-19 risk perception and perceptions of risk related to Ebola virus infection. This suggests that Kenyans may view both Ebola and COVID-19 as substantial health threats, likely due to shared characteristics such as rapid transmission and high mortality rates. Second, a significant positive correlation is observed between COVID-19 risk perception and the fear of job loss, highlighting the close relationship between economic concerns and how Kenyans perceive the risks associated with COVID-19. Job loss can lead to financial instability and reduced access to healthcare, intensifying worries about the virus's impact on livelihoods and overall well-being. Finally, the positive and significant correlation between COVID-19 risk perception and perceptions of injustice underscores the role of social and political factors in shaping how Kenyans perceive the risk of COVID-19. This connection suggests that perceptions of unfairness or inequality in areas such as healthcare access, resource distribution, or access to COVID-19 information can contribute to heightened concerns about the virus's impact.

Column 5 presents the outcomes for South Africa, revealing notable patterns in COVID-19 risk perception. Significantly positive correlations are observed for risk perception concerning being injured in an accident and perceptions of injustice. What stands out is the substantial difference in the magnitude of injustice when compared to all the other countries and the pooled estimates. Several factors may contribute to this noteworthy observation. Firstly, the historical context of South Africa, characterized by social inequalities and the legacy of apartheid, likely amplifies concerns related to injustice in various aspects of life, including healthcare access and resource distribution. Additionally, the socio-economic disparities within the country may further accentuate perceptions of unfairness and inequality, translating into elevated COVID-19 risk perception driven by broader societal issues.

In Tanzania (column 6), we find that COVID-19 risk perceptions are correlated with risks related to HIV/AIDS infection and Ebola virus infection. A possible explanation for this correlation might be the historical context of disease management and government communication. Historically, Tanzania has faced significant health challenges, including the ongoing fight against HIV/AIDS and past encounters with Ebola outbreaks in neighboring countries. In this context, the government's denial of COVID-19 could be consistent with its past approach to health crises, where official communication often downplayed or denied the severity of diseases. Furthermore, the skepticism expressed by President Magufuli regarding COVID-19 vaccines, as well as his doubts about the effectiveness of foreign interventions, could have influenced public perceptions. This skepticism may have eroded trust in the government's response to the pandemic and led to a tendency among the population to question the existence and severity of COVID-19, much like previous diseases.

In Uganda (column 7), we find a positive and significant correlation between COVID-19 risk perception and risks related to Malaria infection, Ebola virus infection, natural disasters, and injustice. Another finding that stands out is the large magnitude of Ebola virus infection. This was expected because of the 2022–2023 Uganda Ebola outbreak. An alternative explanation for this intriguing result could be attributed to deeper socio-political factors, such as perceptions of inequity in access to healthcare resources, social services, or information dissemination, which may amplify concerns regarding COVID-19 in Uganda.

In column 8, we find COVID-19 risk perception in Zimbabwe is positively and significantly correlated with risks related to malaria infection, natural disasters, and political repression. It is interesting to note that Zimbabwe is the only country in our sample where political repression is found to be positive and significant. This finding is consistent with Mwatwara (2022), who argued that government authorities in Zimbabwe used repressive tactics during the pandemic to consolidate President Emmerson Mnangagwa's power. This is evident as the pandemic occurred in a country already experiencing conflict, leading to new conflicts and reshaping existing ones.

4 Conclusion

We have investigated the perceived risks of COVID-19 using unique data from an online survey of 840 individuals across seven African countries. We discovered a multifaceted realm of risk perceptions concerning COVID-19 in Africa, including COVID-19 illness risk, other health-related risks (Malaria infection, HIV/AIDS infection, Ebola virus infection), economic risks (Job loss, Economic distress, Food shortage, Natural disaster), governance risks (Political repression, Injustice, Corruption or fraud), and social risk (Injured in an accident, Domestic violence, Street violence, involvement in armed conflict). Notably, our findings indicate that, when compared to other regions, COVID-19 risk perceptions in Africa appear relatively small. This observation is particularly pronounced in countries like Ethiopia and Zimbabwe, where COVID-19 occupies a lower position in the hierarchy of perceived risks, overshadowed by concerns such as economic distress, corruption or fraud, and injustice. The regression results confirmed the existence of multiple risks associated with the COVID-19 pandemic, such as health risks and governance risks. We found that economic risks are generally not associated with COVID-19 illness risk. Our findings partially explain why individuals in African countries, particularly those facing economic challenges, tend to prioritize other risks over COVID-19.

References

Bruine de Bruin, W., & Bennett, D. (2020). Relationships between initial COVID-19 risk perceptions and protective health behaviors: A national survey. *American Journal of Preventive Medicine, 59*(2), 157–167. https://doi.org/10.1016/j.amepre.2020.05.001.

Dryhurst, S., Schneider, C. R., Kerr, J., Freeman, A. L., Recchia, G., Van Der Bles, A. M., ... & Van Der Linden, S. (2020). Risk perceptions of COVID-19 around the world. *Journal of Risk Research, 23* (7–8), 994–1006. https://doi.org/10.1080/13669877.2020.1758193

Leiserowitz, A. (2006). Climate change risk perception and policy preferences: The role of affect, imagery, and values. *Climatic Change, 77*(1), 45–72. https://doi.org/10.1007/s10584-006-9059-9.

Mwatwara, W. (2022). Pandemic crisis: Old repressions renewed amid anti-COVID-19 lockdown in Zimbabwe, c.2020–2021. *Southern Journal for Contemporary History, 47*(1), 51–77. https://doi.org/10.18820/24150509/SJCH47.v1.4.

Rogers, R. W. (1975). A protection motivation theory of fear appeals and attitude change. *Journal of Psychology*, 91(1), 93–114. https://doi.org/10.1080/00223980.1975.9915803

van der Linden, S. (2015). The social-psychological determinants of climate change risk perceptions: Towards a comprehensive model. *Journal of Environmental Psychology, 41*,112–124. https://doi.org/10.1016/j.jenvp.2014.11.012.

Xie, B., Brewer, M. B., Hayes, B. K., McDonald, R. I., & Newell, B. R. (2019). Predicting climate change risk perception and willingness to act. *Journal of Environmental Psychology, 65*, 101331. https://doi.org/10.1016/j.jenvp.2019.101331.

Christian Samen Otchia Associate Professor of Development Economics at the Graduate School of International Development, Nagoya University, Japan, where he teaches Development Microeconomics and Industrial Development. He is an affiliate member of the African Growth and Development Policy modeling consortium and has extensive experience in industrial policy design and implementation, collaborating with local governments and organizations like FAO and UNECA. His research focuses on the impact of special economic zones on local development through skills and technology transfer. Dr. Otchia holds a Ph.D. in International Development (Nagoya University) and has published in several academic journals.

Kazuyo Hanai Project Assistant Professor at the Institute for Future Initiatives, The University of Tokyo, Japan and Representative Director of NPO RITA-Congo. She holds a PhD in International Cooperation Studies from The University of Tokyo. She researches the role of resources in the conflicts in Africa and the responsibility of global society. In particular, her research focuses on the relations between the conflict minerals issue in the Democratic Republic of Congo and the responsibility of Japanese consumer society. Her main publication is Justice of Resource Issue: Responsibility of Consumers on Conflict Minerals Issue in DR Congo (Toshindo, 2016, in Japanese). She has served as president of JSAS since 2023 and the principal investigator for the JSAS Hitachi project.

Chapter 3
Risk Perceptions, Resilience and Evaluation of Government Policies During the COVID-19 Pandemic in South Africa: A Study of the Middle Class

Chizuko Sato, Scarlett Cornelissen, and Tomohiro Hosoi

Abstract The South African middle-class experience during the COVID-19 pandemic is understudied. This chapter aims to understand the practical wisdom and coping strategies employed by middle-class South Africans during the pandemic and explore the relationship between their risk perceptions and evaluation of the government's performance. The authors conducted a quantitative survey and qualitative interviews targeted to this group. The main findings are threefold. First, middle-class persons were less adversely affected by the COVID-19 pandemic than the poor, while at the same time they suffered stress. Second, middle-class persons showed mixed evaluations of the government's COVID-19 policy. Third, the middle class are not only self-reliant but also providers of support and resilience to the poor during the pandemic. They hold the civic value of supporting others in difficulties, while they criticise governmental policy failure and corruption.

1 Introduction

South Africa recorded the highest number of confirmed cases of COVID-19 infections and casualties on the African continent. According to the World Health Organization (WHO), there were more than four million confirmed cases of infection and

C. Sato (✉)
Institute of Global Studies, Tokyo University of Foreign Studies, Fuchu, Tokyo, Japan
e-mail: satochi@tufs.ac.jp

S. Cornelissen
Department of Political Science, Stellenbosch University, Stellenbosch, South Africa

Stellenbosch University Japan Centre, Stellenbosch, South Africa

T. Hosoi
Global Initiative Center, Gunma University, Maebashi, Gunma, Japan

K. Hanai et al. (eds.), *Practical Wisdom and Resilience Overcoming Downside Risk*,
https://doi.org/10.1007/978-981-96-4455-1_3

the pandemic claimed 102,595 lives.[1] At the same time, the South African government provided socio-economic assistance for their citizens to overcome the difficulties during the pandemic. Scholars have analysed the economic and psychological impacts of the pandemic since its onset, starting with the National Income Dynamic Study—Coronavirus Rapid Mobile Survey (NIDS-CRAM).[2] Many articles show that the poor suffered most severely from the pandemic (Jamieson and Van Blerk 2022; Khambule 2022; Nnaeme et al. 2022; Rwafa-Ponela et al. 2022; Turok and Visagie 2022) and a general decline or loss in income has exacerbated their situation. Others highlighted that the pandemic disproportionally affected women regardless of their income levels, socio-economic backgrounds, and professional contexts (Parry and Gordon 2021; Gouws and Ezeobi 2021; Kriger et al. 2022).

While the lived experiences of the pandemic have been studied, these have been in relation to specific social groups, generally defined by indicators of (income) precarity or vulnerability (Coetzee et al. 2022; Theron et al. 2021). There are comparatively few studies centred on the lived experiences of the middle class and the distinctive forms of precarity as well as coping mechanisms that might have been utilised by this group.[3] Against this background, we focus on middle-class persons, defined by income criteria as well as subjective social status (see Burger et al. 2015; Zizzamia et al. 2016), a group that is relatively understudied in an otherwise large emerging body of scholarship on pandemic and post-pandemic South Africa (e.g. Fourie and Lamb 2023; Turok and Visagie 2022). We assess their risk perceptions and experiences of the COVID-19 pandemic, evaluations of the government policies during the pandemic, as well as the mitigation and coping strategies adopted, by analysing quantitative and qualitative interview data. Through discussion of the middle-class views and experiences during and after the pandemic, we explore not only the sources of resilience of the South African middle class, but also their roles in the society as a provider of resilience. We argue that the South African middle class, while small in terms of its number, plays an important role as a provider to poorer population of the society.

After this introduction, the chapter consists of four sections. The second section provides the context for the study, reviewing the existing literature on the impact of the COVID-19 pandemic in South Africa, identifying the research gap and introducing research questions. The third section discusses the idea of the middle class, problematising its definition in the South African context and highlighting their unique values and positions in society. The fourth section explains our research methodology, data collection processes and the characteristics of our quantitative and qualitative interview data. The fifth section presents the results of our analysis,

[1] WHO Coronavirus (COVID-19) Dashboard, https://covid19.who.int/ (Accessed October 25, 2024).

[2] https://cramsurvey.org/

[3] Gouws and Ezeobi's collection of COVID narratives (2021) and Kriger et al.'s (2022) assessments of the experiences of academics can be considered as contributions towards the study of middle-class experiences, although their research is in relation to specific professional contexts. Jacobs' (2023) study of the psychosocial experiences of a diverse suburban middle-class community is the only that looks at the middle class as a cohesive, albeit heterogenous group.

which are thematically classified into four categories: risk perception and COVID-19 experiences; evaluation of the government policy during the pandemic; resilience and mitigation strategies; and views on the government.

2 Background and Purpose of the Study

Given the unique challenges posed by the pandemic and the wide-ranging nature of its adverse effects, much attention has fallen on popular and institutional responses, mitigation strategies, and coping mechanisms, generally centred on the idea of "resilience" (e.g. Theron et al. 2021; May and Mentz-Coetzee 2021). With its roots in fields such as metallurgy and physics, "resilience," originally understood as the capacity of a system to return to its initial form after a disturbance (Norris et al. 2008), has now been widely adopted in the environmental and social sciences. In ecology, for example, the notion of resilience has been applied to refer to the capacity of a system to absorb change and still function (e.g. Holling 1973). With broad application today, understanding of social/human resilience converges on the idea that it is "the capacity to anticipate, respond, adapt, or transform in response to shocks, uncertainty and change, especially novel systemic changes, in order to facilitate desired outcomes" (Biggs et al. 2021).

Studies on South Africans' pandemic experiences and coping and resilience strategies have addressed various social groups and contexts. Focus has fallen on the lower-income group (Posel et al. 2021; Turok and Visagie 2022); residents of townships and informal settlements (Khambule 2022); those identified as sociologically or psychologically vulnerable (such as poorer youth) and therefore deemed more at risk (Coetzee et al. 2022; Closson et al. 2024; Theron et al. 2021); as well as the livelihood effects in the informal sector (Rwafa-Ponela et al. 2022; Nnaeme et al. 2022). Some of these studies show that while people reported high levels of psychological stress and anxiety (Closson et al. 2024; Coetzee et al. 2022), various inter-personal-level resources, social networks, and other forms of social capital were mobilised (Paredes Ruvalcaba et al. 2023) to help address such stressors.

A large volume of research has assessed specific mitigation tools employed by the South African government, including policy measures such as lockdowns and mobility and gathering restrictions (Parker 2023; Struckmann 2023) and the role of temporary social (so-called COVID) grants in helping address the pandemic's poverty impact (Bhorat et al. 2021; Moses and Woolard 2023; Jamieson and Van Blerk 2022; Seekings 2020). These studies suggest that while aspects of the South African government's policy response—including the implementation and policing of lockdown measures—were negatively evaluated (Baumgardt and Robins 2023; Lamb 2023), the government's social security policy helped mitigate the most severely negative impacts of the pandemic on the poor (Bhorat et al. 2021; Chitiga-Mabugu et al. 2021; Gronbach and Seekings 2021; Khambule and Mdlalose 2022; Moses and

Woolard 2023). Importantly, conditions at household level affected people's mitigation practices and success (Jamieson and Van Blerk 2022; Paredes Ruvalcaba et al. 2023; Posel et al. 2021).

Much research has been conducted on policy responses to the COVID-19 crisis in South Africa (see Fourie and Lamb 2023 for a comprehensive overview). In the assessment of the South African government's strategy against COVID-19, Friedman (2021) has argued that it reflected "first-world" interests and that it was prejudiced towards the elite and suburban, while not adequately geared to ameliorate the needs of the (mainly black African) South African "third world." If Friedman's (2021) observation is right, middle-class South African's satisfaction with the COVID-19 prevention policies would be high, although there has been little systematic investigation of this group's evaluation of government performance amid perceptions of (existential) risk.

Our chapter thus has two objectives. The first is to develop an understanding of the "practical wisdom" and coping strategies of the middle-class South Africans during the COVID-19 pandemic, who may not have been the principal target of the socio-economic/mitigation policies introduced by the government. The second is to explore the interrelationship between people's risk perception and their evaluation of the government's performance during the pandemic. Before addressing these questions, we first need to discuss who the middle-class people in South Africa are and what their common features are.

3 The Idea of Middle Class in the South African Context

There is no strict definition of the "middle class" in South Africa; it is not a homogenous group. A widely cited study by Visagie and Posel (2013) notes that there are two main criteria for defining someone as middle class. The first is based on someone's income. According to this criterion, middle-class citizens earn 50–150% of the national average income. The second criterion is based on consumption level. Visagie and Posel (2013) hold that persons who spend ZAR1400–10,000 per month (2008 prices) can be classified as middle class. Other scholars point to other criteria. Mattes (2015) and Schotte (2017) argue that middle-class persons are highly educated and work full-time.

More recent research by Egan (2021) presents the South African consumer landscape by segmenting the South African population into six categories (poor; working poor; working class; middle class; upper-middle class; top end) by household income levels based on the data collected through the National Income Dynamics Survey Wave five in 2019. According to this categorisation, household income of the middle-class population is between ZAR22,000 and ZAR40,000 per month and four million people (one million households) fall in this category. About 40% of this group has more than one income earner in the household, and they tend to have a higher education. Moreover, "while poorer segments are overwhelmingly Black African, nearly 50% of this segment is made up of other races." (Egan 2021, P. 80).

Because estimations of the middle class based on empirical measures such as income, occupational skills, or even educational levels are problematic (see Burger et al. 2015), some researchers have opted for subjective rather than objective notions of social class. Schotte (2017), for example, notes that it is more valid to consider people's subjective evaluation of their class. They argue that if one thinks of oneself as a middle-class person, one should be classified as middle class. Self-defined social status is important given the assumed links between social status and political values and behaviour (c.f. Norris and Inglehart 2019 and earlier work) on the one hand, and between class and social capital on the other (c.f. Putnam 1993).

Scholars have argued that middle-class persons have distinct characteristics or political behaviour as a class compared to the poor, labour class or elites (Mattes 2015; Kotzè and García-Rivero 2018; Musyoka 2023). Since middle-class persons are relatively satisfied with their material circumstances, their demands have been varied. Therefore, in the South African context, some have argued that the middle-class prizes to a greater extent "higher-order" values such as freedom of speech and anti-corruption (Mattes 2015). Others have noted that the South African black middle class, though also a complex category (Khunou 2016; Southall 2016), has a specific burden, the so-called *black tax*, to financially and materially support their relatives (Mangoma and Wilson-Prangley 2019; Mhlongo 2019), a cultural expectation not necessarily shared within the wider, heterogenous middle-class group of South Africa.

4 Research Methodology and Cohorts of Research Participants

This study involved a quantitative survey and qualitative interviews.[4] The quantitative data was collected from 520 South African people through an online survey in July and August 2023 using a closed-ended and open-ended questionnaire. The respondents were 18 years old and above and lived in two of the largest cities in South Africa: Johannesburg or Cape Town. The quantitative data provided us with information about respondents' perceptions of different risks, risk mitigation/coping strategies, and evaluations of governments' performances during the COVID-19 pandemic.

In general, respondents in this online survey were relatively young (74% were under 40 years old and 92% were under 50 years old), highly educated (69% were graduates of tertiary schools), and middle to high-income earners (median household income fell in the bracket of ZAR11,000–19,999 per month). The survey contained respondents whose monthly household income ranged from "less than ZAR800" to "ZAR100,001 and more." In order to elucidate perceptions and experiences of respondents who broadly fall into the category of middle class, we divided respondents into three groups based on their income levels—lower, middle, and higher, and

[4] In this chapter, we distinguish the research participants in the online survey and in the qualitative interviews, by describing the former as "respondent" and the latter as "participant" or "interviewee".

Table 1 Our sample in the quantitative survey

Category	Monthly income of households	Sample size
Lower income	Up to ZAR7,999	112
Middle income	ZAR8,000 to ZAR49,999	324
Higher income	ZAR50,000 and more	75

Source Online survey 2023

examined whether being in a middle-income group made any difference compared to being in a lower-income group. We followed Egan's (2021) classification of middle-class households with slight modification and included Egan's definitions of working-class households (monthly earnings of between ZAR8,000 and ZAR22,000) and a part of upper-middle class households which earn between ZAR40,000 and ZAR49,999 per month.[5] Based on this income definition, our sample are divided as in Table 1.

Higher educational attainments and income levels of respondents were also reflected in their living areas (70% lived in the suburbs, while 28% lived in townships) and their employment status (55% were full-time employees, 10% were part-time employees and another 7% were self-employed with hired labour). For reasons unknown to us, 70% of respondents were women. Most respondents did not perceive COVID-19 as a higher risk, compared to other risk factors such as economic distress, service delivery failure, and crime. On the government's performance during the COVID-19 pandemic, respondents showed mixed assessments of lockdown policy, while specific aspects of the lockdown regulations such as school closures and restrictions on funerals recorded more negative evaluations.

To gain deeper understanding of individual and household experiences of the COVID-19 pandemic among middle-class South Africans, we conducted semi-structured interviews with 20 self-defined middle-class South African persons on online platforms (Zoom and MS Teams) in December 2023 and January 2024. The research participants for these interviews were recruited through multiple entry points including the researchers' personal networks, advertisements on two Facebook groups whose membership consists of South African nationals who live in Japan or who are interested in Japan, and referrals from interviewees. All the participants in the qualitative interviews met the following criteria: they are South African

[5] We broadened Egan's definition of middle-class households for two reasons. On the one hand, the lower end of Egan's definition of working-class households (ZAR8,000) is the cut-off point to be qualified to receive a child support grant, the largest social grant in South Africa. We think it makes sense to include households not qualified to receive the most common form of social grant in the middle-income category as households which are independent of the state assistance. On the other hand, the upper limit for household income to receive a loan from the National Student Financial Aid Scheme (NSFAS), the major governmental assistance for students in higher education in South Africa, is R600,000 per annum, which is R50,000 per month, and we set this as the upper end of middle-income group in our survey. NSFAS website FAQ, https://www.nsfas.org.za/content/faqs.html#:~:text=For%20a%20bursary%3A%20combined%20household,000%20per%20annum%20before%20deductions (Accessed October 27, 2024).

citizens; between the ages of 18 and 50 years; lived in South Africa in 2020 (March to December); have some experience in the tertiary educational environment; and self-identify as middle class.

Of 20 participants in the qualitative interviews, 12 were women and eight were men. Most of them were in the age cohort of 30 s and 40 s with the youngest 26 years old and the oldest 50 years old at the time of the interviews in December 2023 and January 2024. During the COVID-19 pandemic in 2020, 19 participants lived in one of the metropolitan cities (Johannesburg, Ekurhuleni, Pretoria, Cape Town, or Durban), while one lived in a regional city. Half of them worked in the government or university sector in 2020, while two of each were students and unemployed, and the rest worked in private and non-profit sectors. All of them self-identified as middle class, with some specifically saying that they were upper-middle class based on their income and lifestyle. Nonetheless, about half of participants said that their parents belonged to lower-income to lower-middle class, indicating that they are the first generation in their family to enjoy the middle-class lifestyle in major South African cities.

During the semi-structured interviews, research participants were asked their views/opinions on their socio-economic background; experiences of COVID-19 and lockdown measures; assessment of government policies during the pandemic as well as non-pandemic periods; coping strategies during the pandemic; and the government's role in their lives in general. While the number of participants in qualitative interviews is small, their backgrounds and experiences of the COVID-19 pandemic varied and provided us with rich information. All the qualitative interviews were recorded with the permission of participants, and then transcribed for the purpose of the subsequent analysis.

5 Middle-Class Experiences of COVID-19 in South Africa

5.1 Risk Perceptions and COVID-19 Experiences

As discussed in Chapter 1 of this book, risk perception is here defined as the possibility that something negative occurs that harms some aspect of human value. There are various types of risk that people are likely to have factored into their risk assessment, including health-related risks, livelihood-related risks, safety-related risks, and security-related risks. In this study, we are interested in assessing people's reported risk trade-off, based on their perception of how the COVID-19 pandemic and government policies affected other life risks such as loss of employment or income, and the offset/mitigation measures that were adopted. The latter includes individual-, household-level and interpersonal resources, and social and community networks.

Based on this understanding of risk perceptions and the idea of risk trade-off, we asked respondents about the likelihood of 13 different types of risks occurring in the next six months and how harmful the impact would be if these risks occurred.

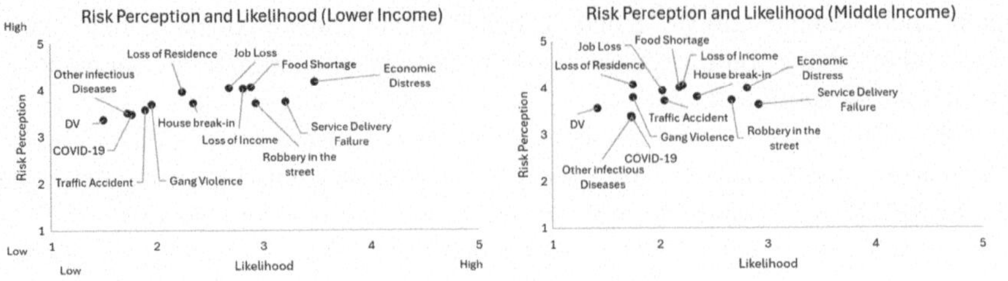

Fig. 1 Risk perception and likelihood of its occurrence: Mean value of respondents by income group (*Source* Online survey 2023)

These risks are grouped into (i) health-related risks (COVID-19 infection; other infectious diseases), (ii) safety-related risks (traffic accident; domestic violence; robbery in the street; house break-in; gang violence), (iii) livelihood-related risks (job loss or retrenchment; loss of income; economic distress/financial problems; food shortage; loss of residence), and (iv) security-related risks (service delivery failure). The respondents were asked to evaluate the probability of these risks materialising to them and their likely impacts by using a five-point Likert scale of one (unlikely, slightly harmful) to five (likely, highly harmful).

Figure 1 shows the results of risk perceptions for lower-income and middle-income groups in the survey. First of all, there is no significant difference between middle-income and lower-income groups in terms of risk perception. Both groups evaluate these events above three on the five-point scale, which means that these events are harmful if they occurred to them. Also, both groups consider economic distress and service delivery failure as the most likely risks materialising in near future. Both groups also consider livelihood-related risks more harmful if they occurred. However, Fig. 1 also implies that lower-income groups could suffer more from harmful events. For example, the likelihood of "economic distress" is higher for the lower-income group than the middle-income group.

Respondents perceived COVID-19 less likely to happen compared to other risks, and also considered its impact less harmful. Since the online survey was conducted in July and August 2023, more than one year after the South African government repealed all the COVID-19 related regulations in June 2022,[6] perhaps there is no surprise that respondents no longer perceived COVID-19 as a significant risk.

Nevertheless, to understand the actual impact of the COVID-19 pandemic on people's lives, we need to investigate whether other risks were triggered or compounded by it, and whether there were any differences among different income groups. For this purpose, we asked respondents whether their living situations changed positively or negatively since the pandemic by using a five-point Likert scale of one (worsened) to five (improved) and the result is shown in Table 2.

In general, both lower-income and middle-income groups answered that their living situations got worsened after the pandemic, regardless of economic aspects,

[6] https://www.gov.za/covid-19/resources/regulations-and-guidelines-coronavirus-covid-19 (Accessed July 30, 2024).

Table 2 Change of living situations after COVID-19 pandemic

	Income level	Cost of living	Job and income	Health	Crime and safety	Relationship		
						Family	Work	Community
Mean	Lower	1.77	1.81	2.73	1.94	3.03	2.66	2.89
	Middle	2.36	2.59	3.08	2.18	3.33	3.07	3.1
	High	2.51	2.71	3.13	2.20	3.48	3.12	3.12
Standard deviation	Lower	1.13	1.11	1.20	1.2	1.34	1.19	1.25
	Middle	1.37	1.82	1.23	1.23	1.59	1.50	1.44
	High	1.40	1.35	1.33	1.33	1.25	1.27	1.33

Source Online survey 2023

or crime and personal safety. In almost all aspects of life, the participants' answers scored less than three points, which was the medium point meaning no change. However, the economic impact of the pandemic on the middle-income group was less severe than on the lower-income group. The differences in "cost of living" and "job and income" are statistically significant between low and middle-income groups. In fact, through our qualitative interviews, we came across many interviewees who remembered that they were positively impacted economically during the pandemic, as we show below. Another notable point from Table 2 is that middle and high-income respondents reported improvements in social capital-related matters such as relationships with family, at workplace and within the community. This point will be elaborated further in the section below on resilience and coping strategies where family relationship features significantly.

The COVID-19 pandemic affected a wide-range of sectors, but there was also difference among sectors. One advantage for middle-class persons during the COVID-19 pandemic was that many of them could work from home or switch to online work, due to the nature of their profession, which allowed them to save on commuting costs like the cost of petrol. Moreover, shift to "work from home" gave some people freedom to manage their time, and they could do extra income-earning activities, or so-called "side-jobs" as shown in the following testimony.

> Honestly, COVID benefited me economically. […] Because remember, I worked from home. I was able to earn income from home and also had a monthly salary from [my employer]. I was also able to work for [another company] for three months, during the work from home thing. So, I was able to do three jobs, and I had two employees from home here to assist me. I had more time on my hands. After COVID, I felt like returning to the office was a loss for me. (*Male in the 40s, Pretoria, December 2, 2023; he was a full-time employee in university sector in 2020.*[7])

[7] The age and the place of residence of respondents and participants are correct at the time of online survey and interviews, while their professions are as of 2020. We have added information on professions only for participants in the qualitative interviews.

Some other participants of our qualitative interviews were similarly able to earn extra income during the "work from home" time of the pandemic, by utilising skillsets acquired through their education and professional training.

Even though middle-income households were relatively spared of negative economic impacts from the pandemic, they reported other hardships like emotional and psychological impacts of isolation and loneliness during the pandemic and "losing loved ones and not being able to mourn them properly." Uncertainty and fear of the unknown prevailed, and people felt various constraints in their lives, evidenced in the frequent use of the phrase "not being able to …" in the free description part of the online survey. These restrictions on people's lives were caused not only by the COVID-19 pandemic, but also by the government policy to contain it.

5.2 *The Evaluation of the Government Policy during the Pandemic*

The South African government's responses to the COVID-19 pandemic were rigorous in two senses. On the one hand, the government introduced strict and wide-ranging restrictions on people's movements and activities in order to prevent the spread of the disease. For more than two months from late March 2020, a nationwide lockdown was implemented, during which all workers deemed to be in non-essential jobs and industries were required to stay home.[8] People were allowed to go out only to do errands deemed to be essential, such as visiting clinics and hospitals, buying medicines and foods at pharmacies and supermarkets, withdrawing cash at banks and ATMs, and receiving social grants (South African Government News Agency 2020). Many economic activities came to a standstill. The police and the army patrolled in the streets, arresting those who did not adhere to the lockdown regulations (see Column 1, "Grassroots voices of COVID-19 and lockdown experiences from South Africa" after the current chapter). Lockdown regulations were somewhat relaxed from June 1, 2020, and people were allowed to go to work, although most of other restrictions such as the ones on gatherings were maintained. With easing lockdown, new restrictions including curfew were also introduced. The strict lockdown had devastating impacts on the South African economy. The GDP in the second quarter of 2020 (April to June) shrank by 16.4% and 2.2 million jobs were lost (Ramaphosa 2020b).

On the other hand, the South African government was exceptional among the African countries discussed in this book for introducing a series of socio-economic measures to ease the negative impacts of the pandemic and lockdown on people's livelihoods. In late April 2020, President Ramaphosa announced that the government budgeted ZAR500 billion for this purpose, amounting to 10% of GDP. These policy measures included debt relief and rescheduling, tax deferral and exemption

[8] Essential jobs and industries included those who worked in hospitals and clinics, police, pharmacies, banks, supermarkets, and on farms.

measures for small- and medium-scale enterprises, temporary unemployment benefits to workers from the Unemployment Insurance Fund (UIF), top-ups to the existing social grants such as pensions and child support grants, the introduction of a new grant for unemployed (so-called COVID-19 grant), and the distribution of food parcels (Ramaphosa 2020a).

Given that these government responses to the COVID-19 pandemic were important parts of people's lived experiences, we tried to find out how people evaluated the government's performance during that time. For this purpose, we asked the respondents how each policy/measure introduced by the government to contain the COVID-19 pandemic affected them by using a five-point Likert scale of one (negatively) to five (positively). The results are shown in Fig. 2. Since there was no significant difference of answers among different income groups, except for the alcohol and tobacco ban, Fig. 2 presents the result of the respondents as a whole. For those who can afford these items or vices, alcohol and tobacco were important to relieve their stresses, and therefore larger percentages of respondents in middle- and high-income groups reported negative impacts of this measure.

Of the 11 policies/measures as shown in Fig. 2, those producing the most negative effects were "unable to mourn death properly" (64.2% said negative), "school closure" (57.7%), "hard lockdown" (56.8%), and "lockdown levels one to four" (54.1%). However, 38.5% of respondents said "lockdown levels one to four" affected them positively. Similarly, 30.7% of respondents said that "hard lockdown" affected them positively. Thus, our survey shows that while respondents were highly critical of specific lockdown regulations, most notably restrictions on funerals and school closure, their assessments of the central element of the South African government's prevention policy, i.e., lockdown, differed, depending on personal circumstances. On the other hand, positive responses outnumbered negative ones only for "vaccination," even though only 38.9% said it affected them positively. Thus, overall,

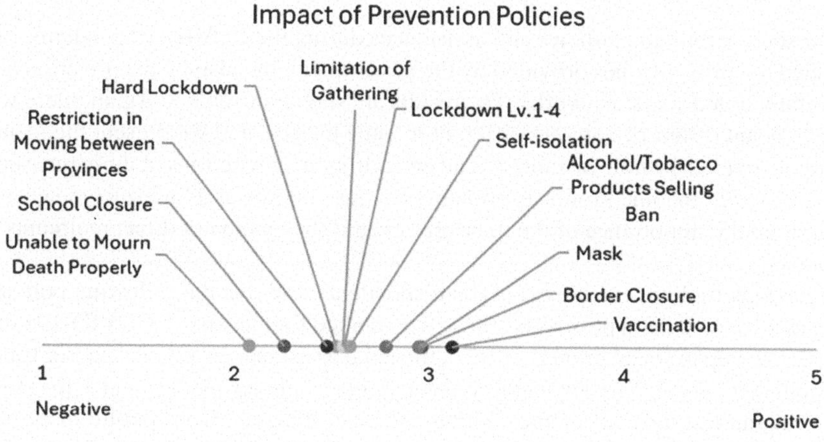

Fig. 2 Impact of government prevention policies (*Source* Online survey 2023)

respondents' lives were made more difficult or inconvenienced by the government's strict prevention polices/measures during the pandemic.

On the effectiveness of the government's prevention policies/measures, more than half of the respondents (52.8%) answered that they were effective, which more than doubled those who said that they were not effective (24.6%). This implies that the South African government has the capacity to implement its policy, as long as it has a will to do so, which is also probably to some extent unique among the African countries discussed in this book. Nevertheless, some participants in the qualitative interviews voiced criticisms on the specific aspects of the government's prevention policies/measures. In particular, several female participants questioned the merit of school closure for children in poorer communities.

> Children losing meals at school [due to school closure] was disastrous. More than 10 million South Africans suddenly lost access to their only source of food for the days that they could count on. That was absolutely disastrous. [...] Government should have had feeding schemes in place rather than closing schools and denying children their one meal of the day. (*Female in the 40s, Pretoria, December 1, 2023; she was a full-time employee in university sector in 2020.*)

Another participant raised the issue of loopholes in the implementation of policies and reminded us of the corruption scandal which must have affected people's assessments of the government's performance during the pandemic.

> I understood the lockdown, but I didn't understand the [ban on the] sale of cigarettes, but then they allowed the black market for cigarettes to thrive. I understood also no alcohol, but not [the ban on] selling in stores, but later on they relaxed that, where you could buy from store, but you can only consume at home. That made more sense. And each time they did explain the reasoning behind each decision that was made, [...but] it wasn't enforced correctly anymore in my opinion. [...] And it didn't help that at the time, our Health Minister, which everybody came to trust in the beginning of COVID, was then implicated in a scandal, which then just destroyed all credibility. (*Male in the 40s, Japan, December 20, 2023; he was between jobs in 2020.*)

For socio-economic policies and assistances during the COVID-19 pandemic, we included not only the ones provided by the government, but also by the private sector and relatives and social networks. The results are shown in Table 3. Again, there was no significant difference among different income groups, and we present the results of respondents as a whole in Table 3. The uniformity in perceptions of these measures across different income groups is probably because middle and high-income groups understood the importance of the measures even if they were not direct recipients of assistance.

Relatively higher percentages of the respondents said that the following policies/measures affected them positively (those who ranked four and five): COVID-19 grant (42.3%); top up to social grants (41.9%); financial assistance by relative and/or friend in South Africa (41.8%); financial assistance by employer (41%), and UIF-TERS (40.4%). Interestingly all of these items are cash transfers from public or private sources. On the other hand, half of participants (48–52% depending on items) chose

Table 3 Impact of socio-economic assistance

Governmental supports							
	Food parcels		Social grants		UIF-TERS	Tax relief for SMMEs	Prohibition of eviction from home
	National and provincial governments	Local government	COVID-19	Top up			
Mean	3.21	3.20	3.46	3.51	3.47	3.43	3.38
Standard deviation	1.22	1.16	1.25	1.17	1.14	1.13	1.17

Supports from private and non-profit sectors						
	Food parcels	Rebates for payment	Stokvel/ saving club	Financial assistance from		
				Employer	Relative or friend in South Africa	Relative or friend abroad
Mean	3.33	3.30	3.24	3.44	3.36	3.24
Standard deviation	1.12	1.21	1.15	1.22	1.26	1.17

Source Online survey 2023
Note UIF-TERS refers to UIF—Temporary Employer/Employee Relief Scheme

the middle point which means "not affected" or "neither positively nor negatively affected" for all the food parcels regardless of the distribution entities.[9]

In all policies/measures, the respondents who said "positively affected" outnumbered those who said negative, but close to one in five respondents answered negatively for the following three items: financial assistance by relative and/or friend in South Africa; food parcels by national and provincial governments; and food parcels by local government. Our interpretation is that this result probably reflects the higher risk perception of "service delivery" failure or governmental corruption as mentioned in the quote above, and that some respondents were on the giving side of assistance to family members and relatives, rather than the receiving side, given that more than half of the respondents were full-time employees and the majority (three-fourths of them) were middle to high-income earners. We will explore the issue of middle class as a provider of assistance in the next section.

In terms of the effectiveness of socio-economic policies and assistance, less than half (46.9%) of respondents said that government socio-economic policies were effective, while 30% said that they were not effective. On the other hand, 57.9% of respondents said that supports provided by civil society, religious, and other organisations were effective, while 23.5% said they were ineffective. Thus, it seems that the non-government sector played an important role to mitigate negative socio-economic impacts on people's lives caused by the COVID-19 pandemic. Nonetheless, while "family" was most frequently mentioned as a source of support to survive during the

[9] In addition to food parcels, the following four items also scored similarly: tax relief for SMMEs; prohibition of eviction from home; stokvel/saving club; and financial assistance by relative and/or friends who live abroad.

pandemic, a considerable number of respondents referred to the role of "government policies" of both prevention and economic assistance that helped them.

> Family support and government interventions [helped me most to live through the COVID-19 pandemic period]. The vaccines helped a lot, and also the lockdown levels helped to save us as a country. More people could have died and the pandemic would have been worse without government interventions and family being careful. (*Female in the 20s, middle-income group, Cape Town, July-August 2023*)

We can only conclude that the respondents' evaluation of government policies during the COVID-19 pandemic was mixed.

5.3 Resilience and Mitigation Strategies

As discussed in Chapter 1, one of the purposes of this book is to compare the "practical wisdom" applied in local contexts as part of people's resilience in different African countries during the pandemic. It also aims to investigate people's strategies to mitigate the fallouts from the pandemic. This chapter looks at the South African middle-class persons' resilience and coping strategies from three different angles during the pandemic. First, we discuss coping strategies adopted by middle-class persons in order to mitigate negative impacts on their lives during the pandemic. Second, we investigate the sources of resilience for middle class, who were largely excluded from the governmental supports. Third, we explore middle class as a provider of resilience, highlighting their social roles and positions in wider South African society.

For the coping strategy, we listed six possible actions people might have resorted in order to mitigate the negative economic impacts of the COVID-19 pandemic and asked the respondents to what extent they have activated these options, by using a five-point Likert scale of one ("not doing") to five ("more than usual"). Six options were: using or depleting household savings; selling off assets; reliance on family support; borrowing money more than s/he can pay back on time; changing the spending priority; and changing occupation. Of these, most used strategy regardless of income level was "changing the spending priority" (60.2%), followed by "using or depleting household savings" (44.5%), "borrowing money more than s/he can pay back on time" (33.1%), and "reliance on family support" (32%). On the other hand, more than half of the respondents said that they refrained from "selling off assets" (53.6%) or "borrowing money more than s/he can pay back on time" (50.6%) more than usual. This implies that they tried to keep what they already have and were worried that they might end up losing their assets if they had borrowed money at that time.

There were some notable differences among different income groups in terms of their coping strategies, as shown in Fig. 3. While using household savings and changing spending priorities are popular ways to overcome difficulties regardless of the income group, reliance on family support shows different tendencies among different income groups. About three-fourths of lower-income groups were supported by relatives more than or as usual during the pandemic. However, about a quarter of

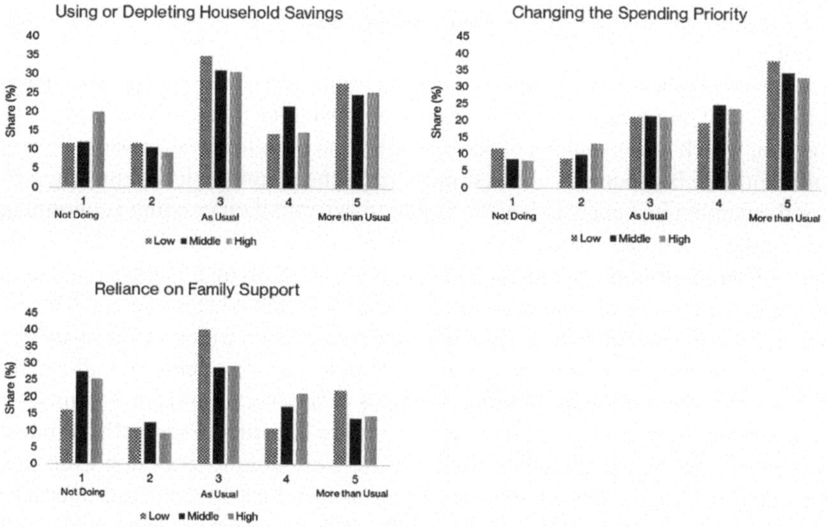

Fig. 3 Coping strategies of different income groups (*Source* Online survey 2023)

middle- and high-income respondents answered that they "did not" gain any support from families. Interestingly, the percentage of middle-income respondents who did not rely on additional family support exceeded that of high-income respondents. It suggests that middle-income respondents had to overcome difficulties on their own account, even in comparison with their higher-income counterparts.

In order to explore wider coping strategies adopted by the respondents, our quantitative survey also asked this question in an open-ended format. While it is difficult to quantify the opinions given in free description style, as many respondents mentioned more than one strategy, careful readings of their answers give us a picture that not only economic, but also social and emotional supports were important for people to survive the pandemic period. In replying to the question of "what has helped you most during the pandemic?", the most frequently mentioned word was "family." Typical examples include: "family, especially my children and wife"; "staying indoors with family, spending lots of time together"; "family has united, we have learned to help each other and support each other."

Another observation is that many respondents mentioned of technology (IT) and entertainment like "internet," "studying online," "social media," "video call" and "Netflix." This was probably because the respondents were relatively young, working people who were able to afford such things. A large number of respondents acknowledged of the specific government policies/measures introduced during the COVID-19 pandemic. Others mentioned of own financial resources and economic stability like "savings" and "working from home." While such phrases as one may find in contemporary self-help books like "staying positive," "keeping healthy and exercising," and "watching motivational speakers" also appeared a lot, others mentioned of more traditional sources of emotional supports such as "prayer," "faith in God" and "religion."

The difference between the middle-income group and the lower-income group in the activation of their economic coping strategies brings us to the second aspect of our discussion, which is the sources of resilience for the middle-class persons. We argue that the middle-class persons showed more resilience than the lower-income group during the pandemic, because they were able to activate their existing economic and social capital when they faced the unprecedented crisis like the COVID-19. Their sources of strength come from the combination of their own acquired skills and positions in the society, arising from their relatively higher educational qualifications which give them better chances to find a formal occupation, which in turn usually can have fringe benefits including "working from home" arrangements and allows them to gain access to institutional supports. As discussed above, several participants in our qualitative interviews categorically stated that they benefited financially or boosted their incomes during the pandemic time. Some were able to grab opportunities to find a side job, usually some kind of contract or task-based jobs using internet, by making most of the newly acquired relative flexibility of working from home, rather than working in the office. Others mentioned that working from home arrangements allowed them to save the commuting costs.

While the middle-class persons were more resilient than lower-income households thanks to their economic situation and social networks, their wealth is not confined to themselves and we cannot ignore their roles as providers of resilience in the South African society as a whole. We see this aspect of middle-class resilience on two levels. On the personal, individual levels, many contemporary middle-class persons, especially the ones who belong to so-called "historically disadvantaged groups," are the first generation in their families who were able to enjoy middle-class lifestyles. Their successes in acquiring professional jobs and career development were based on their own personal drive for education and for betterment. Some of our interview participants, especially those in the middle age of 40 s and 50 s, were government employees, who were able to get promotions by completing additional studies through correspondence after they joined the government sector. The University of South Africa (UNISA), which is the largest tertiary educational institution in Africa specialising in long-distance education, catered for these demands for personal and career developments.

These first-generation middle-class persons often spoke about so-called "black tax" during the interviews. Often the only person in the family who climbed the socio-economic ladder through education and hard work, they feel or they are made to feel that they have obligations to financially support their parents and/or their siblings who are not as successful as they are. However, not everybody embraces this term. Some people are critical of using the word "tax," because of its negative connotations, and argue that it should be understood in a cultural norm of "ubuntu" which means humanity (Mhlongo 2019). One participant explains her situation and opinion about it as follows.

> The actual word, to call it black tax, I do not think it is the right word. However, many of us do feel that obligation to support our families and give back to them. For example, I went to a private school. And, you know, even when they were struggling at home, I remember my sister said something to me: "You better do something with your life because they are taking all the money and paying your school fees." There is that expectation that when you become something, you have to support. (*Female in the 30s, Japan, December 4, 2023; she was an employee in non-profit sector in 2020.*)

Whether out of a sense of obligation or of love and mutual help, many of our interview participants provided extra support to their family members during the pandemic.

> The biggest hardship is not about me but my siblings because it will affect you indirectly. Some of my siblings lost their income because they are also entrepreneurs. They lost their incomes, and also some of them were critically ill. But fortunately, they did not die. So it was very difficult because when your siblings are not working, you have to provide for them. Because you cannot eat when your brother is not eating. […] Even today, even now, because I know my siblings are not working, I have to assist them in a way. It just comes naturally. (*Female in the 50s, Pretoria, December 14, 2023; she was an employee in government sector in 2020.*)

The moral economy of affection is not limited to the black communities in South Africa. One white participant spoke of continuing financial assistance to his former domestic worker after he had to force her retirement due to her old age. He called his action arising from a "white guilt."

> [My housekeeper] turned 70 and I had to let her go. […] Well, during COVID as well, I was sending her money, and I sent her into retirement December a year ago. So, 14 months ago. And I've had to pay for her the whole of last year. So, she's not working for me, but I'm still paying her. […] because I know that she can't survive without getting help from me because what she's getting from the government is not enough. But she also has family members that should be working. And they aren't. […] there's this terminology that we have here, white guilt, that I don't know if white guilt is appropriate or if it's just having a heart. […] I feel that I was somehow responsible for her. (*Male in the 40s, Cape Town, January 19, 2024; he was self-employed in 2020.*)

He was not the only white participant who provided extra assistance or something like a "private pension" to their former domestic employees. We observe that this kind of continued assistance after the end of formal employment relations usually takes place between domestic workers and their former employers. There is something unique or special about domestic work, due to the nature of their jobs which bring unusual levels of intimacy between employers and employees.

Another contribution that middle-class persons make to the South African society is as taxpayers. As of the financial year 2021/22, main sources of tax revenue in South Africa were Personal Income Tax (35.5%), Value-added Tax (25%) and Corporate Income Tax (20.7%) (National Treasury and SARS, 2023, 8). Thus, personal income tax is the main contributor of tax revenue. Since only those who earn more than certain thresholds are liable to pay tax,[10] middle-class and higher-income earners are

[10] This is R95,750 per year if one is working age (younger than 65 years) for the tax year 2024 (March 2023 to February 2024) and 2025 (March 2024 to February 2025). This roughly translates

main contributors of tax revenues in South Africa. The South African government under the African National Congress (ANC) boasts of "pro-poor policies," which is reflected in the fact that 28 million people—45% of total population—received social grants in 2023 (Patel and Sadie 2024). This sort of policies cannot be maintained without a certain level of consensus among tax-paying citizens about their obligations to the wider society, beyond their immediate circumstances. One of our qualitative interview participants articulated her role in the South African society as paying tax. Many interview participants emphasised that the government is for poor people. This statement brings us to the final point of our analysis, which is middle-class persons' views on the role of the government in South Africa.

5.4 *Views on the Role of Government*

We start with the fact that respondents in our survey showed generally low level of trust in all levels of the government. Of the five-point Likert scale of one (no trust) to five (trust very much), 55% of respondents chose one and two as their answers for national government, 54.8% for provincial government and 58.8% for local government. There was no statistically significant difference between lower-income group and middle-income group in terms of the level of trust in any of these three levels of the government. However, there was statistically significant difference between Cape Town residents and Johannesburg residents. The former's trust level was lower for national government and it was higher for provincial government. This could be reflection of the fact that the Western Cape province where Cape Town is situated was governed by a different party from the national government at the time of the survey. However, we also need to add that there was no statistically significant difference in the trust for local government between Cape Town residents and Johannesburg residents. Most of the qualitative interview participants, who self-identified as middle class, also did not differentiate their levels of trust for different levels of the government. While some of them said that their ward councillors were approachable and willing to help them to solve problems in their neighbourhoods, they also added that their ward councillors alone could not change the ineffectiveness of local government.

The research participants' deep scepticism of the government arises from their beliefs that there is widespread corruption in the South African government.

> I never tried to apply for a grant or financing from the government. [...] because, in our mind, we know that there is just so much corruption, you know, that someone will get it. Someone that is a relative of this/that politician or so. There's just so much nepotism, and I want to stay far away from the government. (*Male in the 40s, Pretoria, December 2, 2023; he was an employee in university sector in 2020.*)

into R8,000 per month. The thresholds are higher if one is over 65 years old. https://www.sars.gov.za/types-of-tax/personal-income-tax/ (Accessed August 6, 2024).

The view that corruption is a widespread problem in South Africa was not limited to those who worked in the private or non-profit sectors, and even our interviewees who worked for the government admitted that corruption is a widespread problem. Nonetheless, our interviewees who worked in the government sector tended to differentiate between the policy and the people who implement it, and blamed the latter for not realising the intended outcome of the policy due to the greed and desire for self-enrichment.

> We know very well what we must do as a government. That is why we have developed these excellent policies. But when it comes to implementation, it is a problem. Sometimes, I will say maybe it is a problem because the government is deeply involved in the administration. I mean, for politicians to be really involved in government administration. [...] Some politicians, they come with good intentions and they really improve. But others do not come with good intentions. They come with their own intentions. [...] They are just stealing, you know, if you are given a R100, you take the R90. It is a lot of money, and you leave the people with R10. (*Female in the 50s, Pretoria, December 14, 2023; she was an employee in government sector in 2020.*)

Faced with corrupt, ineffective governments, many of our interviewees resorted to private solutions to solve the problems arising from such situations as service delivery failures. Some installed solar panels on the roof and water tanks in order to cope with the prolonged load-shedding and to prepare for water-shedding that might happen next. Other private solutions available to them include medical aid and private security which can protect or mitigate them from health- and personal safety-related risks. Some contemplated going abroad to look for opportunities and better lives. Others mentioned of fixing potholes collectively as residents on public roads in their neighbourhoods. These private solutions are seen across racial boundaries among middle-class populations. Given that middle-class persons are the backbone of the South African society as the providers of resilience which is important to increase social cohesion and stability of society, and ultimately to realise the "rainbow nation dream" advocated by Nelson Mandela and embraced by general South Africans since the end of apartheid, their retreat into private solutions is not something to be celebrated.

6 Conclusion

While there is substantial research on the experiences of vulnerable populations in South Africa during the COVID-19 pandemic, studies focusing on the middle class are sparse. This study aimed, firstly, to develop an understanding of the practical wisdom and coping strategies employed by middle-class South Africans during the pandemic, and secondly, to explore the relationship between risk perceptions and their evaluation of the government's performance. Through a quantitative online survey and qualitative semi-structured interviews, this study has highlighted the grassroots voices of the South African middle class, contributing to a richer understanding of their experiences during the COVID-19 pandemic.

The findings of this study can be summarised in three main points: middle-class experiences and risk perceptions; their evaluation of government policies; and their coping strategies or practical wisdom.

First, the adverse effects of the COVID-19 pandemic were comparatively less for middle-class persons, thanks to their relative economic stability and skillsets. The quantitative data showed that the pandemic caused greater economic harm to poorer citizens, while middle- and higher-income groups were relatively less affected. Perhaps this is reflected in their risk perceptions after the pandemic. While both middle-income and poor income groups recognised the potential threats of harmful events at almost the same level, the likelihood of them occurring perceived to be less for middle-income group. However, this does not imply that the middle-class persons were unscathed by the pandemic. Social and emotional impacts of the pandemic and the government restrictions, such as those on funerals and alcohol and tobacco bans, caused significant stress across all income levels. Thus, while economically better off, the middle class still faced considerable challenges during the COVID-19 pandemic.

Second, the middle-class persons' evaluations of the government's responses to the pandemic were mixed. Despite the hardships imposed by restrictions on the movements and their daily lives, many respondents in the quantitative survey believed that the restrictions imposed by the government were necessary and effective. They acknowledged the government's efforts during a difficult time, with some stating that the situation could have been worse without these restrictions. The opinions expressed during the qualitative interviews contained more critical assessments of the certain aspects of government policies such as school closure and tobacco bans, but this did not necessarily mean that they were against the lockdown per se. The middle-class persons also expressed support for the socio-economic relief measures aimed at poorer citizens, even though they themselves were not direct beneficiaries.

Third, the study revealed two aspects of middle-class persons' resilience during the pandemic. On the one hand, the middle class demonstrated self-reliance. As they were not the main beneficiaries of the supports provided by the government, they had to rely on their own efforts to cope. Their relatively stable employment allowed them to maintain their income. In addition, they could do extra activities in their home to gain more income or relieve stress. The pandemic forced people to work from home and provided some extra time for those who could switch to work from home. Thanks to their skills and internet access, some middle-class persons could continue to work or conduct business. It not only mitigated stress but also provided more income.

On the other hand, middle-class persons played a crucial role as supporters and providers, both personally and financially, for poorer citizens. Even before the pandemic, many had supported poorer members of their family, especially parents, siblings, and relatives. Participants in the study often felt a responsibility to help the poor, driven by such norm as ubuntu or, in the cases between different population groups, a sense of white guilt or just a compassion. This support, alongside the government's pro-poor policies, helped alleviate the challenges faced by poorer citizens in pre-, during, and post-pandemic. As taxpayers, middle-class participants also expressed strong support for redistributive policies.

This study shows that the middle class is the key for South African society. They are not only a self-sufficient actor, but also providers of support and resilience to poor citizens. From another view, it also means that middle-class citizens compensate for the governmental shortcomings or failures. Indeed, middle-class participants show dissatisfaction towards the government as far as corruption and maladministration are concerned. As members of the middle class, they know that they can opt for private solutions to mitigate the impact of government inefficiency. But they are also aware that their poorer counterparts in the society do not have such option.

7 Column 1

Grassroots voices of COVID-19 and lockdown experiences from South Africa

1. Losing Loved Ones and Unable to Mourn Properly

I lost my family member during lockdown. I had to travel back home, which was very difficult to [do], mov[ing] from one province to another. I had to request [a] permit, which was also a draining drill as I was supposed to have the death certificate before apply[ing] for the permit. I had to arrange for the funeral whilst busy with the permit issues. (Female in her 20s, middle-income group, Cape Town, Online survey respondent in July-August 2023)

I lost my brother, ah, relative, during COVID, and [with] me based in Johannesburg, I could not even travel to attend [his] burial ceremony. He was asthmatic, so we knew COVID was somewhat more associated with such diseases. In African culture, I attend every burial that happens in my family, [it] doesn't matter who. During that time, I could not. I think that was one of the [greatest] hardships that I faced during COVID. (Male in his 30s, Johannesburg, Interviewed December 9, 2023; he was an employee of private company in 2020.)

I think the major thing was the loss of life because we lost quite a lot of family members in my extended family in Durban. Also, colleagues, former colleagues, and relatives of colleagues, we lost quite a lot [of them]. There was a lot of emotional strife. […] And then the additional pain of not burying the family members who died. You know, for us, in African culture, when a person has died, it's a big thing. You want to attend the funeral and prepare for it to get there and all of those things. During the pandemic, the number of people could attend funerals was restricted and limited. So, we could not bury most of the family members who died around the COVID time. That puts another strain emotionally. Sometimes people say you have some sort of closure when you attend a funeral. But when you don't attend the funeral, it kind of feels like it takes longer to heal. (Female in her 40s, Pretoria, Interviewed December 14, 2023; she was an employee in university sector in 2020.)

2. Isolation and Emotional Challenges

It was six months after I moved from Limpopo to the Western Cape and I had not yet settled in, so the lockdown was really hard because I did not even have friends here. Yes, we could not move and visit friends, but not having any familiar face[s around] was hard. (Female in her 30s, middle-income group, Cape Town, Online survey respondent in July-August 2023)

I have lived alone for so long; I am used to being alone. But it was a different kind of being alone when you were not allowed to leave the house. The emotional aspect was difficult because I was suddenly not alone by choice, but I was forced to be alone. (Female in her 30s, Japan, Interviewed December 4, 2023; she was an employee in non-profit sector in 2020.)

I was by myself, which means I was very isolated. Initially, I enjoyed being by myself. I don't mind being by myself. I'd been single for a long time until then, and I was comfortable in my own company. But after a while, it became very pressured because the day[s were] very long. And I think, as you know, we weren't allowed to go out, even to walk a dog. It was very strict here, and they really enforced it. I sometimes snuck out with the dog to just go walk around the block, and the police stopped me, and they sent me back home. Initially, it was good. I was exercising a lot. I was working out. I was very healthy, and I was very fit. But after a while, it got quite depressing. (Male in his 40s, Cape Town, Interviewed January 19, 2024; he was self-employed in 2020.)

3. Lockdown Restrictions and Police Presence in a Township

South Africa is just too much, so I was staying in Umlazi, which is a township, the lockdown was just too much. There were soldiers on the streets. There were casualties; when they tried to control people, people died. [...] Clashes with the army. It was unnecessarily hard, they brought the army, everything was just shut. Also, the black market became a big thing, accessing things through the black market. In townships the black market was thriving. [Author: For alcohol and cigarettes?] Exactly, yes alcohol and cigarettes. [....] there was time when curfew was six o'clock. The army was not in the picture anymore, it was the police. I was stopped by the police. You know you can't stay indoors all day. Six in the evening, they asked me where [I was] going, all of these things. Also, we have this picture. You know townships are busy places, this police van came during their surveillance. People were running everywhere. That kind of picture is very "Apartheid days" when black people were running from the police. It was traumatising in that way. (Male in his 30s, Stellenbosch, Interviewed December 7, 2023; he was unemployed in 2020.)

4. Coping Strategies

It was being with my partner or husband and [I] cannot imagine how it was for people who were alone. Also, the church kept me going with [its] online service. (Female in her 30s, middle-income group, Johannesburg, Online survey respondent in July-August 2023)

I remember that at first, with my husband, we started to [get] a little bit depressed, because work and everything was done at home. We could not do the normal activities that we usually do on the weekends. There was also that worry about our family. But then we adopted a sort of challenge to make the lockdown more fun and started challenging ourselves. There was "Grow with Jo", an exercise and personal trainer on YouTube. We used to take her classes constantly just to make things fun. I could say, at first, it was very worrisome, but we managed to adapt by just bringing in things that would help us to be distracted and not focus on all the news, the deaths, the infections, hot spots and lockdown restrictions, you know, we just found ways to try and adapt. (Female in her 30s, Johannesburg, Interviewed December 13, 2023; she was a government employee in 2020.)

I think what really helped during COVID time, number one, you ha[d] a good support structure. So, you have your family. Number two, we had everything we needed. When I say that, I mean like food, the necessities we had. And then the third thing is, […] I did some volunteer work for an NGO where I was helping with marketing. I still assist with marketing from time to time. There were students that studied in Japan and that went back to Africa and were all affected by COVID-19. It's called Kakehashi Africa. So, we did a lot of educational seminars that we hosted once every month. So, I helped with the facilitation of that. So that was done for more than six months, those seminars. And then in between then, because we had a private gym that I used to go to. So, I used to train as well. (Male in his 40s, Japan, Interviewed December 20, 2023; he was between jobs in 2020.)

My husband and I get along very well, so it was nice to have that time together. We usually don't see each other much. It was fine for us. You get concerns about parents getting COVID, but it was generally positive. We kept exercising, staying healthy, we put the time to good use. It was frustrating not to see family initially during hard lockdown. That was frustrating. Once the hard lockdown was over, we arranged to go out and do walks together and do outside things together. (Female in her 40s, Johannesburg, Interviewed December 5, 2023; she was self-employed in 2020.)

Acknowledgements The authors are grateful to the online survey respondents as well as the semi-structured interview participants for their participation in this study. Financial assistance from the Hitachi Foundation enabled us to conduct both quantitative and qualitative data collection, as well as to organise two workshops in Stellenbosch and Chiba where we discussed the ideas for this chapter. The earlier versions of this chapter were presented at two annual conferences of the Japan Society for Afrasian Studies (JSAS) in 2023 and 2024, and at the 6th South Africa-Japan University Forum (SAJU6) in Stellenbosch in August 2024. We thank participants of these events for their comments and feedback. We also acknowledge all the hard work of three research assistants from Stellenbosch University who transcribed the semi-structured qualitative interviews. This study has been approved by the Research Ethics Committee at Stellenbosch University (Project ID: 29478).

References

Baumgardt, L., & Robins, S. (2023). Slow crises: South Africa's governmental responses to COVID-19 in times of 'crisis within crisis'. In P. Fourie, & G. Lamb (Eds.), *The South African response to COVID-19* (pp.74–94). Routledge. https://doi.org/10.4324/9781003294931-5

Bhorat, H., Oosthuizen, M., & Stanwix, B. (2021). Social assistance amidst the COVID-19 epidemic in South Africa: A policy assessment. *South African Journal of Economics, 89*(1), 63–81. https://doi.org/10.1111/saje.12277

Biggs, R., Pringle, C., Sitas, N., Clements, H., Dube, B., Hamann, M., Malherbe, W., Manyani, A., Preiser, R., Selomane, O., & Waddell, J. (2021). *Resilience: Fostering capacity to navigate shocks, change and uncertainty*. CST Policy Brief. http://www0.sun.ac.za/cst/wpcontent/uploads/2021/11/CST-Resilience_digital-1.pdf

Burger, R., Steenekamp, C.L., Van den Bergh, S., & Zoch, A. (2015). The emergent middle class in contemporary South Africa: Examining and comparing rival approaches, *Development Southern Africa, 32*(1), 25–40. https://doi.org/10.1080/0376835X.2014.975336

Chitiga-Mabugu, M., Henseler, M., Mabugu, R., & Maisonnave, H. (2021). Economic and distributional impact of COVID-19: Evidence from macro-micro modelling of the South African economy. *South African Journal of Economics, 89*(1), 82–94. https://doi.org/10.1111/saje.12275

Closson, K., Zharima, C., Kuchena, T. M., Dietrich, J. J., Ogilvie, G., Raj, A., Beksinska, M., & Kaida, A. (2024). Relationship impacts of the COVID-19 pandemic and lockdown restrictions on young women and men in Durban and Soweto, South Africa. *Culture, Health and Sexuality, 26*(6), 734–746. https://doi.org/10.1080/13691058.2023.2243300

Coetzee, B. J., Gericke, H., Human, S., Stallard, P., & Loades, M. (2022). How young people experienced COVID-19 disease containment measures in the Western Cape, South Africa: A qualitative study including the perspectives of young people, their parents, teachers and school counsellors. *Psychology and Psychotherapy: Theory, Research and Practice, 95*(2), 383–401. https://doi.org/10.1111/papt.12374

Egan, P. (2021). The South African consumer landscape. In J. Lappeman, P. Egan, G. Rightford, & T. Ramogose (Eds.), *Marketing to South African consumers* (pp.69–85). UCT Liberty Institute. https://openbooks.uct.ac.za/uct/catalog/view/29/43/1401

Fourie, P., & Lamb, G. (2023). *The South African response to COVID-19: The early years*. Routledge. https://doi.org/10.4324/9781003294931

Friedman, S. (2021). *One virus two countries: What Covid-19 tells us about South Africa*. Wits University Press.

Gouws, A., & Ezeobi, O. (Eds.) (2021). *COVID diaries: Women's experience of the pandemic*. Imbali Academic Publishers.

Gronbach, L., & Seekings, J. (2021). Pandemic, lockdown and the stalled urbanization of welfare regimes in Southern Africa. *Global Social Policy, 21*(3), 448–467. https://doi.org/10.1177/14680181211013725

Holling, C. S. (1973). Resilience and stability of ecological systems. *Annual Review of Ecology and Systematics, 4*, 1–23.

Jacobs, S. (2023). 'We can manage this Corona disaster': Psycho-social experiences of a diverse suburban middle-class community in South Africa: Interview-based study. *Societies, 13*(4), 90. https://doi.org/10.3390/soc13040090

Jamieson, L., & Van Blerk, L. (2022). Responding to COVID-19 in South Africa–Social solidarity and social assistance. *Children's Geographies, 20*(4), 427–436.

Khambule, I. (2022). COVID-19 and the informal economy in a small-town in South Africa: Governance implications in the post-COVID era. *Cogent Social Sciences, 8*(1). https://doi.org/10.1080/23311886.2022.2078528

Khambule, I., & Mdlalose, M. (2022). COVID-19 the state coordinated responses in South Africa's emerging developmental state. *Development Studies Research, 9*(1), 192–205. https://doi.org/10.1080/21665095.2022.2098791

Khunou, G. (Ed.) (2016). *South Africa's emergent middle class*. Routledge.

Kotzè, H., & García-Rivero, C. (2018). The evolution of the middle class during nearly two decades of democracy in South Africa. *Politikon, 45*(3), 387–407. https://doi.org/10.1080/02589346.2018.1466846

Kriger, S., Walters, C., & Jansen, J. (2022). How COVID reconfigured family relationships: Explaining the work of academic women through the lens of complexity theory. *Perspectives in Education, 40*(3), 62–77. https://doi.org/10.18820/2519593X/pie.v40.i3.5

Lamb, G. (2023). Police legitimacy and the SAPS's policing of the COVID-19 pandemic. In P. Fourie, & G. Lamb (Eds.), *The South African response to COVID-19* (pp.136–155). Routledge.

Mangoma, A., & Wilson-Prangley, A. (2019). Black tax: Understanding the financial transfers of the emerging black middle class. *Development Southern Africa, 36*(4), 443–460. https://doi.org/10.1080/0376835X.2018.1516545

Mattes, R. (2015). South Africa's emerging black middle class: A harbinger of political change? *Journal of International Development, 27*(5), 665–692. https://doi.org/10.1002/jid.3100

May, J., & Mentz-Coetzee, M. (2021). Re-imagining resilient food systems in the post-COVID-19 era in Africa. *Sustainability, 13*(19), 1–13. https://doi.org/10.3390/su131910752

Mhlongo, N. (Ed.) (2019). *Black tax: Burden… or ubuntu?* Jonathan Ball Publishers.

Moses, E., & Woolard, I. (2023). The role of temporary social grants in mitigating the poverty impact of COVID-19 in South Africa. In P. Fourie, & G. Lamb (Eds.), *The South African response to COVID-19* (pp.156–177). Routledge. https://doi.org/10.4324/9781003294931-9

Musyoka, J. (2023). South Africa's black middle classes between 2009 and 2018. *Journal of Contemporary African Studies, 41*(1), 75–85. https://doi.org/10.1080/02589001.2022.2030466

National Treasury & South African Revenue Service (SARS). (2023). *Tax statistics 2022 highlights.* https://www.sars.gov.za/wp-content/uploads/Docs/TaxStats/2022/TStats-2022-Highlights-booklet-A5.pdf

Nnaeme, C., Patel, L., & Plagerson, S. (2022). Livelihood activities and well-being outcomes of cash transfer beneficiaries in Soweto, South Africa. *Development in Practice, 32*(1), 29–38. https://doi.org/10.1080/09614524.2021.1911950

Norris, F. H., Stevens, S. P., Pfefferbaum, B., Wyche, K. F., & Pfefferbaum, R. L. (2008). Community resilience as a metaphor, theory, set of capacities, and strategy for disaster readiness. *American Journal of Community Psychology, 41*(1–2), 127–150. https://doi.org/10.1007/s10464-007-9156-6

Norris, P., & Inglehart, R. (2019). *Cultural backlash.* Cambridge University Press.

Paredes Ruvalcaba, N., Kim, A. W., Ndaba, N., Cele, L., Swana, S., Bosire, E., & Moolla, A. (2023). Coping mechanisms during the COVID-19 pandemic and lockdown in metropolitan Johannesburg, South Africa: A qualitative study. *American Journal of Human Biology, 35*(12). https://doi.org/10.1002/ajhb.23958

Parker, W. (2023). The rough and the smooth: South Africa's uneven response to COVID-19. In P. Fourie, & G. Lamb (Eds.), *The South African response to COVID-19* (pp.39–55). Routledge. https://doi.org/10.4324/9781003294931-3

Parry, B. R., & Gordon, E. (2021). The shadow of pandemic: Inequitable gendered impacts of COVID-19 in South Africa. *Gender, Work & Organization, 28*(2), 795–806. https://doi.org/10.1111/gwao.12565

Patel, L., & Sadie Y. (2024, May 14). *Over 26 million South Africans get a social grant. Fear of losing the payment used to be a reason to vote for the ANC, but no longer—study.* The Conversation. https://theconversation.com/over-26-million-south-africans-get-a-social-grant-fear-of-losing-the-payment-used-to-be-a-reason-to-vote-for-the-anc-but-no-longer-study-229771

Posel, D., Oyenubi, A., & Kollamparambil, U. (2021, March 3). Job loss and mental health during the COVID-19 lockdown: Evidence from South Africa. *PLoS ONE, 16*(3). https://doi.org/10.1371/journal.pone.0249352

Putnam, R. (1993). *Making democracy work: Civic traditions in modern Italy.* Princeton University Press.

Ramaphosa, C. (2020a, April 21). *Statement by president Cyril Ramaphosa on further economic and social measures in response the Covid-19 epidemic Union Buildings, Tshwane.* Department of Science, Technology and Innovation, Republic of South Africa. https://www.dsti.gov.za/index.php/media-room/media-room-speeches/other/3054-statement-by-president-cyril-ramaphosa-on-further-economic-and-social-measures-in-response-the-covid-19-epidemic-union-buildings-tshwane-21-april-2020

Ramaphosa, C. (2020b, October 15). *Address by president Cyril Ramaphosa to the joint sitting of parliament on South Africa's economic reconstruction and recovery plan. South African Government.* https://www.gov.za/news/speeches/president-cyril-ramaphosa-south-africa%E2%80%99s-economic-reconstruction-and-recovery-plan-15

Rwafa-Ponela, T., Goldstein, S., Kruger, P., Erzse, A., Karim, S. A., & Hofman, K. (2022). Urban informal food traders: A rapid qualitative study of COVID-19 lockdown measures in South Africa. *Sustainability, 14*(4), 2294. https://doi.org/10.3390/su14042294

Schotte, S. (2017). *The anxious and the climbers: Ambivalent attitudes towards democracy among South Africa's middle class* [GIGA Working Papers 304]. Hamburg: German Institute of Global and Area Studies (GIGA). https://hdl.handle.net/10419/162812

Seekings, J. (2020). *Bold promises, constrained capacity, stumbling delivery: The expansion of social protection in response to the Covid-19 lockdown in South Africa* [Working Paper 456]. Centre for Social Science Research (CSSR), University of Cape Town. https://humanities.uct.ac.za/cssr/bold-promises-constrained-capacity-stumbling-deliverythe-expansion-social-protection-response-covid

South African Government News Agency. (2020, March 23). *President Ramaphosa announces a nationwide lockdown.* https://www.sanews.gov.za/south-africa/president-ramaphosa-announces-nationwide-lockdown

Southall, R. (2016). *The new black middle class in South Africa.* James Currey.

Struckmann, C. (2023). COVID-19 in South Africa: History, impact, and government response—An overview. In P. Fourie, & G. Lamb (Eds.), *The South African response to COVID-19* (pp.13–38). Routledge. https://doi.org/10.4324/9781003294931-2

Theron, L., Levine, D., & Ungar, M. (2021). Resilience to COVID-19-related stressors: Insights from emerging adults in a South African township. *PLoS One, 16*(12). https://doi.org/10.1371/journal.pone.0260613

Turok, I., & Visagie, J. (2022). The divergent pathways of the pandemic within South African cities. *Development Southern Africa, 39*(5), 738–761. https://doi.org/10.1080/0376835X.2022.2098089

Visagie, J., & Posel, D. (2013). A reconsideration of what and who is middle class in South Africa. *Development Southern Africa, 30*(2), 149–167. https://doi.org/10.1080/0376835X.2013.797224

Zizzamia, R., Schotte, S., Leibbrandt, M., & Vimal, R. (2016). *Vulnerability and the middle class in South Africa* [SALDRU Working Paper]. https://www.opensaldru.uct.ac.za/handle/11090/846

Chizuko Sato Professor at the Institute of Global Studies, Tokyo University of Foreign Studies, Japan. Her research focuses on land reform, rural development and cross-border migration in southern Africa. Her recent publications include Transnational Social Protection in Southern Africa: Labour Migration to South Africa from Mozambique and Malawi (edited volume, IDE-JETRO, 2024, in Japanese), and 'Land Tenure Reform in Three Former Settler Colonies in Southern Africa' in S. Takeuchi, ed., African Land Reform under Economic Liberalisation: States, Chiefs, and Rural Communities (Springer, 2022).

Scarlett Cornelissen Professor in the Department of Political Science at Stellenbosch University, South Africa, and director of Stellenbosch University Japan Centre. Her research centres on Africa's international relations and the political economy of Africa-Asia relations. Recent book publications include Migration and Agency in a Globalizing World: Afro-Asian Encounters (co-edited with Yoichi Mine) and The Routledge Handbook of Africa-Asia Relations (co-edited with Pedro Amakasu Raposo and David Arase). She is a current co-editor of Geopolitics and a former co-editor of Review of International Studies.

Tomohiro Hosoi Lecturer at the Global Initiative Center, Gunma University, Japan. He obtained a PhD in Advanced Social and International Studies from the University of Tokyo. He has studied South African politics, public administration in Africa and African international relations. His recent work includes 'METI and Japanese scramble: re-definition of Japan's African policy under the second Abe administration and future of African summit diplomacy' (The Pacific Review, 2024).

Chapter 4
Peasants Survive Again: Risk Perception and Implications for COVID-19 Resilience in Urban and Rural Areas of Zimbabwe

Rangarirai Gavin Muchetu and Walter Chambati

Abstract Risks related to agricultural production, market access, and public health measures have persisted in rural areas despite decades of development. This chapter examines differing perceptions of Zimbabwe's rural and urban populations regarding their COVID-19 experiences, focusing on how these views shaped responses to government containment measures. A questionnaire (N = 175) and Online Focus Group Discussions (N = 69) collected data from Harare (urban), Goromonzi (peri-urban), and Kwekwe (rural). Results show how lockdowns disrupted agricultural activities by limiting access to inputs/output markets, thereby increasing the vulnerability of rural populations to economic shocks. Containment measures also bred corruption as people bribed their way out of the restrictions. There was increased domestic violence, disrupted education, rising crime rates, and economic downturns. Pandemic resilience manifested as community solidarity and informal support networks (some online). Comparatively, urban populations were more adept at adopting digital solutions for work and education, while rural communities faced significant challenges due to limited access to technology and information, resulting in a clear digital divide. The chapter, therefore, advocates for community-centered strategies that recognize differences in the needs of rural and urban areas.

Keywords Lockdowns · Curfews · Downside risks · Market access · Perceived risks

R. G. Muchetu (✉)
College of Intercultural Communication, Rikkyo University, Toshima, Tokyo, Japan
e-mail: rgmuchetu@rikkyo.ac.jp

W. Chambati
College of Graduate Studies, University of South Africa, Pretoria, South Africa
e-mail: wsschambati@gmail.com

K. Hanai et al. (eds.), *Practical Wisdom and Resilience Overcoming Downside Risk*,
https://doi.org/10.1007/978-981-96-4455-1_4

1 Introduction

The COVID-19 pandemic significantly impacted rural farming communities worldwide, disrupting essential activities like crop and livestock production, petty trading, and labor exchange. These activities rely on the free movement of people, goods, and services, which were severely restricted during the pandemic. This amplified pre-existing rural challenges, directly affecting rural communities through health risks and indirectly via containment measures established by the government. The disruptions in Southern Africa were particularly severe, exacerbating unresolved rural, peasantry, land, financial, and agrarian questions (Mazwi et al. 2021). The impacts varied geographically and by social class across third-world nations. Countries such as Zimbabwe and Zambia, already facing high levels of food insecurity, experienced heightened vulnerabilities. In contrast, nations with more robust social support systems, like South Africa and Botswana, fared relatively better (Seko et al. 2023, p. 420).

This chapter examines the personal experiences of rural and urban populations during the pandemic, focusing on three key objectives. First, it presents authentic grassroots voices, reflecting people's fears and beliefs about COVID-19 during and after the pandemic. Second, it explores how perceptions influenced interactions with the virus and the effectiveness of government containment measures. Lastly, it investigates resilience mechanisms and how communities exercised agency against these measures. A mixed-methods approach was used, gathering data through a structured questionnaire ($N = 175$) and three online Focus Group Discussions (FGDs) ($N = 69$) via WhatsApp. These discussions highlighted the harsh realities communities face and underscored the varied impacts of global crises on different regions, demonstrating the need for nuanced responses that address specific vulnerabilities.

This chapter differentiates rural and urban socio-economic practices in the proceeding sections, highlighting their effect on risk perception. It identifies specific downside risks faced by agricultural communities and urbanites. The chapter then scrutinizes changes in livelihood options due to these risks, providing narratives as evidence. Next, strategies for fostering resilience are discussed. The comparative analysis explores both settings' differing impacts and adaptation strategies, offering insights and lessons learned. Finally, the paper summarizes findings, proposes implications for future pandemic preparedness, and makes recommendations for policymakers.

2 Overview of Livelihoods in Rural and Urban Areas

This chapter examines the implications of COVID-19 on rural and urban livelihood practices, focusing on how people perceived, experienced, and withstood the direct/indirect effects of the pandemic. Agriculture is discussed as a livelihood source akin to paid work for urban residents. Rural farmers play a vital role in the economy,

Industry	Agriculture
Continuous production: Uninterrupted processes facilitated by technology.	**Discontinuous production** ➔Driven by natural factors and seasonality.
Simultaneous process ➔ Processes can run in parallel or be synchronized.	**Sequential process**➔ One step follows the other due to natural growth cycles.
Flexible location ➔ Materials transported to centralized factories.	**Fixed location**➔ Bound to fields; workers and machines must move to production sites.
Adjustable Constraints➔ Relies on pre-processed raw materials.	**Biological Constraints**➔ Relies on nature, with uncertainties like weather and soil quality.
Durable products ➔ Can be stored and transported over long periods.	**Perishable products** ➔ Short shelf life, requires immediate use/sale.

Fig. 1 Production outcomes between the city and the rural areas. *Source* Adapted from Bernstein 2016, p. 172

providing employment, preserving culture, and maintaining indigenous knowledge (Mubangizi 2023, pp. 4–5). The bulk of the research for this book focuses on urban areas, which faced the brunt of the direct biophysical effects. However, this chapter provides the rural perspective as a comparison. How we define rural and urban areas influences governance and service delivery, impacting resource allocation. Urban areas are characterized by high population density, extensive infrastructure, and a mix of residential, commercial, and industrial functions. Despite increasing urbanization, rural populations still comprise about 60% of most African countries; for Zimbabwe, the figure is 67% (WB 2023). Rural areas are characterized by low population densities, poor infrastructure, and predominantly agriculture.

Agricultural activities range from commercial farming on private lands to subsistence farming on communal lands (see Moyo et al. 2015; Muchetu 2018, pp. 72–78). Nevertheless, these two localities are driven by different socio-economic motivations, significantly impacting how they have withstood crises such as the 2007/8 global financial crisis. In particular, the nature of production processes and outcomes puts urban and rural areas in sharp contrast, perhaps with each of these localities having advantages and disadvantages over each other (see Fig. 1). Although we do not focus on urban agriculture in this paper, it still exists and shapes COVID-19 perceptions and resilience mechanisms. Urban agriculture, which involves producing and distributing food within or near cities, primarily aims to provide food for personal consumption or generate income, especially for peri-urban farmers with more land (Baumgartner and Belevi 2001, pp. 2–6).

2.1 Conceptualizing Peasant Responses to Crises

It is crucial to discuss the notion that agricultural participants in rural areas are not homogenous but manifest through varying degrees of integration into the conduits of agricultural supply chains. The bulk of literature on Zimbabwean (and African) agrarian studies points to the persistence of small-scale producers, often emphasizing their peasant nature (Boltvinik 2016, pp. 57–59; Moyo 2016, pp. 9–12 & 23–24).

Moyo (2016, pp. 6–8), based on variables such as land ownership, market orientation, labor use, asset accumulation, and other things, differentiated farmers into three groups. First were better-off/capitalist/market-oriented family farms that employ more hired labor than family labor and sell larger quantities of produce to markets. Second, the middle/semi-subsistence family farms neither hire out nor sell labor and produce most of their food requirements while selling some produce to meet family needs. Lastly, the poor/near-landless family farms, which primarily sell labor to other farms and non-farm entities, often do not produce enough food to meet family requirements and, hence, fall below the poverty line. Mazwi et al. (2021, p. 11) estimated their numbers as 13.3%, 36.9%, and 49.8%, respectively—the middle and poor classes overwhelmingly outnumbered the capitalist farmers.

We must highlight these clusters because they affect how people view risk and respond to agrarian crises. Notably, a theory of peasant reactions to crises has been developed, derived from empirical data on how peasants have historically navigated the past five global financial crises (Van de Ploeg 2010, p. 1). There is a discernible pattern in which peasants tend to cope with crises by disengaging from markets and concentrating solely on subsistence production until the crisis subsides. Consequently, farmers who are deeply integrated into agricultural markets, maintaining strong farm-to-city linkages, are more susceptible to adverse impacts from such shocks due to their market dependency. In the context of Zimbabwe, these shocks would predominantly affect the better-off classes and the poorer/landless groups.

The central concept in this chapter is the theory of peasant poverty (Boltvinik 2016, p. 62), which serves as a framework for understanding the devastating effects of global market shocks on peasant livelihoods and the strategies through which they have historically built resilience. The theory underscores the dual impact of agricultural seasonality on peasant farming, illustrating a dynamic that both sustains peasant agriculture and perpetuates peasant poverty. This interplay is deeply embedded within capitalist agricultural systems, where seasonality leads to peaks in labor demand during sowing and harvest periods, with peasant producers providing essential labor during these critical times. Their willingness to work during peak periods is crucial for capitalist agriculture, which relies on this flexible, low-cost workforce. Without it, agricultural firms would struggle to find workers willing to perform labor-intensive tasks, threatening the viability of agricultural production. Moreover, peasant farming stabilizes capitalist systems by (i) ensuring continuous food production for their family, even during economic disruptions (farmers revert to auto-consumption), (ii) acting as a buffer (or subsidizing the markets through their labor) against market volatility (Chayanov 1991; Boltvinik 2016, pp. 54–55). This ensures their persistence.

However, the same seasonality that sustains peasant farming also perpetuates their poverty. Peasants earn wages only for the specific days they work, which fails to meet their broader economic needs and leads to irregular, insufficient incomes. Concentrated earnings during peak agricultural periods cause financial instability, forcing peasant families to seek alternative income sources during off-seasons. This instability makes it difficult for them to achieve economic security. Additionally, their dependence on seasonal agricultural cycles limits opportunities for economic diversification, trapping them in a cycle of poverty (Boltvinik 2016, pp. 79–81). Thus, agricultural seasonality functions as a double-edged sword. While it preserves peasant farming by supporting capitalist agriculture, it also entrenches poverty by undervaluing their contributions and keeping their incomes low. This interdependence perpetuates a system where peasants rely on selling seasonal labor, maintaining their agricultural production role, and ongoing economic insecurity.

These concepts informed our primary theoretical inquiry, elaborated in the introduction. We asked: Can the 2019–2023 COVID-19 curfews and lockdowns be conceptualized as a form of prolonged seasonality? To what extent did farmers revert to subsistence production (auto-consumption) during this period? How did they diversify their livelihoods without functional markets and reduced labor demand (resilience)? We analyzed these questions through a comparative perspective of urban and rural areas.

2.2 *Government of Zimbabwe Lockdowns: A Timeline*

Before discussing the risks in detail, it is essential to review the COVID-19 timeline. The first Zimbabwe case was recorded on March 20, 2020 in the tourist city of Victoria Falls, and the following day, two more confirmed cases were recorded in Harare, including that of Zororo Makamba. All the infected people were returning from traveling to the United Kingdom. Zororo Makamba was a media personality, journalist, and TV show host. He was also the son of a prominent broadcaster, businessman, politician, and philanthropist, James Makamba.

On March 23, Zororo Makamba passed away, becoming Zimbabwe's first recorded COVID-19 death and sending panic and fear across all Zimbabweans. His death changed people's perceptions and caused many citizens to feel threatened by COVID-19, leading to acceptance of its reality. Seven days later, President E.D. Mnangagwa announced a 21-day national lockdown to curb the further spread of the virus. Further lockdowns were extended in phases, with varying levels of restrictions. Early lockdowns included strict measures, while later phases allowed gradual reopening of businesses, with tighter restrictions reintroduced as cases spiked. By mid-2021, localized lockdowns were enforced, and the focus shifted toward vaccination, leading to eased restrictions. In 2022, the government began relaxing measures further, permitting most activities with ongoing emphasis on vaccination and social distancing (Verituszim, 2023). By March 2023, minimal restrictions were maintained, and in August 2023, all COVID-19 measures were lifted, marking the official end of the pandemic emergency. Appendix A.1 presents more details.

3 Downside Risks in Agriculture During COVID-19

Risk refers to the potential variability or uncertainty associated with agricultural production processes. This uncertainty is an intrinsic aspect of agriculture due to the unpredictable weather and the possibility of damage from diseases or pest infestations, which can significantly impact agricultural production. Such uncertainties become even more pressing in the context of climate change, which heightens the frequency and severity of adverse shocks like droughts, heat waves, and pest invasions, resulting in crop failures (Chavas 2019, pp. 1–2). Before the COVID-19 pandemic, farmers in both peri-urban and rural areas had to deal with these risks annually. Never had a direct threat to people's health as significant as COVID-19 existed because it came with numerous socio-economic "downside risks."

Farmers were accustomed to managing these risks through traditional methods, crop diversification, and other strategies to mitigate the effects of unpredictable events on their income and livelihoods. However, the onset of COVID-19 brought a direct threat to people's health, disrupting not only the physical ability of farmers to work but also the socio-economic environment they operated in. The perception of COVID-19 as a significant health threat exacerbated the existing downside risks in agriculture by introducing additional layers of uncertainty that affected farmers' resilience mechanisms. Overall, all respondents to our survey reported following some COVID-19 protocols at some point during the pandemic. However, the decision to strictly or occasionally adhere to protocols was affected by several variables, all elastic to perception. Respondents reported adhering to protocols mainly due to the fear of contracting the virus itself (94.9%, with 54% of them strictly adhering). However, there were no statistical differences.

Interestingly, knowing the COVID-19 symptoms—read as access to information—positively affected strict adherence (50.9% compared to 26.9%), which was statistically significant. The same was observed for those who believed that COVID-19 was a punishment from God. Of the people who viewed COVID-19 through the spiritual realm, the number of respondents who did not adhere strictly to protocols (27.4%) was more than double the number who did (12%) (see Table 1).

These measures disrupted supply chains, restricted access to grocery markets for the urbanites, and affected the availability of agricultural inputs like seeds and fertilizers, further heightening the vulnerability of farm households to income loss. Furthermore, the perception of COVID-19 as a high-risk event likely diverted attention and resources away from pre-existing agricultural risks. Farmers who might have otherwise invested in resilience mechanisms to cope with climate-induced shocks (like irrigation systems, pest-resistant crops, or storage facilities) instead prioritized immediate health safety measures and food requirements, reducing their capacity to handle agricultural uncertainties. Thus, the perceived severity of COVID-19 amplified the downside risks by creating additional barriers for farmers, not only through health directly but also by disrupting socio-economic systems crucial for maintaining agricultural production and resilience.

Table 1 Factors affecting adherence to government COVID-19 protocols

Opinion/Reason for Adherence	Adherence to COVID-19 protocols					
	Always		Sometimes		Aggregate	
	No.	%	No.	%	No.	%
I felt at risk of contracting C-19.	95	54.3	71	40.6	166	94.9
I knew the C19 signs & symptoms.	89	50.9	47	26.9	136	77.7*
I could not access food markets.	31	17.7	43	24.6	74	42.3
I believe C-19 is God's punishment to us.	21	12.0	48	27.4	69	39.4*
I got infected once	14	8.0	12	6.9	26	14.9
Average family members that were infected.	3		10.2		6.6	

Source Fieldwork Data (2024), N = 175
* Statistically significant difference at 95% CI

3.1 *Rural Communities*

The curfews and lockdowns significantly disrupted social interactions, mental health, economic productivity, and access to essential services, forcing people to face heightened insecurities and rely on limited resources. Despite some government support, the crisis highlighted the need for better preparedness to mitigate adverse effects in the future.

Loss of Market Access as COVID-19 Downside Risk

Movement restrictions and curfews made it challenging for farmers to obtain essential agricultural inputs like seeds, fertilizers, and chemicals necessary for production. Accessing these inputs improved agricultural productivity and sustainability. Also, accessing markets to sell their produce was severely limited, disrupting the entire supply chain. Based on the FGDs data, inputs like chicken stock feed were not easily obtainable, negatively impacting livestock rearing activities.

> The lockdown really affected the farmers a lot, setting them back. Fertilizers, seeds, and other inputs could not be easily accessed, and this mostly affected us here in Goromonzi because we make horticultural products like tomatoes and vegetables. Some tomatoes rotted away in the fields because they could not be brought to the markets easily [21/9/2022, 17:34:55, Madzipa, 55y/o male, farmer, Goromonzi].

> COVID-19 affected the farmers, especially during the curfews, because it was not easy to travel from one place to another, and they wanted to go to the hardware store to buy

> fertilizer and chemicals. It was not easy to obtain a pass from the police [21/9/2022, 21:48:37, Matamba, 69y/o male, farmer, Goromonzi].

Rural agricultural communities faced several downside risks regarding market access during the COVID-19 pandemic. Many farmers experienced considerable losses as they could not access marketplaces where they traditionally sold their produce. For instance, as participants highlighted, the inability to access markets led to the rotting and spoiling of produce, resulting in financial losses.

> As a farmer, my produce rotted because my marketing place was closed. I lost a lot [21/9/2022, 19:15:46 Mago, 40y/o male, Goromonzi].[1]

> I failed to travel from one place to another to perform some business activities. My perishable commodities decomposed due to movement restrictions, and markets were closed [23/9/2022, 20:57:05, Saka, 53y/o male, teacher, Goromonzi].

> I had planted a lot of vegetables. I was expecting a bumper harvest and a lot of money through sales, but that didn't happen because of the lockdown; I couldn't sell my vegetables [21/9/2022, 22:25:47, Gochai, 40y/o male, farmer, Kwekwe].

The need for letters or passes to travel through roadblocks presented significant challenges. As Kajese from Goromonzi mentioned, farmers could not transport their produce to markets or obtain necessary supplies from other regions—their constant worry about navigating roadblocks added to their stress and operational difficulties. Farmers lost income due to unsold produce, while input shortages meant they could not produce optimally for future market periods. Because of the curfews, those who could get travel letters and access markets also had limited time to sell their products, as reported by Johanne from Kwekwe. Goods and services became more expensive due to scarcity and opportunistic price hikes by traders. As Kumema from Kwekwe pointed out, "…in the market, some traders sold commodities at costly prices because no one else could go out to the next town to buy. Other people would hide commodities to create scarcity so that they could inflate the prices. It is just that human beings are so corrupt we capitalize on a crisis" [22/9/2022, 18:34:57, 49 y/o female, self-employed]. Rural farmers, therefore, faced increased costs for essentials while having reduced income due to market access issues. These compounded risks severely impacted rural agricultural communities, making it imperative for governments and organizations to develop more robust support mechanisms during future crises.

Agricultural activities in developing countries, including Zimbabwe, heavily rely on labor-intensive production systems (see Chambati 2011). Movement restrictions and reduced working hours during the COVID-19 pandemic severely impacted agricultural productivity and income, as farmers had to dismiss workers early, leading to reduced production hours. Increased theft ensued as idle individuals turned to illicit activities, targeting crops and homes. Restrictions also hindered farmers' ability to travel for those essential goods purchases that are not produced on-farm (sugar, salt, oils).

---

[1] The names of participants in the FGDs have been changed to protect their identity.

Psychological stress among farmers grew due to operational uncertainties. At the same time, youths faced rising drug addiction due to job cuts and school closures, further diminishing the labor force and harming the social fabric of rural communities. The stress of losing produce, not knowing when markets would reopen, and dealing with logistical issues took a toll on farmers. The personal risk of contracting the virus, as seen from the experiences shared by participants like Mago and Mai Mpositori from Goromonzi, also exacerbated the mental health burden and trauma. Muponesi's experience summed up other sources of stress and trauma that farmers experienced.

> Talking about lockdowns, OMG, this was the most disturbing thing. It left many of my colleagues who work in the city jobless because they were laid off. That was more traumatizing than other aspects of COVID-19 because the thought of losing your job and the inability to move around looking for alternative income sources is the most challenging thing. There were food shortages, and the prices increased tremendously for the little available. With such problems, the family looked up to the father, and the trauma increased and the father would end up taking it all on the family or the wife, so domestic violence skyrocketed. A relative called me many times and told me that they were not on good terms with their spouses, and I could not go there to mediate because of lockdowns […]. I once watched a relative being stigmatized because people thought that the relative had COVID. I also had to reject a relative who had tested positive for the COVID-19 virus. Rejection and stigmatization hence affected not only my relatives but myself as well because I had to make that difficult decision to reject them. This was traumatizing. Even now, when I think about that time, I feel ashamed [21/9/2022, 23:32:52, Muponesi, 41y/o male, Farmer/Carpenter, Goromonzi].

3.2 *COVID-19 Shocks on Urban Life*

Due to travel restrictions, curfews, and banning informal trading activities, many families who depended on day-to-day trading faced severe economic hardships, leading to increased poverty as they lost their income sources. Companies faced operating challenges due to movement restrictions and low business volumes, resulting in unemployment. These newly unemployed individuals had to search for alternative livelihoods, further aggravating their financial struggles.

Harsh lockdown and curfew regulations disproportionately affected those working in the informal sector, who require free movement for their livelihood. The restrictions pushed many families into poverty as their daily operations were severely curtailed.

The lockdown measures and curfew hours also made it difficult for people to access supermarkets. Public transport limitations and the absence of nearby shops in certain areas forced people to walk long distances for groceries. Working individuals faced significant constraints as supermarkets would close by the time they finished their daily shifts, leading to frustration and challenges in acquiring daily necessities.

> We were affected because we are a low-income nation. The majority live hand-to-mouth daily. What will happen to a person who survives on selling fruits and vegetables if a lockdown is imposed for 21 days? That means disaster to that person and his entire dependents. If the economy had been in good shape, the severity or impact of those restrictions would have been low [21/9/2022, 09:38:02, Kukumba, 39y/o male, self-employed, Harare].

Corruption was the biggest challenge to implementing policy in urban areas, significantly undermining efforts to enforce regulations effectively. Before implementing the regulations, the government should have anticipated or addressed public transport availability issues hindering market access. The poor enforcement or abuse of quarantine measures for individuals arriving from outside the country (the Zororo Makamba case, see The Herald 2020), compounded by corruption at road checkpoints, heightened the risk of COVID-19 transmission within urban areas. Law enforcement officials often accepted bribes, allowing some individuals to bypass the restrictions. This corruption not only compromised the effectiveness of the regulations but also increased risks for those who complied, highlighting how deeply corruption impeded policy implementation in urban areas.

> The regulations seemed harsh, but they were for our own benefit. Humans sometimes lack discipline, so we need constant monitoring. That's why the police and army were deployed to ensure everyone adhered to the COVID-19 regulations. However, the police and army let down the government initiative to curb COVID-19, as they were now involved in corrupt activities. They accepted brides to let people pass through roadblocks [21/9/2022, 09:46:31, Muriri, 33y/o male, Health officer, Harare].

> […] other top government officials were allowed to go about their business as they pleased [without restrictions]. At hospitals, you would need a COVID-19 certificate before they even attended to you, even if it was just a routine checkup. The police were taking advantage of people at roadblocks, charging them for passage. So, basically, [government restrictions were ineffective] because of corruption [21/9/2022, 09:32:29, Katamba, 29y/o male, IT specialist, Harare].

Healthcare and safety concerns were more significant in Harare during the COVID-19 pandemic. Despite lockdown directives, some public spaces, such as vegetable markets (e.g., Mbare Musika), were allowed to operate, albeit without proper enforcement of COVID-19 protocols (masks and social distancing). This created hotspots and increased the risk of virus transmission. Furthermore, insufficient awareness and ineffective monitoring allowed people to continue business as usual in crowded and unsafe conditions, heightening the public health risk. These issues underscored the downside risks that urban communities in Harare faced concerning supply chain disruptions during the pandemic.

Psychological Breakdowns and Trauma

Restrictions on movement and activities hindered the ability to engage in regular social and recreational activities, such as going to bars or attending social events, exacerbating the sense of frustration and isolation. Participants in the Harare FGD highlighted various mental and emotional problems caused by lockdowns, curfews, and the overall uncertainty brought by the pandemic. The disruption of daily routines, such as the inability to conduct regular business or access public transport, fostered feelings of anxiety and helplessness. Moreover, the pressure to vaccinate amid fears propagated by social media conspiracy theories exacerbated these psychological stresses, with some individuals feeling coerced and doubting the efficacy of the vaccines. This mental turmoil not only affects personal health but can also lead to broader societal issues, such as increased poverty and reduced resilience in facing ongoing challenges, ultimately compounding the difficulties communities face during and after the pandemic. Ms. Olise highlighted the effect on stress and anxiety every time they thought of COVID-19:

> […] I was pregnant, and the lockdown was an inconvenience because I couldn't go to the Ante-Natal Clinic for checkups before and even after I gave birth. So, after giving birth because of the lockdown, they discharged us within hours after birth. I could not take my baby to the usual baby clinic checkup. My newborn daughter fell ill as well, and we were asked to go to a bigger Harare Hospital, but I also feared meeting people at the hospital since anyone could be a potential COVID-19 carrier. I chose not to go there. I ended up losing my newborn daughter. COVID-19 destroyed my life [almost sobbing at the end of the audio] [21/9/2022, 00:34:43, Olise, 32 y/o female, Customer Service, Harare].

The majority of the FGD participants reported getting psychological trauma from their experience with the pandemic, especially those who relied on social media for information and updates. Social media was a triple-edged sword that simultaneously informed, disinformed, and misinformed the public. Over 90% of all the FGD participants were traumatized by using social media platforms during the pandemic.

> Social media increased my fear of the COVID-19 pandemic. I remember the first video I saw was of Zororo's [Makamba] girlfriend, and it terrified me. Then, the daily statistics from Econet[2] sent through text messages didn't help either. All I saw was the number of people dying, so I eventually stopped opening them [22/9/2022, 12:11:47, Pamunda, 37y/o female, Pensions settlement clerk, Harare].

> Social media made my fears worse. Seeing reports of the rate at which it was spreading made me anxious, especially when people would start posting messages about losing a loved one or their experiences while being in isolation. I feared it happening to me [23/9/2022, 17:46:25, Xanthe, 26y/o female, Feminist Knowledge leader, Harare].

> Social media was a poison. It said we could use Bute[3] to cure COVID-19. We ended up having Bute/snuff on standby in our homes to prepare for COVID-19 [23/9/2022, 18:45:13, Chamisa, 35y/o female, health and environmental safety manager, Harare].

> I realized later that the more news I saw about COVID […], the more I panicked. […] at one point, I got into a supermarket […] it was full; I didn't even buy the bread because I was now feeling swamped, running short of breath, and sweating profusely. So, I then later decided to quit viewing any information that had to do with COVID-19 […] because I realized that now it's affecting my mental health. […] [22/9/2022, 08:12:02, Claire, 31y/o female, town planner, Harare].

4 Perceived Versus Real Risks of COVID-19

Perceived risks are those that people believe exist based on personal evaluations, experiences, or societal influences. Non-scientific factors like media coverage may influence perceived risks, whereas actual risks rely on scientific data and factual

---

[2] Econet Wireless is a mobile and internet service provider in Zimbabwe.

[3] Bute is snuff made from ground tobacco which people smoke/sniff through their noses.

analysis, leading to different behavioral impacts. For example, during COVID-19, perceived risks contributed to the extent to which individuals overestimated the danger of everyday activities based on media portrayals and anecdotal evidence, leading to behaviors like avoiding public places or excessive fear of infection and vaccines (Shrader-Frechette 1990, pp. 342–344).

In contrast, experts quantitatively assess actual risks using statistical models and empirical data, providing objective measures of the likelihood and consequences of hazards. For COVID-19, this means calculating the real probability of virus transmission based on factors such as local case rates, effectiveness of safety measures, and vaccination coverage (Shrader-Frechette, 1990, pp. 345–346). The critical differences between perceived and actual risks lie in subjectivity versus objectivity, the influence of emotions versus scientific data, and varying interpretations of risk definitions, often resulting in public behaviors that may not align with the real threat level.

4.1 Rural Perception of COVID-19 Risks

Rural perceptions evolved from skepticism to acceptance, influenced by misinformation, personal experiences, and adaptive behaviors. Initially, many participants doubted the virus's existence, seeing it as a foreign problem until high infection and death rates hit their communities. Social media fueled confusion and skepticism with conspiracy theories and exaggerated reports about the virus and vaccines. Widespread fear, amplified by alarming videos and misinformation about vaccine side effects, led to anxiety and reluctance to get vaccinated. However, as infection rates declined and participants saw the virus's effects on friends and family, their perceptions shifted to acknowledge the reality of COVID-19. For instance:

> […] it was really a difficult decision whether to take the vaccines or not. COVID-19 myths were dispelled later, but most of us used a wait-and-see approach. We only got the vaccine after seeing what effects it had on others, even though we saw how devastating the disease had been to our friends. We also had access to information about daily infections, which should have pushed us to get the vaccine, but we waited until others had taken it and not died [22/9/2022, 13:22:10, Matadza, 39 y/o male, teacher, Goromonzi].

Despite initial resistance to lockdowns and preventive measures due to their impact on daily life, individuals gradually adapted, using home remedies and traditional practices. Trusted information sources also shifted from social media to government officials, local health officers, and traditional media outlets. Overall, rural perceptions of COVID-19 risks transitioned through a complex interplay of misinformation, personal experiences, and behavioral adaptations.

4.2 *Urban Perception of COVID-19 Risks*

On the other hand, urban perceptions also evolved through a complex mix of fear and confusion. However, the effect of social media on urbanites' perspectives was particularly intense. Initially, widespread fear stemmed from alarming statistics and exaggerated stories shared via social media and news sources, heightening anxiety about the virus. Social media amplified these fears with conspiracy theories and misinformation, leading to vaccine hesitance and distrust in health communications. For instance:

> It is true that many people do not believe in the vaccination process, especially in Africa, particularly Zimbabwe. The reason is that people were just forced to get vaccinated by the government and employers without being told of the benefits and consequences of doing so [20/9/2022, 12:11:48, Kukumba, 39y/o male, Self-employed, Harare].

> I don't believe in the vaccination process because some medical companies developed viruses so that they can also develop a cure or vaccine for them. In this case, it brings in more money to their pockets. I believe this virus results from either politics or capitalists who benefit from the lower classes, as always [22/9/2022, 10:13:50, Claire, 31y/o female, Town planner, Harare].

As COVID-19 cases declined, perceptions shifted toward a more optimistic view of controlling and eventually eradicating the virus. Despite initial resistance, urban populations adapted to new health measures, such as wearing masks and social distancing. Over time, improved information from trusted sources helped reshape understanding and increase compliance with health guidelines. Thus, while early perceptions were marked by fear and misinformation, evolving communication led to a more measured acceptance of health protocols.

5 Rural Versus Urban Experiences: Comparative Analysis

5.1 *Impact on Agricultural Livelihood Practices*

Perceived risk during the pandemic had significant implications for agricultural production in urban and rural areas, highlighting the disparities between these settings. Farmers faced challenges in accessing necessary inputs. This resulted in reduced agricultural production, increased transaction costs to secure alternative markets, and substantial post-harvest losses. The fear associated with the virus and its effects created a traumatized environment, making it hard for farmers to focus on agricultural activities. Some individuals initiated small backyard projects, such as rearing chickens and starting vegetable gardens, to respond to market conditions and food availability instability.

On the other hand, while affected similarly to rural farmers, peri-urban farmers sometimes enjoyed a relative advantage as they capitalized on intercity movement restrictions. They could sell goods to those stuck at home while maintaining health protocols. The fear of financial loss drove peri-urban farmers to smuggle goods into the city despite governmental restrictions. Urban consumers faced challenges as essential goods became overpriced due to scarcity, further complicating food security. Urbanites often experienced fear from both the virus and enforcement actions from law enforcement, affecting their morale and perception of risk. For example, 105,000 people had been arrested by the end of April 2020 for violating lockdown protocols (BBC 2020). With time, farmers were added to the essential service provider list, and they could enter the city markets after obtaining a travel letter.

5.2 *Significant Differences in COVID-19 Experiences Between Urban and Rural Areas*

Urban areas encountered substantial challenges related to access to services, education, and employment during the pandemic. In contrast, rural areas exhibited a combination of skepticism regarding the severity of the virus and a sense of communal resilience, even amidst restrictions. Urban residents reported more pronounced disruptions due to lockdown measures, notably concerning restrictions on their freedoms. Meanwhile, rural inhabitants often perceived daily life as continuing uninterrupted (minus intercity travel), though with increased exposure to downside risks compared to their urban counterparts (see Table 2). Therefore, the threat for rural area dwellers was not coming from COVID-19 itself but from the downside risks associated with the consequences of government containment measures.

In urban areas like Harare, participants faced challenges accessing grocery stores due to curfews and reduced public transport, causing frustration. Lockdowns severely impacted entrepreneurs and self-employed individuals, initially seen as a break but later leading to economic hardship and increased domestic violence. Education was disrupted, and limited access to devices hindered the shift to online learning, affecting students' learning outcomes. Social isolation was also significant, as participants felt a loss of spiritual connection due to restrictions on attending church. The effects were perceived differently in rural areas (Goromonzi & Kwekwe). Although some participants struggled with strict health measures, some found daily life largely unaffected, particularly those not integrated into farm-city markets. The inter-village movement continued, and there was skepticism about COVID-19's existence, citing bustling city markets such as Mbare Musika, where restrictions were disregarded. Despite government measures, communal gatherings persisted, reflecting a community-oriented approach that contrasted with the urban experience of isolation.

Table 2 Summary of urban and rural areas COVID-19 experiences

	Urban areas (Harare)	Rural areas (Goromonzi & Kwekwe)
Access to services is a challenge. (groceries, public transport)	Big challenge	Small challenge
Understand the rationale of health system response (lockdowns, roadblocks)	Low Higher understanding	High Low understanding
Belief in the virus's existence	High (experienced high infections)	Low (only seen after it affected livelihoods)
Impact on employment and business (work, school, farming)	High	High
Effect of education	Negative (online learning proved difficult to implement)	Negative (online impossible to implement)
Social isolation	High (inability to go to church)	Lower (rural life continued to some extent)
Community engagement	Low (people afraid of the virus)	Higher (people still moved a little more freely)

Source Created by author (2024) based on Fieldwork Data (2024).

6 Resilience in Agricultural Communities

Resilience is defined as the capacity of individuals and communities to respond to change (immediate unanticipated shocks or more gradual processes), such as rural depopulation, aging, political change, or loss of essential services. It encompasses the ability to absorb shocks and adapt to changing circumstances while maintaining functionality and relationships within the system (Adger 2000; Mackay and Petersen 2015; Moberg and Hauge Simonsen 2011). COVID-19 represents one of the biggest such unanticipated shocks, albeit globally.

This chapter discussed several challenges rural and urban populations face, which we grouped into three major categories (Health and Safety Concerns, Economic and Employment Challenges, and Social and Mental Health Issues). As discussed in the FGDs, people found a way to overcome and persevere through the pandemic for each of these challenges (see Fig. 2). More details are provided in Muchetu (2023). Figure 2 summarizes the resilience mechanisms employed by rural areas in Zimbabwe in response to various COVID-19 challenges. Urban and rural communities adapted through such strategies as boosting immunity through local remedies, utilizing trusted information sources, diversifying income sources, and enhancing communication with loved ones. Detailed differences between urban and rural resilience are summarized in Appendix A.2.

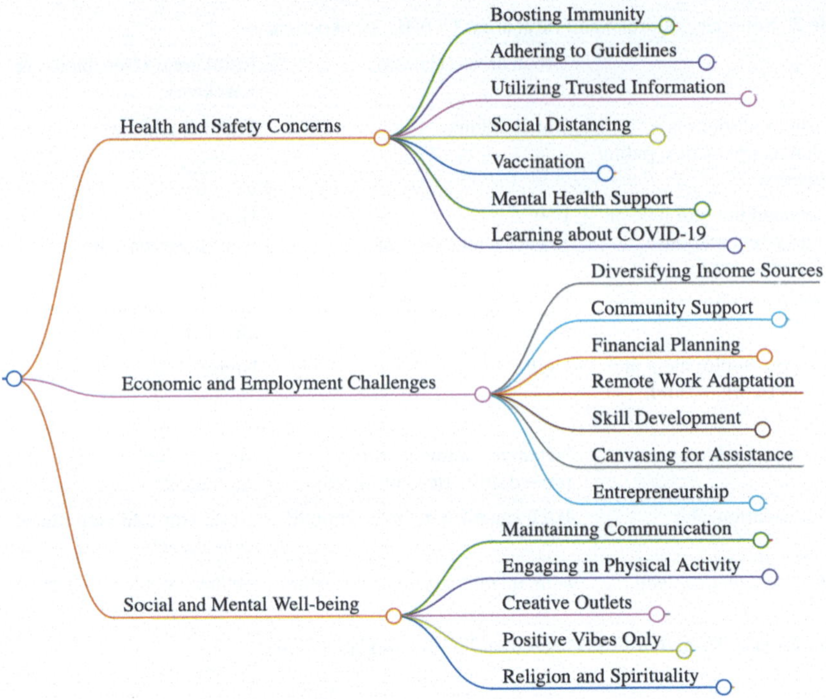

Fig. 2 Mind map of community resilience in urban and rural areas of Zimbabwe. *Source* Created by author (2024) based on Fieldwork Data (2024).

Of interest in these resilience approaches is using local/Indigenous methods to prevent or cure COVID-19. Almost all participants agreed that Lippia Javanica—Zumbani (a shrub local to Zimbabwe; see more in Muchetu 2023, p. 54) was extremely helpful in mitigating the pain one would feel if or when infected by the COVID-19 virus. Others highlighted steaming using various natural essential oils (gumtree leaves) and imported Chinese Tsunami® ointment.

As envisaged in the theory of peasant economy, peasant farmers revert to auto-consumption for subsistence in times of crisis. FGDs revealed that urban and rural area dwellers used several techniques, including reducing the amount of food they ate, monetizing hobbies, and farming for their food in backyard gardens. In urban areas, people with a backyard could grow vegetables for local neighborhood sales, filling the gap left by locked-down, out-of-city vegetable suppliers. For instance, they grew vegetables as a hobby and a way to monetize their hobbies (growing leafy vegetables in Avondale and growing beetroot in Southview; Fig. 3). However, this phenomenon was primarily practiced in rural areas as those farmers had access to larger land sizes (relative to urbanites) as a fallback for reduced livelihoods outside the farm.

Few respondents reported accessing government food programs, and others accessed government COVID-19 allowances. The budget for these was significantly

Fig. 3 Harare respondents engaged in backyard gardening. *Source* Photos shared by respondents in Fieldwork Data (2024).

lower, and they only targeted people who lived in extreme poverty. Other countries, such as South Africa and Botswana, had robust financial assistance for more enormous proportions of their populations.

Lastly, FGD participants highlighted payment of bribes as a legitimate source of agency and, to some extent, resilience against what they assumed to be unrealistic government blanket restrictions. This phenomenon was particularly true for people living in the urban Harare area. For instance,

> Several people lost their jobs because companies could no longer operate, worsening the impact of COVID-19. The newly unemployed had to move around in search of livelihoods, even outside curfew times, further worsening their plight as they encountered overzealous police officers who asked for fines and bribes [21/9/2022, 09:47:15, Ngoni, 27y/o male, self-employed, Harare].
>
> Some restrictions were necessary, and some were not. I think the 'Essential Service' certificates/letters[4] were unnecessary. Those letters led to corruption, with people buying letters stamped by government offices to access the CBD. The government went on to ban public transport, creating a nightmare for the public. When ZUPCO[5] was given the monopoly to transport people, it got overwhelmed. However, the government ignored this, and people suffered for long hours looking for transport, breaking the curfew rule. Which led to more corruption as people were subjected to paying fines or bribes for breaking the curfew [21/9/2022, 09:51:27, Isabel, 32y/o female, Pensions administrator, Harare].

---

[4] The state designated some industries as essential services (hospitals, pharmacies, armed forces, supermarkets), and workers in these industries were allowed to travel if they had a letter confirming that they worked in such an industry.

[5] The Zimbabwe Passenger Company—ZUPCO is a public transportation company wholly owned by the government of Zimbabwe and operates both urban and long-distance routes.

However, as Nene from Kwekwe highlighted, not all government workers were corrupt, especially in rural areas.

> [...] at first, I really didn't want to vaccinate, and I didn't even want to hear about vaccination. I tried to go to the hospital to bribe someone to get a vaccination card even though I wasn't vaccinated, but they refused. The hospital personnel then told me that it was so easy for them to render a vaccination card to me, but they were not doing that because COVID-19 is real. They explained that if they gave me a card without being vaccinated, I would not be protected against the COVID-19 virus, and if by chance I got infected, I would die [21/9/2022, 21:01:42, Kumema, 49y/o female, self-employed, Kwekwe].

7 Conclusion

This study examined the multifaceted impacts of curfews and travel restrictions on agriculture, focusing on travel and logistics issues, workforce reductions, and the resulting social and economic repercussions (downside risks). Farmers faced significant challenges obtaining essential inputs like fertilizers due to travel restrictions and difficulties procuring travel passes. This logistical bottleneck and reduced working hours led to a substantial drop in productivity and income, particularly in rural areas heavily reliant on agricultural output—with little to no monetary savings. Social consequences included increased teenage pregnancies among girls with idle time due to school closures and a rise in drug use among boys facing job cuts. The enforced curfews disrupted social activities, leading to isolation, especially in rural communities known for their close-knit nature. Health concerns saw people turning to vitamins and heavily relying on local remedies for immunity and curing COVID-19.

The study confirms earlier works of Boltvinik (2016), Moyo (2016), and van der Ploeg (2010). Critical distinctions between agricultural and industrial production shape how urban and rural populations respond to crises like COVID-19. Agriculture is discontinuous and seasonal, leading rural communities to view disruptions as temporary breaks like natural cycles, fostering acceptance and adaptability. In contrast, urban areas rely on continuous industrial processes that suffer from abrupt halts, creating economic uncertainty and the need for rapid adjustment. Agricultural work follows a sequential, phased approach, aiding rural adaptability to pandemic-related changes, while industrial work relies on synchronized processes, making staggered shifts challenging. The production location also varies. Agriculture occurs in open fields, reducing virus transmission risks, whereas industrial production is concentrated in factories, increasing contagion potential. However, agricultural products are perishable/time-sensitive, meaning those that had produced (market-oriented) but could not access markets suffered greatly. These differences underscore the varying resilience strategies between rural and urban populations during the pandemic.

These production-related differences indicate that rural and urban communities had to adopt different strategies for resilience. Rural populations, accustomed to seasonal shifts and environmental variability, may have relied on their flexibility and self-reliance to navigate pandemic disruptions. Their ability to work in isolated conditions and familiarity with nature's capability could have fostered a more adaptable response. In contrast, urban areas needed to develop new methods to handle the sudden, large-scale interruptions brought about by the pandemic, such as adjusting to remote work, reconfiguring factory layouts for social distancing, and implementing stringent health protocols. Therefore, the resilience of urban populations depended on their ability to quickly innovate and restructure systems to maintain continuity, even when traditional industrial processes were disrupted.

8 Column 2

Grassroots voices from Zimbabwe

1. **Shifting perception on COVID-19: The story of Isabel *(Female, 32-year-old, from Harare, Interviewed September 23, 2022)***

Initially, I thought the virus was just a joke. I didn't believe that there was COVID-19. I didn't care about the police or anything, but then people we knew started dying due to COVID-19. Then the reality struck that the virus might be real. And then, as time went on when the numbers of COVID-19 infections and deaths were decreasing, it was now more about the restrictions than the fear of COVID-19 because maybe we were now used to people dying or people getting COVID-19 and then recovering. So, in the end, it was now more about the police and the restrictions rather than the fear of COVID-19, but at first, it was the fear of people that you knew dying. Yes, COVID-19 does exist, just like other pandemics, such as the Spanish flu of 1918 and the 1968 Flu pandemic, which killed more than one million people. COVID-19, caused by SARS cov2, has wreaked havoc worldwide, killing more than 2 million people, so yes, it does exist. I think our government was even more relaxed (they also didn't believe it existed) until the death of Zororo Makamba, which sent the elites into a panic. (Before Zororo's death) …they (elites) thought COVID-19 was coming only for the poor.

I couldn't understand how Europe was the worst affected by COVID-19. How, with all their best healthcare, could they not minimize the impact of the pandemic, compared to Zimbabwe, which was ill-prepared to fight the virus? True, they actually expected Africa to be the worst affected and have high mortality, and when that didn't happen, they came up with theories such as Africa has a young population and that most Africans live in rural areas and travel less to explain why Africa wasn't most affected.

I didn't understand how quickly someone went from being healthy to dying within days of being infected by COVID-19. I still don't understand the long-term effects of COVID-19 because I personally suffered from COVID-19. My body has not returned to normalcy. Will there ever be a cure for COVID-19? [However,] I don't believe that the vaccine works and am very scared that we might have introduced dangerous substances into our bodies in the long run through the vaccine. That is why I will not be taking any of the booster shots. It's quite a surprise how, after being vaccinated, one still got COVID-19, and then they tell you that, had you not been vaccinated, you would have become worse or critical. That didn't sound right to me at all. Statistics show that about 3% of children might get measles even after vaccination, depending on one's immune system. However, with COVID-19, almost all the people who were vaccinated still contracted COVID-19. Hence, I have reservations about whether the vaccine worked or not. Besides, we still have lots of unvaccinated people who never got infected.

Yes, I got vaccinated. I got the Sinopharm vaccine, which the Zimbabwe government was providing then. I didn't trust any of the vaccines. Had it not been for my employer, who was threatening retrenchment for those not vaccinated, I would not have been vaccinated. I had no choice. The government was pushing on one end, and the employer said those coming to work must be vaccinated. If you don't come to work, it means no pay, so you either get vaccinated or stay at home. I checked the price of buying a vaccination card, which was too expensive, so I was jabbed. In Zimbabwe, people bought those vaccination cards (through corruption). Haha, Zimbabweans are afraid of injections in general unless they are really sick. People also didn't want to be jabbed with things they didn't understand; they were just forced to do it because of work. I think the virus just died a natural death. I personally regret getting the first jab.

Lockdowns were great at the beginning. It meant not going to work. I needed that break, but it wasn't so nice as the lockdowns continued. Staying at home for weeks wasn't so nice after all. We needed to hang out, go to places, go shopping, and all, but we couldn't. Lockdowns led to a lot of domestic violence in households. The lockdown greatly affected businesses, especially for entrepreneurs/self-employed people who couldn't get into town to sell their stuff. However, others mastered online marketing during this period.

Education was severely affected because primary kids lost out a lot due to COVID-19. Although online lessons were introduced, it was challenging for children because they now required special devices. In many cases, they had to rely on their parents' phones, which brought some further depression, given the fact that the parents also wanted to use the phones. Most of the teachers had never done online teaching, and little training was available at a fast pace to make online learning efficient. They just ended up sending exercises through the WhatsApp platform and then later sending the answers. Thus, online learning basically became the duty of the parent to teach, describe, explain, and mark/grade work for their kids. Not every parent had the skills, time, and patience to do this, frustrating both parents and kids. With lost incomes, data was also expensive for parents who ended up abandoning the online lessons.

Some restrictions were necessary, and some were not. I think 'Essential Service' letters were not necessary at all. A lot of time was wasted on roadblocks while police were checking the authenticity of those letters, with some people being sent back home if their letters did not meet the police 'standards.' Those letters led to corruption, with people buying letters stamped by government offices to access the CBD. The government went on to ban public transportation, creating a nightmare for the public. It got overwhelmed when Zimbabwe United Passenger Company

(ZUPCO) was given a monopoly to transport people. However, the government ignored this, and people suffered long hours while looking for transport, breaking the curfew rule. So, we had to walk many kilometers and wait in long queues for transport, thereby breaking curfew rules. This led to arrests and having to 'negotiate' [pay bribes] with the police so that they let us go. This led to more corruption as people were subjected to paying fines or bribes.

Not being allowed to attend church was also a big source of frustration. I really missed church, and after a while, I felt spiritually lost. I think a lot of people felt this way, too. However, I think that banning social gatherings, churches, and funerals was good because it did reduce the number of infections. Also, mandatory wearing of masks and sanitization was good as it mitigated the spread of the virus. I feel that the government took too much time to close our borders and allow people from high-risk countries to fly into the country. If a lockdown had been instituted on time, we could have recorded very low COVID-19 infections. Also, there was no proper quarantine for those coming from outside the country. People would just land at the airport and go straight home, while others would pay bribes so they wouldn't go into quarantine. Zimbabwe was ill-prepared for COVID-19.

Lastly, I think social media increased the fear of COVID-19. I remember specifically in December 2021, when COVID-19 had infected me. At that time, Zimbabwe was recording a huge number of new infections and deaths, and Econet (a cellular service provider) was sending daily statistics. I was so terrified and afraid that I was going to die that I also ended up not opening those Econet messages. I remember there was actually an outcry from citizens to the extent that Econet stopped sending the messages. COVID-19 was all about being mentally positive. Now, if you were affected psychologically, it meant one could get worse because the only thing in your mind would be the fear of death. When I got sick/infected, I had to stop watching the news and reading anything related to COVID-19 deaths.

2. **Dealing with restrictions, curfews, and vaccines: The Story of Muponesi** ***(Male, 41-year-old, from Goromonzi, Interviewed September 21, 2022)***

The curfews disturbed my life a lot, starting with my social life; I could not see or visit relatives, which frustrated me. After work, we visited relatives and friends and had dinner together or watched soccer. The curfew disturbed that. It also affected business and production because we used to finish work later, but we had to dismiss at 1500 h due to curfew. We had to work for 6 h instead of 8 h. So, as a farmer, I was most affected. Production was greatly affected and, by extension, income. We also had the psychological trauma of not knowing what tomorrow was going to be like. We were all traumatized by COVID-19 and the restriction measures. Sometimes, there would be an ongoing program or project, and you could not finish that project because of [sudden] policy changes. Regarding the issue of vaccines, there was uncertainty about how the cure would be found because no treatment was available in the beginning. There was no hope at all. However, we were also concerned about the side effects when the vaccines became available. It was difficult to know whether these vaccines were good for us. If you remember, after the first vaccines were introduced, it was discovered that some batches had side effects such as headaches, numbness, death, and so on. When I had the confidence to take the vaccine, there wasn't enough for everyone, and we had to wait in the queue to get the first shot.

Talking about lockdowns, OMG, this was the most disturbing thing. It left many of my colleagues who work in the city jobless because they were laid off. That was more traumatizing than other aspects of COVID-19 because the thought of losing your job and the inability to move around looking for alternative income sources is the most difficult thing. There were food shortages, and the prices increased tremendously for the little that was available. With such problems, the family looked up to the father, and the trauma increased and the father would end up taking it all on the family or the wife, so domestic violence skyrocketed. A relative called me many times and told me that they were not on good terms with their spouses, and I could not go there to mediate because I feared they might be infected, or if not, then the lockdown roadblocks would stop me. I once watched a relative being stigmatized because people thought that the relative had COVID. I also had to reject a relative who had tested positive for the COVID-19 virus. Rejection and stigmatization hence affected not only my relatives but also myself because I had to make the difficult decision to reject them. This was traumatizing. Even now, when I think about that time, I feel ashamed. I also had to deal with kids who were now spending time at home and ended up taking drugs. Some local girls and boys lost hope of finishing school and got pregnant, and some got married. There have been a lot of dropouts, and the pass rate has dropped significantly; even up to now, some kids are half-baked upon graduation.

I was one of the lucky ones to receive some subsidy from the government for COVID-19 relief. Others were not so lucky. The number of thieves also increased greatly because people wanted to make ends meet. The restrictions that were in place stopped me from going to church to exercise my freedom of religion. Sometimes, you need some time with others to be lifted spiritually. We could not fellowship with each other, and it was a challenging time. The restrictions also stopped us from attending funerals and sending our loved ones off. We could not do body-viewings or lay wreaths; at times, we were not even allowed to bury them by ourselves. That was very traumatic. The restrictions also separated me from my family. When the restrictions were announced and when intercity travel was banned, my kids were still at boarding school. I missed my kids and was constantly worried about their health. I ran several scenarios in my head, which worsened the trauma.

One could not easily access inputs like chemicals needed to produce agricultural products. We could not get chicken stock feed for my chicken production, but we lost out in terms of production and time. We could also not access markets for outputs. The government needs to be ready for such illnesses in the future instead of setting up the funds later when the pandemic hits; the government should already have the funds in place. It needs to set aside these funds to take care of natural disasters and pandemics such as this one so that people are not too severely affected. I should stress that.

3. **Psychological trauma: The Story of Olise** ***(Female, 32-year-old, from Harare, Interviewed September 21, 2022)***

Alright, I want to share the negative side because this one somehow outweighs the positive aspect. You know, apart from going to work, I am a [peri-urban] farmer; though I don't produce on a large scale, I had injected a lot of capital into it. I can say that, as a family, my husband and I had saved a lot of capital, and then we went to look for a piece of land along Mazvikadei dam (123 km from the Harare CBD), and then we started growing tomatoes under irrigation. We had about two hectares of butternut. But remember that the first lockdown was introduced around the 30th of March in 2020, and that was the time we had really put a lot of our finances on the ground, paying people to work for us so that the project would be a success. We invested a lot of money there, you know, buying herbicides, clearing the land since it was a new piece of land, and investing in generators, fuel, and other farming equipment. So, when the first lockdown was introduced, my husband was at the farm and could not come to the city.

The tomatoes started to ripen, and if you recall, Mbare market was also closed at some time. You know, each and every day, we would have a scotch cart full of ripe tomatoes but no one to sell to. We couldn't take them anywhere; we couldn't take them to Mbare market, and we couldn't even take them to any nearby marketplaces like Banket or Chinhoyi because there was no one there. You know, during the first lockdown, everything was so strict, and we lost so much money, the money that we had injected into that project. It was a big loss that was so severe that even if I try to recall it, I am traumatized. When the time to start selling tomatoes arrived, we began by selling the tomatoes in 20-L buckets, and no one really wanted to buy the tomatoes, so we ended up having to sell 10-L buckets of tomatoes at US$1. Some of the tomatoes were getting rotten. There was no way of selling the tomatoes at the market in Harare because the central market (Mbare) was closed. We had about 3 hectares of tomatoes, so you can imagine the loss. I also had butternut.

When we started planting the butternuts, we spoke to different hotel procurement officers, such as [*name withheld*]. Because of the lockdown, there was no business, and hotels shut down, so we started harvesting and eating the butternuts at home until they started to rot. We also had no transport to bring the butternuts to Harare because our utility truck developed mechanical problems, so my husband was the only one who visited the farm by public transport. I remember the first day that lockdown started, my husband walked on foot from Westgate to Lochinvar (about 17 km) because he could not get transport. The restrictions were really too much, especially the 6 am-6 pm curfew.

At the same time, I was pregnant, and the lockdown was an inconvenience because I couldn't go to the antenatal clinic for checkups before and even after I gave birth. So, after giving birth, because of the lockdown, they discharged us within hours after birth. I could not take my baby through the usual baby clinic checkup routine. My newborn daughter fell ill as well, and we had to go to the big Harare Hospital, but I also feared meeting people at the hospital since anyone could be a potential COVID-19 carrier. I chose not to go there. I ended up losing my newborn daughter. COVID-19 destroyed my life.

Appendices

See Appendix A.1.
See Appendix A.2.

Appendix A.1 A timeline of COVID-19 lockdowns in Zimbabwe

Year	Date	Event
2020	Mar 30	The first 21-day nationwide lockdown is instituted
	Apr 19	Two-week extension to May 3
	May 3	Indefinite extension with partially relaxed restrictions (highly restricted business reopening)
	Jun	Introduction of phased easing of lockdown measures, with businesses reopening gradually. Lockdown phases from 1 (few restrictions) to 4 (strictest)
	Jul 22	Tighter lockdown restrictions to curb a surge in cases (imposition of a dusk-to-dawn curfew)
	Aug	Gradual easing of lockdown, but curfew and other restrictions remained in place
	Sep	Schools began reopening in phases
2021	Jan 5	Strict Level 4 lockdown because of a spike in cases (no most activities and intercity travel
	Feb 15	Lockdown extended (some easing, e.g., reopening of schools for final-year students)
	March	Continued easing of restrictions (reopening of more businesses and schools)
	Jun 14	A localized lockdown was imposed in areas like Kwekwe due to a surge in cases
	July 6	Spike in cases, reintroduction of stricter nationwide lockdown (6:30 PM to 6:00 AM curfew and the suspension of intercity travel)
	August	Gradual easing of restrictions began (vaccination being emphasized)
2022	Jan	Easing of lockdown measures (lifting of the curfew and reopening of all schools)
	April	Further easing of restrictions (businesses and gatherings allowed under specific conditions)
	June	Encourage vaccination while maintaining minimal restrictions
	August	Government declared lockdown would remain, but largely relaxed (focus on vaccination)
	Dec	Further relaxation (most activities returning to normal, but with masks and social distancing)
2023	March	Maintenance of minimal restrictions (focus on vaccination and public health measures)
	June	Lifting of nearly all COVID-19 restrictions (vaccination & personal health safety)
	August	The end of the COVID-19 emergency, ending all remaining lockdown measures

Source Derived based on Veritaszim various updates (2020–2023)

Appendix A.2 Community resilience approaches in urban & rural area Zimbabwe

Type	Approach	Location	
		Urban Areas	Rural Areas
Health and safety concerns	Boosting immunity	Vitamin C&D supplements; consultations with health professionals	Local remedies (Zumbani, steaming); cleaner lifestyle
	Adhering to guidelines	Remote work; reconnect with family; online socializing; mindset shifts	Using available resources + bribes
	Utilizing trusted info	Trusting Radio; TV & state bulletins; limiting use of social media; compare/discuss info from various sources; relying on first-hand experience	
	Social distancing	Modified greetings (no handshake or hug but fist/elbow); accept social distance laws; avoid crowds; home-based care instead of hospitals when sick; online education	Caution at funerals (no handshakes)
	Vaccination	Follow church/employer mandates; fear of the virus; compare to previous virus epidemic vaccines; disputing misinformation	Communication with overseas family; trust in the government
	Mental health support	Online group discussions (WhatsApp); routine changes (exercise, meditation, gardening); seeking professional help	Family/ community connections
	Avoiding infection	Own COVID-19 research; regular testing; use of traditional remedies; sharing experiences	Traditional remedies; sharing experiences
Economic and employment challenges	Diversifying income sources	Exploring alternative income (e-commerce & delivery); monetizing hobbies (crafts & gardening); monetizing social networks (selling to friends and family); online trading	monetizing social networks (friends & neighbors)
	Community support	Utilizing technology for connections (WhatsApp; Zoom, Twitter/X, Facebook)	Solidarity (food, info, experiences); Social networks (SNS)
	Financial planning	Reduce non-food spending; limited movement; money saved from outside entertainment; financial management (more time to plan)	Reduce non-food spending; reduce food quantities

(continued)

Appendix A.2 (continued)

Type	Approach	Location	
		Urban Areas	Rural Areas
	Remote work adaptation	Setting up home workspaces; new time management (work from home, side hustles, family time, self-care); utilization of technology (work, communication, research)	
	Skill development	Online courses or Webinars; reading; self-directed research learning (about COVID-19 & beyond)	
	Canvasing for assistance	Sharing needs on SNS; utilization of local organizations/centers (shelter/food, etc.)	Government/ NGO assistance programs
	Entrepreneurship	Shifting to online (marketing & consumer engagement—WhatsApp); taking online entrepreneurial courses	Explore new opportunities (crossing borders, travel letters)
Social and Mental Health Issues	Maintaining Comms	With friends and family; video calls; virtual parties; utilization of social media	Talking to neighbors
	Engaging in physical activity	Home exercises (stairs, push-ups—gyms were closed); jogging around the neighborhood; virtual fitness challenges (Zumba, yoga)	
	Creative outlets	Engaging in arts and crafts; doing more hobbies as a form of expression and stress relief; involving family in one's hobbies	Involving family in one's hobbies
	Positive vibes only	Accepting reality mindset; trying to stay positive always; ignoring things that stress the mind	
	Religion and spirituality	Pray to the lord to deliver us from the pandemic; leave everything in the hands of God become more religious	Both God & spirituality

Source Compiled by the author (2024), based on Fieldwork Data (2024).

References

Adger, W. N. (2000). Social and ecological resilience: Are they related? *Progress in Human Geography*, *24*(3), 347–364. https://doi.org/10.1191/030913200701540465

Baumgartner, B., & Belevi, H. (2001). A Systematic Overview of Urban Agriculture in Developing Countries. https://bit.ly/3DfnNYY

BBC. (2020, July 16). *Coronavirus: Zimbabwe arrests 100,000 for "violations" of measures.* BBC Africa News. https://www.bbc.com/news/world-africa-53462259
Bernstein, H. (2016). Agriculture/Industry, rural/urban, peasants/workers: Some reflections on poverty, persistence and change. In J. Boltvinik, & S. A. Mann (Eds.), *Peasant poverty and persistence of the peasantry in the 21st century: Theories debates, realities and policies.* ZED books.
Boltvinik, J. (2016). Poverty and persistence of the peasantry: Background paper. In J. Boltvinik, & S. A. Mann (Eds.), *Peasant poverty and persistence of the peasantry in the 21st century: Theories debates, realities and policies.* ZED books.
Chambati, W. (2011). Restructuring of agrarian labor relations after Fast Track Land Reform in Zimbabwe. *The Journal of Peasant Studies, 38*(5), 1047–1068. https://doi.org/10.1080/03066150.2011.632088
Chavas, J. P. (2019). Adverse Shocks in Agriculture: The Assessment and Management of Downside Risk. *Journal of Agricultural Economics, 70*(3), 731–748. https://doi.org/10.1111/1477-9552.12312
Chayanov, A.V. (1991). *The Theory of Peasant Cooperatives. In Library: Second World series* (2nd ed.). Ohio State University Press.
Mackay, M., & Petersen, K. (2015). Rural Community Resilience: Research Stocktake and Annotated Bibliography. Lincoln University.
Mazwi, F., Muchetu, R. G., & Mudimu, G. T. (2021). Revisiting the trimodal agrarian structure as a social differentiation analysis framework in Zimbabwe: A Study. Agrarian South: *Journal of Political Economy, 4*(10), 60–73.
Moberg, F., & Hauge Simonsen, S. (2011). What is Resilience: An Introduction to Social-ecological Research. Stockholm Resilience Centre.
Moyo, S. (2016). *Family farming in sub-Saharan Africa: its contribution to agriculture, food security and rural development.* [Working paper, 150]. Sam Moyo, African Institute of Agrarian Studies. https://www.fao.org/3/a-i6056e.pdf
Moyo, S., Chambati, W., Mazwi, F., & Muchetu, R. G. (2015). Inter-district household survey: Follow up to the baseline survey.
Mubangizi, B. (2023). What is 'Rural' in South Africa, and Why Does it Matter? *African Journal of Governance and Development, 12*(2), 1–6. https://doi.org/10.36369/2616-9045/2023/v12i2a1
Muchetu, R. G. (2018). Agricultural Land-Delivery Systems in Zimbabwe: A Review of Four Decades of Sam Moyo's Work on Agricultural Land Markets and their Constraints. *African Study Monographs, 57*, 65–94.
Muchetu, R. G. (2023). COVID-19: A Perfect Storm of Downside Risk for Farmer's Markets and Livelihoods in Zimbabwe [Conference Paper]. *Japan Association for African Studies: 60th JAAS Annual Conference*, 41–46. https://bit.ly/3WtFBpk
Seko, B. B. M. B. S., Prisca, K., Jotham, K., Zhao, C., Hermane, G., & Babuna, P. (2023). The Economic Impact of COVID-19 on Africa and the Countermeasures. *Open Journal of Business and Management, 11*(02), 416–436. https://doi.org/10.4236/ojbm.2023.112023
Shrader-Frechette, K. S. (1990). Perceived Versus Actual Risks: Managing Hazards through Negotiation. *RISK: Health, Safety & Environment, 1*(4), 341–363. https://scholars.unh.edu/risk
The Herald. (2020, March 24). *Zimbabwe records first Coronavirus death: Breaking News.* Zimpapers Online. https://www.herald.co.zw/zim-records-first-coronavirus-death/
Van der Ploeg, J. D. (2010). The peasantries of the twenty-first century: The commoditization debate revisited. *Journal of Peasant Studies, 37*(1), 1–30. https://doi.org/10.1080/03066150903498721
Veritaszim. (2023). National Lockdowns. https://www.veritaszim.net/taxonomy/term/984?page=5
World Bank. (2023). *Rural population (% of total population) - Sub-Saharan Africa.* Metadata. https://bit.ly/4fkRypP

Rangarirai Gavin Muchetu Assistant Professor at the College of Intercultural Communication at Rikkyo University, Tokyo, Japan. He obtained his Ph.D. from Doshisha University, where he studied Japanese agriculture, drawing lessons for Zimbabwean policymakers. Thus, his research focuses on international agrarian issues, particularly the interplay between state policy and the socio-economic relations of rural dwellers. His recent publications include *After Radical Land Reforms: Restructuring Agricultural Cooperatives in Zimbabwe and Japan (2021, Langa RPCIG)* and 'South-South Cooperation in Agriculture: Impacts of Brazil's More Food International Program on Post-Land Reform Social Organizations in Zimbabwe (2022, *Agrarian South: Journal of Political Economy*).

Walter Chambati Executive Director of the Sam Moyo African Institute for Agrarian Studies, Harare, Zimbabwe. He is also a Research Fellow at the College of Graduate Studies, University of South Africa. He obtained a Ph.D. in Public Administration from the University of South Africa. Earlier degrees, a BSc (Hon) in Agriculture (Economics) and Master of Management were awarded by the Universities of Zimbabwe and Witwatersrand, respectively. His research mainly examines agrarian transformation in Africa. Recent publications include Labour Questions in Global South (Springer Press, 2021) and Farming and Working under Contract: Peasants and Workers in Global Agricultural Value Systems (Tulika Press, 2022).

Chapter 5
Politicization of COVID-19 in Uganda: A Critical Reflection on Government Interventions and Citizens' Perceptions

Vick Lukwago Ssali, Wakiko Ohira, Denis Musinguzi, and Nakabuye Juliet Musoke

Abstract The COVID-19 outbreak in Uganda coincided with the 2021 general elections. Facing strong opposition, Yoweri Museveni was standing at a critical juncture whether he would mark his 35th year as the president. This chapter situates COVID-19 in Museveni's regime. It examines how Museveni and his party, the National Resistance Movement (NRM), instrumentalized the pandemic, how citizens perceived the government interventions, and their consequences for Uganda's political future. We argue that, although the instrumentalization of the pandemic might have worked favorably for the ruling party to win the elections, the government interventions revealed the shortcomings of the semi-authoritarian regime—the skewed relationship between the central and local government and incapabilities of local governments—that might challenge Museveni's regime in the future.

Keywords Government interventions · Local governments · Politicization · Resilience · Risk-perception · Semi-authoritarianism

1 Introduction

Between the outbreak of COVID-19 and March 2023, Uganda—a landlocked country in East Africa—had confirmed 170,255 cases and 3630 deaths (Johns Hopkins University and Medicine 2023). The numbers are significantly low despite only 43%

V. L. Ssali (✉)
Department of English Language and Cultures, Aichi Gakuin University, Nisshin, Aichi, Japan
e-mail: vicks62@dpc.agu.ac.jp

W. Ohira
Center for Global Education and Discovery, Sophia University, Chiyoda, Tokyo, Japan

D. Musinguzi · N. J. Musoke
School of Arts and Social Sciences, Uganda Martyrs University Nkozi, Mpigi, Uganda

K. Hanai et al. (eds.), *Practical Wisdom and Resilience Overcoming Downside Risk*,
https://doi.org/10.1007/978-981-96-4455-1_5

of the population receiving at least one vaccination dose.[1] This low infection rate may be attributed to Uganda's lessons from several outbreaks of Ebola virus disease as well as the Ugandan government's strict measures against COVID-19. Soon after the World Health Organization (WHO) declared a pandemic on March 11, 2020, and even before Uganda registered a single death, President Yoweri Museveni announced a nationwide lockdown. The country closed its borders, set a curfew, restricted gatherings of more than five people, suspended business, stopped public transportation, and closed all schools.[2] The government also ordered people to follow the Standard Operating Procedures (SOPs) for COVID-19, such as washing hands, wearing a mask, and keeping a distance.

The government announced the first COVID-related death on July 23, 2020 (Mumbere 2020; Busari and Dean 2020). However, by the same date, twelve people had died at the hands of the armed forces enforcing curfews (BBC News, July 23, 2020). Ugandan citizens started to notice that the disease was not killing as many people as the strict measures and their implementing bodies—the army and the police. Moreover, the outbreak of COVID-19 coincided with a heated moment in political campaigns and elections for the president, members of parliament, and local government officials in January 2021. Although the total lockdown might have mitigated the spread of the unprecedented disease, the dominant view among the people was that the government was instrumentalizing the pandemic as a political tool to offer an undue advantage to the ruling party—the National Resistance Movement (NRM)—and constrain the activities of opposition parties during the campaign and election process.

Indeed, there are some examples of harassment and arrests of opposition members. For instance, during the first lockdown, an opposition member of parliament, Francis Zaake, provided food relief to members of his constituency and was arrested and tortured for engaging in negligent acts likely to cause the spread of coronavirus (Human Rights Watch, April 28, 2020; Uganda Police Force, April 24, 2020). Also, citizens criticized the lockdown because they faced many difficulties, such as unemployment, domestic violence, and teenage pregnancy, to list a few. However, we need to critically examine how the government interventions to COVID-19 played a role in further consolidating Museveni and the NRM's power.

The NRM government, led by Museveni, emerged as a celebrated force of liberation in 1986 (Ssali 2023). Initially, it garnered widespread support for bringing stability to the country, with many Ugandans viewing Museveni's takeover as a

[1] For example, Japan shows one of the highest percentages of the population receiving at least one dose of vaccinations: 83%. However, the number of confirmed cases and deaths are incomparable to those of Uganda: 33,320,438 cases and 72,997 deaths (Johns Hopkins University and Medicine 2023).

[2] Originally, the nationwide lockdown was to continue for 14 days. However, this closure of schools and institutions of higher learning ended up as the "world's longest lockdown," lasting more than 83 weeks (Muhumuza 2022).

much-needed relief from turmoil. However, since the country transitioned into elective politics in 1996, there has been a noticeable shift. Museveni's regime has gradually adopted elements of authoritarian control such as (1) limited political competition—while multi-party elections may exist, opposition parties are often marginalized or suppressed, and the ruling party maintains a firm grip on power; (2) restricted civil liberties—freedom of speech, assembly, and association is often curtailed, with dissenting voices facing harassment, censorship, or imprisonment; (3) the weak rule of law—legal institutions exist, yet they are often subservient to the ruling party, and selective enforcement of laws is common, particularly against political opponents; and (4) concentration of power—political power concentrates in the hands of the president, the NRM, and a small group of elites, often with little to no checks and balances (Tripp 2010; Mwenda 2007; Ssali 2023).

The general elections in January 2021 were crucial for the NRM and Museveni. People's distrust in the NRM has increased because of its authoritarian characteristics. According to Afrobarometer, when asked "how much [they] trust the ruling party," those who responded "not at all" increased from 11% in 2005, just before the country conducted the first multi-party elections in fifteen years, to 25% in 2019.[3] Also, Museveni's vote share decreased from 76% in 1996 to 61% in 2016 (The Electoral Commission 2007, 2016).[4] Furthermore, in the 2021 elections, the NRM and Museveni faced a new opposition party—the National Unity Platform (NUP) led by Kyagulanyi Robert Ssentamu, also known as Bobi Wine, the "strongest challenger to Mr[.] Museveni" (Chibelushi 2024). The NUP was registered as a political party in August 2019 and has gained support, particularly in the central region. Museveni's regime was at a critical juncture when COVID-19 outbroke: Was he going to mark his 35th year as the president, or would Ugandan citizens give their verdict that they are tired of authoritarian rule and choose the opposition forces? Thus, Museveni's handling of COVID-19 and how the citizens perceived the government interventions were of the utmost importance for the elections.

Given this context, interesting questions arise: How did Museveni and the NRM instrumentalize the pandemic? How did the citizens perceive the government interventions? And, what are the consequences of the government interventions for Uganda's political future? This chapter makes three interlocking arguments based on in-depth semi-structured interviews in 2022 and 2023. First, Museveni and the NRM took clear advantage of the government interventions, particularly restricting public gatherings during the campaigns for the general elections. Second, the citizens recognized that the central government unfairly managed the election campaigns; however, they also commended the government's handling of the pandemic to prevent the spread of COVID-19 and protect people's lives. Third, although citizens commended the central government, they showed their disappointment with local governments'

---

[3] Respondents selected one answer among five multiple-choice answers: a lot, somewhat, just a little, not at all, and don't know/haven't heard enough to say.

[4] Interestingly, when the country transitioned from "no-party democracy" to multi-party elections in 2006, Museveni scored the lowest: 59%. In other years prior to the latest election in 2021, he scored 69% in 2001; 69% in 2011.

response to the pandemic: the pandemic revealed a heavily centralized authority—local governments' dependency on the central government and their incapabilities. Taken together, the instrumentalization of the pandemic may be reflected in the result of the presidential election, where Museveni won with 58% of the total vote and the NRM remained the dominant party.[5] However, in the long term, citizens' growing dissatisfaction with local governments might influence future elections.

This chapter is organized as follows. First, we explain our method. Second, we describe our conceptual framework and explain how we situate Uganda's COVID-19 experiences in Museveni's regime. Third, we critically examine how the government instrumentalized the pandemic, how citizens perceived the government interventions, and their consequences for Uganda's political future. We argue that, although the instrumentalization of the pandemic might have worked favorably for the ruling party to win the elections, the government interventions revealed the shortcoming of the semi-authoritarian regime—heavily centralized authority and incapacities of local governments, which might challenge Museveni's regime in the future.

2 Method

To answer the research question—how the government interventions to COVID-19 played a role in further consolidating Museveni and the NRM's power—our team conducted 172 semi-structured interviews in nine districts in three regions: Central (13 respondents in Kampala; 12 in Wakiso and Mpigi; 21 in Mukono; and 23 in Mubende), Western (28 in Mbarara; and 22 in Ishingiro), and Eastern (25 in Mbale; and 28 in Jinja). We conducted the interviews in two phases: between October and December 2022 and between July and September 2023. Interview questions were divided into five sections. Section A asked about the basic information of the respondent—such as age, ethnicity, and political orientation. Section B asked about the government interventions—what kind of interventions/restrictions the respondent observed, whether they received any relief supplies from the government, and how they evaluated the central/local government handling of the pandemic. Section C asked about the observed relationship between government interventions and political campaigns in the 2021 general elections. Then, Section D asked about the respondent's experience during the first lockdown in 2020 and the second lockdown in 2021. Finally, Section E asked how the respondent and their family survived the severe lockdowns.

We qualitatively examine the answers to several questions. First, the respondents' political orientation—whether they support the NRM, the NUP, other opposition parties, independent candidates, or have no interest in politics—is crucial to examining how citizens perceive the government interventions in the pandemic. If they support the NRM, they may favorably evaluate the government interventions. They

[5] Ssentamu received 35% of the total vote (The Electoral Commission 2021). Establishing a direct link between pandemic-related measures and electoral results is beyond the scope of this chapter.

may on the other hand unfairly criticize the government interventions if they support the NUP or other opposition parties. Among the respondents, 70 stated that they support the ruling NRM party, 60 expressed no interest in politics, 17 said they support the main opposition party, NUP, 10 supported independent candidates, 11 expressed their support for other opposition parties, and 4 respondents did not wish to disclose their political orientation. While 70 respondents indicated support for the NRM and 60 claimed disinterest in politics, it is important to consider the potential for response bias. Given the context of the interviews, it is plausible that some individuals may have overstated their support for the ruling party or claimed disinterest in politics due to concerns about the interviewer's intentions or the perceived consequences of their responses. We kept this possible distortion in mind when interpreting the data.

Regional differences and ethnic affiliations play a crucial role in shaping political orientation, as evidenced by the results from Mbarara District, President Museveni's home. In this district, 78% of respondents expressed support for the ruling NRM party. Mbarara is predominantly inhabited by Banyankole, Museveni's ethnic group, who are known to offer strong backing to his leadership.[6] However, it is important to recognize that not all respondents in this region may have been entirely sincere when expressing support for the NRM. Some may have overstated their allegiance due to social pressures or concerns about how their political orientation would be perceived.

Second, we examine whether respondents observed any instrumentalization of the pandemic in the process of campaigns for the 2021 general elections. For instance, if they noticed that the government officials, the army, or the police restricted an opposition party candidate's campaign while the NRM members conducted campaigns without any restriction. Third, we look into how severely respondents were affected by the first and second lockdowns and how they overcame their difficulties. We repeated the same set of questions about the first lockdown in 2020 and the second lockdown in 2021—their location during the lockdowns, whether their children attended school or had access to online learning tools, and their biggest problems. We consider the differences between the answers about the first lockdown and the second. Fourth, we scrutinize their perceptions of government interventions, particularly their evaluation of the central and local government.

The three foci of our examination are how the government instrumentalized COVID-19, how citizens perceived the government interventions, and the consequences for Museveni and the NRM in relation not only to the 2021 general elections but also to their power consolidation for the foreseeable future. There are limitations to our fieldwork. First, we could not conduct the research during and immediately after the lockdowns. Thus, respondents needed to reflect on their memories, which might differ from realities. Moreover, we could not collect answers from the northern region of Uganda. The northern region is often home to opposition parties. We must also consider the northern districts' physical distance from Kampala, which

[6] Banyankole means the people of Ankole, the ancient Ankole Kingdom and the region also referred to as Nkole.

COVID-19 affected severely, particularly during the second lockdown. Citizens in the northern region may have different tendencies in their answers. Recognizing these limitations, our chapter contributes to understanding the ramifications of the unprecedented disease and Uganda's political dynamics.

3 Framework: Centralization of Decentralized Local Councils

This study situates the government's COVID-19 interventions in Museveni's semi-authoritarian or "hybrid regime" as described by Tripp (2010, p. 1). According to Tripp (2010), a hybrid regime is a political system that exhibits characteristics of both authoritarianism and democracy. While there are some semblances of democratic institutions, such as multi-party elections and a legislature, they are often manipulated or controlled by a highly centralized authority in the president. Tripp (2010, p. 1) reiterates that Museveni and the country's leaders "adopt the trappings of democracy, yet they pervert democracy—sometimes through patronage and largess, other times through violence and repression—for the sole purpose of remaining in power." Fifteen years have passed since Tripp made this observation, and Museveni's regime has acquired even more authoritarian characteristics to consolidate his power. Museveni removed presidential term limits in 2005, and to run in the 2021 presidential election, he amended the constitution in 2017 to remove age limits for presidential candidates. His regime is one of the longest-running in Africa.

Museveni has instrumentalized many things besides amending the constitution to remain in power. Instrumentalization of local governments is crucial to our examination of the COVID-19 interventions and citizens' perceptions of them. Uganda's local government system is called Local Councils (LCs). The origin of LCs is Resistance Councils (RCs). The National Resistance Army led by Museveni established RCs in the early 1980s to support their guerrilla warfare against the preceding regime. After taking power in 1986, he quickly implemented a decentralization reform based on RCs. Although RCs in the early 1980s were limited to the central region, Museveni began placing RCs across the country. The 1995 Constitution renamed RCs as LCs. LCs are placed at each administrative level: LC5 at the district level, LC4 at the county level, LC3 at the sub-county level, LC2 at the parish level, and LC1 at the village level.[7]

The 1997 Local Governments Act clearly states that the aim of decentralization is to "ensure good governance and democratic participation in, and control of, decision making by the people" (The Government of Uganda 1997). However, Museveni and the NRM gradually centralized the formerly decentralized LCs and deprived them of the power to function as a body to provide goods and services and a place to ensure citizens' decision-making.

[7] In urban areas, there are five levels of administrative units: city, municipal, town, ward, and zone. City is equivalent to a district in urban areas.

What lies under the centralization of LCs is the increasing number of districts under Museveni's regime. There were only 33 districts in Uganda when Museveni came to power. The parliament added six districts in 1991, and shortly after the 1996 presidential election, it added another six in 1997. Adding a few districts every two to three years doubled their number: there were 111 districts by 2010. Furthermore, the parliament has added new districts every year since the presidential election in 2016. As a result, at the time of writing there are 146 districts, including 11 cities. The number of districts has more than tripled under Museveni's regime. The number of lower administrative units—from villages to counties—has also dramatically increased. There are several reasons for the increase of administrative units, such as bringing local government services nearer to the people in a remote area. However, the Development Network of Indigenous Voluntary Associations (DENIVA)—a non-governmental advocacy organization based in Uganda—argues that "the best explanation for district creation is that the new districts are being used as patronage" (DENIVA 2011, p.29). Many scholars back this view (Green 2010, Awortwi and Helmsing 2014; Vokes and Wilkins 2016; Titeca 2018; Mwenda 2007; Makara 2010; Ohira 2023).

As the number of LCs increased, Museveni gradually centralized the decentralized LCs through several means. First, LCs are financially dependent on the central government: 96% of LCs' revenues comes from the central government. This is the highest dependency rate in Sub-Saharan Africa, followed by 90% in Tanzania, 89% in Rwanda, and 75% in Mali (Organization for Economic Co-operation and Development and United Cities and Local Government 2019). In 2005, a year before the 2006 presidential election, the government decided to eradicate the Graduated Personal Tax—the primary source of local revenues—owing to its unpopularity. However, the percentage of the national budget allocated to LCs has decreased from 23% in FY2011/12 to 11% in 2019/20 (MoFPED 2012; Ggoobi and Lukwago 2020; National Planning Authority 2020).[8] LCs must implement decentralized services—such as education and health care—with a smaller budget allocated to each district.

Second, the central government controls key positions at the local level. The 1997 Local Governments Act allows the president to appoint a Resident District Commissioner (RDC) who represents the president and the government in each district (GoU 1997). In addition, before 2005, a District Service Commission (DSC)—consisting of an elected district chairperson and other members—appointed a Chief Administrative Officer (CAO) at each district. However, the constitutional amendment in 2005 reverted the right to appoint CAOs to the central government. As LCs become more accountable to the central government rather than the local people through financial recentralization (Ohira 2023), CAOs are more loyal to the central government, which appoints and deploys them (Nabaho 2013).

By the 2006 elections, LCs had become key in consolidating the NRM's power across the country, as they functioned as local governance bodies and as a means to maintain political control and monitor opposition activities at the community level. Many LC leaders have been either direct members of the NRM or closely aligned

[8] FY stands for Financial Year.

with the party. The party uses its control of local governance structures to mobilize support during elections, often blurring the lines between state resources and party politics. Furthermore, LCs lack competent and qualified human resources to provide decentralized services. In other words, LCs have neither economic resources nor political autonomy. The relationship between the central and local government is highly entangled (Grossman and Lewis 2014; Lewis 2014; Lambright 2011; Ohira 2023).

The COVID-19 outbreak occurred in this context, where Museveni uses LCs to consolidate his and the NRM's power. Behind the instrumentalization, LCs' function as a service delivery body deteriorates or stagnates: How could they effectively function to mitigate the pandemic? Considering that citizens' distrust in and disapproval of LCs has increased, citizens' evaluation of local governments' COVID-19 interventions is highly relevant in examining the consequences of government interventions for Uganda's political future. According to a 2002 Afrobarometer survey, to the question of whether "[they] approve or disapprove of the way [local government councilors] have performed their jobs over the past 12 months," 53.7% of the respondents selected "approve," and only 4.8% selected "disapprove" on a five-point Likert scale. Fifteen years later, in response to the same question, the percentage of respondents who selected "approve" declined to 45.5%, while those who selected "disapprove" increased to 24.8%. Furthermore, Afrobarometer (2002, 2017) shows citizens' growing distrust in local governments: To the question "how much [they] trust [their] elected local governments," those who responded "not at all" and "just a little" increased from 22.1% in 2002 to 40.6% in 2017. The number of respondents who selected "somewhat" and "a lot" decreased from 77.2% to 53.8%.

Thus, taken together with the citizens' increasing distrust in the NRM and Museveni's decreasing vote share, citizens' evaluation of both central and local government handling of COVID-19 is crucial to understanding the current political dynamics in Uganda. Under these circumstances, this study also interrogates the critical claim that political power has tended to be increasingly concentrated in the hands of the president, the ruling NRM party, and a small group of elites. If this is the case, decisions regarding pandemic response would often have been centralized, with little input or oversight from other branches of government, civil society, or the public.

4 Discussion

4.1 Instrumentalization of the Pandemic

> When those in the ruling party and the government were campaigning, it was like there was no COVID-19. But, if the opposition parties were campaigning, like this man, Bobi Wine and Katumba 'Oyee', … , those were beaten all the time that they were breaching presidential

> directives on COVID-19. But, those in government used to do their campaigns without a problem. They did not handle it properly. It was their political game to win elections.[9]

The Electoral Commission released a press statement on October 22, 2020, outlining the campaign period and polling dates for the 2021 general elections. In the press release, the Electoral Commission listed seven guidelines. For instance, to prevent the spread of COVID-19, "processions and public/mass rallies remain banned" (Electoral Commission 2020). However, candidates were "allowed to organize/hold campaign meetings, in a regulated manner, preferably outdoors, with limited attendance of a maximum of seventy (70) persons, to enable the observance of the 2-m social distancing rule for the persons attending the meeting" (Electoral Commission 2020). Were these guidelines fairly applied to all candidates regardless of their political party?

To understand how the ruling party instrumentalized the pandemic and how citizens perceived the government's handling of political campaigns under COVID-19, we asked two questions: (1) How were the government interventions managed in the process of political campaigns for general elections?; (2) How did the interventions or restrictions affect the activities of different political parties during the campaign process? For the latter question, except for 18 respondents who observed that the government—or implementing bodies such as the police and the army—fairly applied the guidelines to all candidates, most respondents perceived that the government used the guidelines as "an excuse" to prevent opposition candidates from campaigning.[10]

Opposition parties receive stronger support in central districts—Wakiso, Mpigi, Mukono, and Kampala. For instance, in Wakiso, all seven elected members of parliament (MPs) belong to the opposition parties, the NUP and the Forum for Democratic Change (FDC). In Mpigi, two MPs were elected, and they are both opposition members from the NUP and the FDC, respectively. In Mukono, among the four MPs, three belong to the NUP, and one belongs to the Democratic Party (DP). In Kampala, among the nine elected MPs, only one MP is independent, and the rest belong to the NUP. Thus, as a result of the 2021 parliament elections, the NRM secured no seat in the parliament in Wakiso, Mpigi, Mukono, and Kampala. Notably, in those four central districts, the respondents perceived that the government unfairly applied the guidelines.

In Wakiso and Mpigi, ten respondents among 12 (83%) described the unfair management of political campaigns. For instance, even though the guidelines allowed a campaign meeting of 70 people, a respondent observed that "if [opposition candidates] gathered more than ten people, [the police] would just put them in prison, beat, and teargas them."[11] Another respondent observed that being jailed, abducted,

---

[9] Interview with a 51-year-old Muganda in Kampala. This respondent supports no political parties. The question was "How were the government interventions managed in the process of political campaigns for general elections?" Katumba 'Oyee' refers to Katumba John, the youngest presidential candidate in the 2021 elections.

[10] Interview with a 27-year-old Muganda, Kampala.

[11] Interview with a 50-year-old Muganda, Wakiso.

or beaten was not the case with NRM candidates. Even though some respondents did not directly complain about the jailing or beating of opposition candidates in Wakiso and Mpigi, they noted that opposition candidates could not hold their campaign meetings while the NRM freely conducted theirs.

In Mukono, where opposition candidates secured all four parliamentary seats, seven out of 21 respondents (33%) clearly stated that there was no discrimination among political parties or that they did not notice any discrimination. Three of the seven respondents claimed to be NRM supporters; four expressed no political affiliations. However, a NUP supporter described the electoral process as follows:

> Chaos. Here, they were like a bush war. They were harassing our voters and beating the youths. All leaders were clad in military attire and moving around in the names of enforcing SOPs and security. But, even at night, when people were indoors, they were being harassed. You could get calls at night from our campaigners being tortured for campaigning.[12]

Three NRM supporters also witnessed how the NRM freely conducted campaigns while the police or the army oppressed opposition candidates. For instance, an NRM supporter said, with chuckles, "… of course, NRM candidates managed to do their campaigns but not opposition."[13] Furthermore, respondents with no political affiliation in Mukono described how the government took advantage of the guidelines: "People in power used it to their advantage to make campaigns and barred the oppositions much."[14]

Among the central districts where we conducted interviews, it was only in Mubende that the NRM secured three seats in the parliament (Uganda Elections Data Portal, 2021a). In Mubende, seven out of 23 respondents said they were NRM supporters; five were opposition supporters; nine had no political affiliation; two did not wish to reveal their political orientation. Then, 12 respondents out of 23 (52%) said they had observed unfair application of the campaign guidelines:

> It was brutal to the opposition. You also saw how the opposition was treated. People like Amuriat. How can you stop one from campaigning and even beat his supporters wherever they go and call that democracy? Even here in Mubende, people from the opposition were beaten all the time whenever [soldiers] saw them and even just walking on the streets.[15]

A statement by an NRM politician at a local council in Mubende is worth noting. To the question of how the interventions or restrictions affected the activities of different political parties during the campaign process, the respondent stated that:

> Of course, we had the power and resources to do our campaigns on TV and radio stations. How could you allow your opponent to do campaigns against you? That is when we also used the chance of restrictions in place. But, for us, we could go everywhere to make campaigns.[16]

---

[12] Interview with a 60-year-old Muganda in Mukono. NUP supporter.

[13] Interview with a 37-year-old Muganda in Mukono. NRM supporter.

[14] Interview with a 30-year-old Muganda in Mukono. No political affiliation.

[15] Interview with a 37-year-old Muteso in Mubende. Opposition supporter. Patrick Oboi Amuriat is the president of the Forum for Democratic Change. Amuriat competed the 2021 presidential election and received 337,689 (3.3%) of the total valid votes (The Electoral Commission 2021).

[16] Interview with a 50-year-old Munyankole in Mubende.

The NRM took clear advantage of the government interventions, particularly restricting public gatherings during the campaigns for the general elections. However, compared with the other four districts in the central region—Wakiso, Mpigi, Mukono, and Kampala, a smaller percentage of respondents in Mubende where the ruling party had more supporters observed unfair application of the campaign guidelines to opposition candidates.

This applies to the eastern and western regions. In Mbale, the NRM candidates secured all three parliament seats. In Jinja, an NRM and an independent candidate won two parliament seats, representing the district. In the western region—where Museveni has a solid support base—an NRM and an independent candidate won two parliament seats in Mbarara, and three NRM candidates and one independent candidate won four parliament seats in Isingiro. Thus, both in the eastern and western districts where we conducted interviews (Mbale, Jinja, Mbarara, and Isingiro), no opposition member could win a parliamentary seat (Uganda Elections Data Portal 2021b, 2021c, 2021d, 2021e).

In Mbale, among 25 respondents, 11 (44%) claimed to be NRM supporters; eight (32%) said they support independent candidates; three (12%) expressed their support for opposition parties; three did not show interest in politics. Six out of 11 NRM supporters in Mbale perceived that the government had fairly managed the political campaigns. A respondent in Mbale noted that "[he thought] it was equal. It was free and fair for everybody."[17] On the other hand, two NRM supporters, three opposition supporters, and five other respondents (40%) observed that the management of electoral campaigns was unfair:

> Yes. They were affected because now these other parties were not allowed to move freely because of the pandemic or the virus. [Opposition candidates] were not allowed to reach out to their people freely. They were negatively impacted. The ruling party had an advantage because they were already in power. They had the control, and still they remained with their support.[18]

Although a smaller percentage of respondents in the districts where the NRM members became MPs perceived the government's unfair management of political campaigns, those interview statements show that the government's authoritarian characteristics were apparent across the Central, Eastern, and Western regions: the government interventions were not only to prevent the spread of COVID-19; the ruling party instrumentalized the guidelines to exclude opposition candidates from the campaign process.

4.2 *Citizens' Perception of the Central and Local Government*

The NRM retained their support despite their unfair management of the election campaigns. When it comes to evaluating the central government's handling of

---

[17] Interview with a 43-year-old Gishu in Mbale. The respondent is an NRM supporter.

[18] Interview with a 38-year-old Japadhola. A NUP supporter in Mbale.

COVID-19, the majority of the respondents did not even mention the unfair election campaigns.[19] They focused on whether or not the government has protected people's lives. Remarkably, our interview data in phase two (conducted between July and September 2023) tells us that the respondents—regardless of their political affiliation—perceived that the central government managed the pandemic fairly well. For instance, an opposition supporter in Isingiro contended that the government interventions saved people's lives: "Government tried especially with restrictions. People feared for their lives and adhered to government guidelines. This minimized infections and deaths."[20] Also, a respondent in Mbarara who supports the FDC stated that "the central government did well because the percentage of deaths in other countries was higher than in Uganda."[21] Citizens believe that the number of COVID-19 deaths remained low because the government imposed strict measures, and they even appreciate the central government.

The point here is that even opposition supporters who strongly condemn the government intervention during the electoral campaigns commend the central government's handling of the pandemic.[22] This is particularly true after the second wave of COVID-19. During the first wave in December 2020, citizens in Uganda did not take the disease seriously. However, during the second wave in July 2021, Uganda was recording more than 100 deaths per day, and the citizens found out how severe the disease was. During the second wave, people were talking about their family members and friends who were in a serious condition or had died. The streets were empty, as people feared the disease.[23] We asked respondents the same set of questions about the first lockdown—before and during the first wave—and the second lockdown—during the second wave—to articulate their perceived risks. During the second wave, respondents perceived both the risk of contracting COVID-19 and losing their lives and other risks, such as losing jobs and not having enough money to buy food for families. When we asked the respondents to reflect on their experiences during the two lockdowns, the unfair management of election campaigns was irrelevant to their perception of the risk of losing one's life.

An interesting finding is that most respondents had a lower evaluation of their local government's handling of COVID-19 than that of the central government. The interview data shows that the local government only followed the central government and took no initiative to protect people's lives. For instance, a respondent in Mubende stated that:

[19] We asked the following question: How do you evaluate the central government's handling of the COVID-19 pandemic?

[20] Interview with a 34-year-old Munyankole. A NUP supporter in Isingiro.

[21] Interview with a 28-year-old Munyankole. A FDC supporter in Mbarara.

[22] In other words, it is likely that NRM supporters commend the central government's handling of the pandemic.

[23] Ohira, one of the authors, was in Uganda and conducting research for another project in June and July 2021.

> The local government was only following orders from the president. Local government was stripped of its powers, and the army was doing most of the work, such as distributing food in the communities. Yet, they did not know the locals.[24]

Another respondent in Mbarara observed that "local government had very little say in COVID-19 matters, as decisions were made from the top."[25] A similar statement by a respondent in Mubende expresses the top-down relationship between the central and local government:

> For me, I saw everything being managed by the central government. Our mayors did not do anything. Everything was left to be managed by RDCs [Resident District Commissioners] at the local level. Everyone had to go to them for permission, and they told you where to go. […] The mayor had no role to play and no say at that time. Not even local council leaders.[26]

The respondents' perceptions of the central government interventions are two-fold: They realize that the ruling party politicized government interventions to COVID-19, particularly the restriction of public gathering, during election campaigns. At the same time, the government interventions did mitigate the risks of people contracting COVID-19 and losing their lives. However, their perceptions of local government interventions differ.

We argue that COVID-19 revealed how heavily centralized the Ugandan government had become. An interview with the mayor of Jinja city, a NUP member, shows how difficult it was to coordinate between the ruling party and the opposition party at the local level during the pandemic.

> But for Jinja City, I should say we tried because with the little resources we had, and remember, given our political situation in Uganda, you find a situation whereby the mayor is NUP, and now you have the RDC who is the president's representative [in a district], which is NRM, you have the police and other organs [who follow president's order].[27]

Some citizens in Jinja also experienced how the conflicting relationship between the ruling and opposition members at the local council prevented the local government from providing relief during the lockdowns.

> There was a lot of politics at the local government level. People support different parties. And, you could go to the sub-county, and someone [an elected politician at the LC3] tells you that you did not elect them! He does not even care about you, but [he cares] only about his family and those who elected him! That was not good.[28]

---

[24] Interview with a 57-year-old Muganda. An opposition supporter in Mubende.

[25] Interview with a 33-year-old Munyankole. A FDC supporter in Mbarara.

[26] Interview with a 51-year-old Muganda in Mubende. This respondent supports no political parties.

[27] Interview with a 43-year-old Musoga. The respondent belongs to the NUP and is the elected mayor of Jinja City. RDC refers to a Residence District Commissioner.

[28] Interview with a 38-year-old Musamya in Jinja. The respondent supports no political parties.

The same respondent observed that the central government handled the pandemic well but criticized the local government for doing "a shoddy job."[29] Another respondent in Jinja also thought that the central government managed COVID-19 well yet described the LC's handling of the pandemic as "very selective."[30]

Certain citizens faced situations where they were denied access to relief supplies during the lockdowns because of their political orientation. This made citizens realize that the country's politics penetrate the local level. Respondents were disappointed that politics can affect people's lives. How does the disappointment influence future elections in Uganda? Surprisingly, 60 respondents (35%) described themselves as apolitical: they do not support political parties and show little interest in the country's politics. After experiencing the pandemic, a respondent said, "I do not vote anymore" because he was disappointed that the local government did nothing for them during the pandemic.[31] As Sect. 3 of this chapter argues, Museveni's instrumentalization of LCs led to their stagnation as a service delivery body. COVID-19 further revealed the skewed relationship between the central and local government, and it may accelerate citizens' disappointment and their loss of interest in politics. Museveni's regime is indeed at a critical juncture.

5 Conclusion

Museveni and the NRM took clear advantage of the government interventions—particularly restricting public gatherings—and controlled election campaigns. At the same time, people perceive that strict government interventions prevented the spread of COVID-19 and protected people's lives. Thus, the central government left impressions of strength and decisiveness. However, the pandemic simultaneously revealed the skewed relationship between the central and local governments, and citizens witnessed local governments' lack of autonomy and incapabilities. It can also be argued that although Museveni's government won the 2021 general elections, people's disappointment with the local governments might influence future elections.

It is necessary to also situate these citizens' perceptions within the broader context of the unique challenges faced by African countries. The COVID-19 pandemic has profoundly affected the African continent, revealing both vulnerabilities and resilience within its diverse nations. For example, African countries, including Uganda, faced significant challenges due to their already inefficient healthcare system and a high burden of communicable diseases, such as malaria, HIV/AIDS, and tuberculosis. The pandemic exacerbated existing issues, highlighting the system's inability to respond to such a crisis adequately. The strain on resources, limited medical infrastructure, and shortage of healthcare professionals made it difficult to manage the surge in cases effectively, ultimately worsening the public health situation. At the

---

[29] Ibid.

[30] Interview with a 36-year-old Musoga in Jinja, a NUP supporter.

[31] Interview with a 58-year-old Musoga in Jinja. The respondent supports no political parties.

same time, Africa's low COVID-19 mortality rate despite the fragile health care system showed the continent's resilience.

Like many other African countries, Uganda also faced severe challenges in education. With widespread school closures, millions of children and youths were deprived of formal education. While some children and youths had access to education through the internet and digital devices, showing their resilience amid the difficult situation, vulnerable families were left behind. The digital divide became more pronounced as many students lacked access to the necessary technology for remote learning, exacerbating educational inequalities. Findings from this research are interspersed with these challenges, as well as the innovation and adaptations within the education sector that these challenges spurred.

In addition to the lack of access to adequate healthcare and education, the measures taken to control the spread of the virus and the socio-economic consequences of the pandemic led to several human rights concerns across the African continent. The pandemic saw increased restrictions on freedoms, including the right to move and assemble. Like many other governments in Africa, the government of Uganda imposed harsh lockdown measures that disproportionately affected populations. Additionally, as the results of our interviews have shown, the economic downturn resulting from the pandemic exacerbated poverty, food insecurity, and unemployment.

Data from the interviews show that to cope with government repression and ineffective local leadership, Ugandan communities formed mutual aid networks, relied on traditional medicines, and engaged in informal economies. Families stood out in aiding each other to share essentials such as food and the meager finances they had left; many turned to herbal remedies and traditional healers when healthcare was inaccessible, and stories were told of professionals such as teachers who resorted to selling charcoal and chapati or driving "boda bodas"[32] to ensure their survival. Although repressive politics and inaction by local government leaders could have undermined people's confidence in the Ugandan government, the pandemic highlighted the resilience and solidarity of grassroots communities. Finally, by focusing on political intervention, we hope this chapter will be a timely addition to the more specific legal, democratic, and human rights perspectives on the COVID-19 pandemic.

6 Column 3

Grassroots voices from Uganda

1. **Grassroots' risk-perceptions**

[32] A "boda boda" is a motorcycle taxi or bicycle taxi that is a common mode of transportation in Uganda and other East African countries.

Story from a 35-year-old male taxi driver from Mbale (Interviewed August 27, 2023)

It [the lockdown] all came very abruptly. People were found unsuspecting. Drivers were caught up in places they could not return from. Many cars were restricted. It was a sudden shock. My biggest problem was a sudden loss of income. Also, when the time came to take children back to school, they had lost TWO years. A child who was in P1 could not just go on to P3. They would not cope. They had to start from zero. Children had gone back to zero academic wise. As a parent I had to try every day not to show them my sadness because they were too young to understand what the lockdown was about. They had promised to bring us TVs and radios (to help children learn), but nothing was accomplished. Even the masks supplied were not enough for all of us. Life was tough. You could even fail to secure an item of 1000 shillings [about 30 cents of a dollar] for your family. The second lockdown found us a little prepared. We knew how to survive. When the first lockdown ended we learned that if you get 2000 shillings, you save at least 200. That could help in emergencies. If you had 100,000 shillings then you could decide to buy corn flour and stock it for your people to survive on for some time. But children left school again. They really went back academically for the collective two years. There was a lack of income, and children were stuck at home. Work was strictly restricted. Even when we [taxi drivers] were allowed back on the road, the number of passengers was restricted to seven or eight.

Story from a 24-year-old female nurse from Jinja (Interviewed 21 August 2023)

My child had to stay at home without going to school. As for me, it was the inability to work while at the same time I had just secured a loan from the bank. During the lockdown, the banks suspended payment, alright, but I had to use the money for survival rather than the intended purpose, and after the lockdown it was difficult to get back the money and pay. My bigger family was greatly affected by the loss of the father, which coincided with the lockdown. It was not the normal way we would handle mourners. The family in the village though benefitted from the kindness of the villagers who brought them food after the loss of my father. Many of my family had to rush to go back. We went back home, but did not know how to survive under the circumstances. There was no work, and no income. When the second lockdown came, the biggest problem was still the inability to work. I could try means like selling fried cassava, but still very few people could afford to buy it. You invested say 20,000 shillings in it, but getting it back was a struggle. As for my daughter, besides getting sick, she did not really know what we were going through as she was only five. In any case she missed a lot of learning as she could not even afford online learning. My bigger family was greatly affected. One of my sisters, for example, lives and works in Sudan, but she could not go back and spent the second lockdown at my place, where she even gave birth to a baby.

2. **Grassroots' Coping Mechanisms**

Story from a 56-year-old male farmer from Mbale (Interviewed 26 August 2023)

Lockdowns taught me as an individual, first, to take money seriously when you have it. Do not overspend. If you have 10,000, save 2000 [shillings]. Because things can happen any time. Even family expenditures must change. If you were consuming 4 kg, reduce and save, do not eat as you want. We also learned to resort or revert to herbals, lemons, etc., as preventives and health support. Families did the same and advised each other about using the same herbs and other unconventional or traditional methods. In the case of need, we also ran to neighbors and friends who had more basic supplies like maize flour for posho. But also, richer people such as our MPs brought flour and other supplies for us to share.

Story from a 58-year-old female farmer from Jinja (Interviewed 21 August 2023)

When we did not feel well, with fevers for example, we used local herbs. We used local medicines; for we could not access hospitals, and we had no money. Also, as family members, we used to check on each other via telephone. To comfort each other. In the community, we mainly kept each in their homes. From there we would call out loud and check how our neighbors were doing. On a few occasions we took what we had and put it on our neighbors' doors in case they have a need. Yes. There was that kind of reciprocation sometimes.

Acknowledgements The authors express their gratitude to the semi-structured interview respondents for their participation in this study. An earlier version of this chapter was presented at a workshop in Kampala, and we are deeply thankful to the workshop participants for their invaluable comments and feedback. Finally, we acknowledge the Uganda National Council for Science and Technology, from whom we obtained a research permit (Research Registration Number: SS1999ES) for this study, and extend our heartfelt thanks for their support.

References

Afrobarometer. (2002). *Uganda, Round 2*, available at https://www.afrobarometer.org

Afrobarometer. (2017). *Uganda, Round 7*, available at https://www.afrobarometer.org

BBC News. (2020, July 23). *Uganda - where security forces may be more deadly than coronavirus.* https://www.bbc.com/news/world-africa-53450850

Awortwi, N., & Helmsing, A. H. J. (Bert). (2014). Behind the façade of bringing services closer to people: The proclaimed and hidden intentions of the government of Uganda to create many new local government districts. *Canadian Journal of African Studies, 48*(2), 297–314. https://doi.org/10.1080/00083968.2014.905260

Busari, S., & Dean, S. (2020, July 24). *Uganda reports its first death from Covid-19.* CNN News. https://edition.cnn.com/2020/07/24/africa/uganda-first-covid-19-death/index.html

Chibelushi, W. (2024, July 23). *Crackdown on Uganda's opposition ahead of protests.* BBC News. https://www.bbc.com/news/articles/cn09e0599jwo

Ggoobi, R., & Lukwago, D. (2020). Financing local governments in Uganda: An analysis of the draft national budget estimates for FY2020/21 and proposals for re-allocation. *ACODE Policy Research Paper Series No.97*. https://www.acode-u.org/uploadedFiles/PRS97.pdf

Green, E. (2010). Patronage, district creation, and reform in Uganda. *Studies in Comparative International Development, 45*, 83–103. https://doi.org/10.1007/s12116-009-9058-8

Grossman, G., & Lewis, J. I. (2014). Administrative unit proliferation. *American Political Science Review, 108*(1), 196–217. https://doi.org/10.1017/S0003055413000567

Human Rights Watch. (2020, April 28). *Uganda: Opposition leader reported tortured by police: pandemic restrictions no excuse for abuse.* https://www.hrw.org/news/2020/04/28/uganda-opposition-leader-reported-tortured-police

Johns Hopkins University and Medicine (2023, March 10). https://coronavirus.jhu.edu/region/uganda

Lambright, G. M. S. (2011). *Decentralization in Uganda: Explaining successes and failures in local governance.* FirstForumPress.

Lewis, J. I. (2014). When decentralization leads to recentralization: Subnational state transformation in Uganda. *Regional and Federal Studies, 24*(5), 571–588. https://doi.org/10.1080/13597566.2014.971771

Makara, S. (2010). Deepening democracy through multipartyism: The bumpy road to Uganda's 2011 elections. *Africa Spectrum, 45*(2), 81–94. https://doi.org/10.1177/000203971004500204

Ministry of Finance, Planning and Economic Development (MoFPED). (2012). *National budget framework paper FY2012/13-FY2016/2017.* https://budget.finance.go.ug/sites/default/files/National%20Budget%20docs/National%20Budget%20Framework%20Paper%202012-13.pdf

Muhumuza, R. (2022, January 10). *Uganda's schools reopen, ending world's longest lockdown.* The Associated Press. https://apnews.com/article/coronavirus-pandemic-health-uganda-east-africa-kampala-71560307f0c892b556fa8cbb53c03171

Mumbere, D. (2020, July 23). Uganda coronavirus: First death registered, cases reach 1,079. Africanews.com. https://www.africanews.com/2020/07/23/uganda-coronavirus-hub/

Mwenda, A. M. (2007). Personalizing power in Uganda. *Journal of Democracy, 18*(3), 23–37. https://doi.org/10.1353/jod.2007.0048

Nabaho, L. (2013). Recentralization of local government chief administrative officers appointments in Uganda: Implications for downward accountability. *Commonwealth Journal of Local Governance, 13/14*, 17–29. https://doi.org/10.5130/cjlg.v0i13/14.3721

National Planning Authority. (2020). *Third national development plan* (NDPIII) *2020/21–2024/25.* https://www.npa.go.ug/wp-content/uploads/2023/03/NDPIII-Finale_Compressed.pdf

Ohira, W. (2023). *Institutional transformation of traditional authorities: The Bunyoro Kitara Kingdom and Museveni's regime* [Unpublished doctoral dissertation]. The University of Tokyo.

Organization for Economic Co-operation and Development (OECD), & United Cities and Local Government (UCLG). (2019). *2019 report of world observatory on subnational government finance and investment: Key findings.* https://www.sng-wofi.org/publications/2019_SNG-WOFI_REPORT_Key_Findings.pdf

Ssali, V. L. (2023). *Power back to the people: The relevance of ethnic federalism in Uganda.* Langaa RPCIG.

The Development Network of Indigenous Voluntary Associations (DENIVA). (2011). *The dynamics of district creation in Uganda.* https://www.asclibrary.nl/docs/371324653.pdf

The Electoral Commission. (2007, August 8). *Ugandan presidential elections. 9 May 1996. Final results.* https://www.ec.or.ug/sites/Elec_results/Nat_Res_1996.pdf

The Electoral Commission. (2016, February 22). *Presidential elections, 2016. Final results.* https://www.ec.or.ug/sites/default/files/docs/01-Summary_PRESIDENT_1_Final22-FEB-2016.pdf

The Electoral Commission (2020, October 22). *Progress of implementation of activities under the roadmap for 2021/2021 general elections* [Press statement]. https://www.ec.or.ug/sites/default/files/press/Press%20Statement%20on%20Campaign%20Period%20and%20Polling%20Dates%20for%202021%20General%20Electionsver.1.pdf

The Electoral Commission. (2021). *Presidential elections 2021. Final results.* https://www.ec.or.ug/ecresults/2021/Summary_PRESIDENT_FINAL_2021.pdf

The Government of Uganda. (1997). *Local Governments Act.*

Titeca, K. (2018). More is less? Decentralization and regime control in neoliberal Uganda. In W. Jörg., G. Martiniello., & E. Greco. (Eds.), *Uganda: The dynamics of neoliberal transformation* (pp.111–126). Zed Books.

Tripp, A. M. (2010). *Museveni's Uganda: Paradoxes of power in a hybrid regime.* Lynne Rienner Publishers.

Uganda Elections Data Portal. (2021a). *Results for 2021 parliament election in Mubende.* https://uganda.electionsdataportal.org/result/Parliament/2021/District/1-031

Uganda Elections Data Portal. (2021b). *Results for 2021 parliament election in Mbale.* https://uganda.electionsdataportal.org/result/Parliament/2021/District/3-026

Uganda Elections Data Portal. (2021c). *Results for 2021 parliament election in Jinja.* https://uganda.electionsdataportal.org/result/Parliament/2021/District/3-008

Uganda Elections Data Portal. (2021d). *Results for 2021 parliament election in Mbarara.* https://uganda.electionsdataportal.org/result/Parliament/2021/District/2-027

Uganda Elections Data Portal. (2021e). *Results for 2021 parliament election in Isingiro.* https://uganda.electionsdataportal.org/result/Parliament/2021/District/2-062

Uganda Police Force. (2022, April 24). *Arrest and detention of Hon.* Francis Zaake. https://upf.go.ug/arrest-and-detention-of-hon-francis-zaake/

Vokes, R., & Wilkins, S. (2016). Party, patronage and coercion in the NRM's 2016 re-election in Uganda: Imposed or embedded? *Journal of Eastern African Studies, 10*(4), 581–600. https://doi.org/10.1080/17531055.2016.1279853

Vick Lukwago Ssali Lecturer who teaches English and The Cultures of British Commonwealth Countries at Aichi Gakuin University in Japan. He holds a master's in teaching English as a Foreign/Second Language from the University of Birmingham in the UK, and a Ph.D. in Global Studies from Doshisha University, Japan. He is the founding president of the Japan Society for Afrasian Studies (JSAS).

Wakiko Ohira Assistant Professor at the Center for Global Education and Discovery, Sophia University, Tokyo, Japan. She holds a Ph.D. from the University of Tokyo. Her research focuses on political history and local politics in Uganda, and her latest research project examines the Uganda-China relationship at the sub-national level. Her publications include 'Roles of traditional authority in securing customary land rights: Case study of Bunyoro region, western Uganda' (*Africa Report*, 2020).

Denis Musinguzi Senior Lecturer, School of Arts and Social Sciences (SASS), Uganda Martyrs University, Kampala, Uganda, where he has served as Dean of SASS and Head of Department, Governance, Peace and International Studies. He is a former IDRC-UPEACE Ph.D. Fellow and has contributed chapters to academic books and articles to refereed journals. He has served as an external examiner for different universities at the national and international level, and as a development consultant for different local and multinational organizations.

Nakabuye Juliet Musoke Lecturer at Uganda Martyrs University for Law courses in the School of Arts and Social Sciences (SASS) and in the Faculty of Business Administration. She holds a Master of Laws (Makerere University), a postgraduate diploma in Legal Practice (Law Development Center-Makerere) Uganda; a Bachelor of Laws (Hons) Degree from Catholic University of Eastern Africa (CUEA), Kenya, and currently a Ph.D. student at the University of Ghent (Belgium). She has served in different administrative capacities of church institutions and contributed to journals locally and internationally.

Chapter 6
We Hustled, We Emerged Stronger: Students' Resilience in Countering the Risks of the COVID-19 Pandemic in Kenya and Tanzania

Laban Kithinji Kinyua, Odomaro Mubangizi, and Maureen Obare

Abstract This chapter analyses college-level students whose studies were disrupted by counter-COVID-19 protocols in Kenya and Tanzania. Using a political ethnographic account of rural and urban students, we consider the ramifications of the education-related disruptions establishing tangible impacts on everyday livelihoods. The students employed "hustling" as a strategic practice to cope with and manage the compounded precarities exacerbated by the COVID-19 pandemic. Therefore, hustling, especially characterised by digitalisation, diversification, and social engagement, was not just a survival tactic but also an agentic effort that turned precarious circumstances into opportunities for both individual and communal advantage. This study contributes to the broader literature on work politics by offering a novel empirical exploration of how student workers transformed precarious conditions into avenues for social change and personal growth during a global crisis.

Keywords Hustling · Recovery and Resilience · Youth · Pandemic · Politics

1 Introduction

The COVID-19 pandemic profoundly impacted countries across the globe, disrupting economies, healthcare systems, and social structures. The responses to pandemic-induced disruptions varied significantly, reflecting different political, social, and

L. K. Kinyua (✉)
African Studies Center, Tokyo University of Foreign Studies, Fuchu, Tokyo, Japan
e-mail: labsgithinji@gmail.com

O. Mubangizi · M. Obare
The Proposed Hekima University, Nairobi, Kenya
e-mail: odomaro@phekimauniversity.org

M. Obare
e-mail: maureen.a.obare@gmail.com

K. Hanai et al. (eds.), *Practical Wisdom and Resilience Overcoming Downside Risk*,
https://doi.org/10.1007/978-981-96-4455-1_6

cultural contexts. These responses highlighted existing inequalities and vulnerabilities in Kenya and Tanzania, particularly among students. The government's initial response included strict curfews and lockdown measures to control the spread of the virus (Were 2020; Janssens et al. 2020). Instances of heavy handedness and police brutality marked the Kenyan government's enforcement of curfews and lockdowns. A tragic example is the case of two brothers in central Kenya who lost their lives during a curfew enforcement incident. Benson Njiru Ndwiga and Emmanuel Mutura Ndwiga were both university students who had decided to set up a meat kiosk business in Mbuinjeru trading centre with the help of their parents during the pandemic. They met their death at the hands of the police, who were ensuring curfew orders (Warah 2021; Munene 2021).[1] This case underscores the paradoxical tension between state coercion and public protection, illustrating how students disproportionately bore the brunt of punitive measures while the powerful elite got away with it because of their power and influence. It is also a reminder of the zealousness of young people during the pandemic who committed to improving their livelihoods during the hardest of times.

Tanzania's response to the COVID-19 pandemic was initially characterised by President Magufuli's denialist stance, which dismissed the virus as a legitimate threat. This political approach significantly influenced societal attitudes towards the pandemic, leading to widespread scepticism and a lack of adherence to global public health measures and well-known standard operating procedures. During Magufuli's rule, Tanzanians were called upon to pray against the pandemic while also being urged to use "traditional" methods to cure COVID-19. However, the transition to President Samia's leadership marked a shift towards conventional public health strategies, reflecting a change in the governmental approach amidst ongoing uncertainties. This change resulted in Tanzania aligning with global standards and measures to curb COVID-19 (Macdonald et al. 2023; Macdonald and Molony 2023).

Despite radical differences in their strategies to curb the spread of COVID-19, both Kenya and Tanzania experienced disruptions induced by the COVID-19 preventive and mitigation protocols. Among these disruptions were state-imposed regulations dictating the conduct of social, religious, cultural practices in Kenya and Tanzania, changes in the school system (from 8-4-4 to competency-based curriculum) in Kenya, change of school calendar in Kenya and Tanzania, political competition in 2022 in Kenya, shift from campus-based classes to digitally driven online learning in Kenya and Tanzania, and regime change in Tanzania. These disruptions shaped and reshaped how students lived, leaving long-lasting impacts on their livelihoods. Although for the purpose of this chapter we focus on education, all of these disruptions had ripple effects on the students.

Disruptions in education in Kenya and Tanzania were largely a result of both the alteration of the schooling calendar and the shift of classes to digital spaces. Beyond mere academic interruptions, these disruptions reverberated across socio-economic

[1] In addition to accounts from media reports, we also relied on accounts of the local residents who had first-hand experience of how the two young students met their death during the field research in Kianjokoma Embu in August 2022.

dimensions, amplifying pre-existing inequalities and constraining educational opportunities for vulnerable students.[2] In both countries, schools were closed, forcing educators to devise ways to implement continued learning. Universities and colleges in Kenya encouraged students to take classes online. In Tanzania, learning was also migrated to digital spaces. There were critical challenges in migrating learning to digital spaces, mainly the availability of digital gadgets and an Internet connection among the students. Perhaps because of this, there was a spike in internet and mobile phone use in the two countries.[3] This expansion of an already thriving digitalisation catalysed by the demands in education-related disruptions resulted in digital spaces becoming critical to the livelihoods of the youth, shaping their activities during the pandemic.

While there was a concurrent migration of education to digital spaces in Kenya and Tanzania, the two countries had different political climates. Tanzania held its elections in October 2020, with President Magufuli declaring that COVID-19 had been eliminated from Tanzania. Following these announcements, the National Election Commission (NEC), during the campaign period, mentioned the virus only intermittently, therefore the campaigns continued with little to no COVID-19 precautions in place (Bol et al. 2020). Kenya's election was held in August 2022, but the campaign atmosphere started around 2020 following the fallout between President Uhuru Kenyatta and his deputy, now President, William Ruto. Kenya's elections had two main candidates: the son of the founding vice-president, Raila Odinga, and William Ruto who presented himself as a "commoner." Ruto's political mobilisation phrase became "hustler nation," appealing to the masses by antagonising his opponents as "dynasties" (Opalo 2022). Although it is not entirely possible to credit the origin of the term "hustler" to Ruto, the notions of hustling resonated with the young people, who already during the pandemic had learnt critical schemes of overcoming the downsides of the pandemic through establishing small ventures they labelled "hustles".

Hustling, therefore, came to have a simultaneous meaning. On the one hand, it meant aligning to a particular political worldview, and on the other hand, endeavouring to maximise entrepreneurial skills in Kenya. In Tanzania, however, hustling only described the entrepreneurial activities emerging from the effects of the first phase of the pandemic among young people. Unlike the neighbouring Kenya, there was no political environment claiming its use for political mobilisation.

We use the term hustling to indicate coping mechanisms that demonstrated the resilience of youths, particularly students, in Kenya and Tanzania during the COVID-19 pandemic, elucidating the complex dynamics of societal resilience. College-level

[2] Scholars have addressed the abrupt closure of educational institutions in response to the pandemic, highlighting that the closure of universities significantly disrupted academic schedules and posed challenges to ensuring continuous learning. It caused uncertainties among students regarding degree completion and disrupted faculty's ability to deliver course content effectively. A study by Oyoo et al. (2020) examines the impact of academic fatigue on student engagement and learning outcomes in Kenya's higher education system.

[3] For data on digital use see (Digitala 2023) for Kenya, and for Tanzania see (Mwananziche et al. 2023).

students in Kenya and Tanzania navigated the crisis and emerged stronger as they strategised within politicised crises that had tangible impacts on their everyday livelihoods. The testimonials and narratives of the students from both Kenya and Tanzania that we collected during the various stages of fieldwork emphasised the critical role of minor strands of work that supplied their fiscal needs, alleviating their present challenges, while also at times shaping their future trajectories. This is exemplified by Makau's assertion during the interview, who stated, "see…we hustled pretty hard, and that's how we are still stronger."

While considering the disruptions that occurred during the COVID-19 pandemic as a direct consequence of the pandemic or an indirect consequence of the state measures in attempts to contain the spread of the pandemic, this research is concerned with the primary question: "What ramifications did the abrupt changes have on students' educational and daily lives during the pandemic and in the long term?" This research question is set in the context of increasing digital learning platforms as one of the protocols to counter the spread of COVID-19.

We answer this primary question using field data, analysed qualitatively, and collected in rural and urban areas of select parts of Kenya and Tanzania. The research design used a diverse range of data collection methods, employing both in-person and digital strategies to garner a comprehensive understanding of the COVID-19 disruptions in Kenya and Tanzania's higher education. We used structured and unstructured techniques incorporating traditional questionnaires, conversations, online surveys, and the study of daily life narratives. Specifically, we relied on field visits, conducting field visits in Embu, Dar-es-Salam, and Nairobi counties in December 2021; February and August 2022; February and August 2023; and February and August 2024. Field visits provided a firsthand understanding of the local context and allowed researchers to interact directly with the study population. During these field visits, researchers held face-to-face conversations with stakeholders. These discussions followed a semi-structured format, providing guided but flexible dialogue in which participants could share their experiences and insights related to the research topic. This approach allowed structured data collection, capturing specific and quantifiable information related to the impact of COVID-19 on higher education. Ethnographic techniques provided a holistic and grassroots comprehension of the effects of the COVID-19 pandemic on students' daily lives. Other methods of collecting and analysing data were geared towards making sense of daily life narratives at the grassroots level with college-level students. In this pursuit, we sought to capture stories, jokes, daily conversations, and rumours that people engage in on a daily basis, especially about the pandemic. Thus, strategic places for carrying out and collecting data were *matatu* (minibuses), *nduthi* (motorbike rides), evening hangout sheds for coffee and snacks, and participation in private and public gatherings. While the data was collected from specific counties, it captured students from around the two countries, including Dar-es-Salaam, Arusha, Siaya, Nairobi, Kiambu, Kisumu, Baringo, Elgeyo Marakwet, Embu, Kirinyaga, Meru, and Nyeri. This broad geographical representation adds diversity to this study and enhances the generalisability of its findings. The diverse geographical representation in the data allowed researchers to understand how students from different regions experienced COVID-19 disruptions in higher education, highlighting the unique challenges faced by students in specific countries and providing a more nuanced understanding of the pandemic's impact on higher education across Kenya and Tanzania.

2 Definitions and Theoretical Premise

Although Kenya and Tanzania adopted different strategies to cope with the pandemic, our research established a clear thematic emphasis on the livelihoods of college-level students, particularly those entrenched in informal urban spaces and rural areas. The response from the college-level students was largely on an engagement with income-generating activities that we have identified as "hustling". This term was politically inspired and popularised in Kenya and was used for political mobilisation in Kenya's 2022 elections.[4] This resonated with most people who transformed their struggles into income-generating small-scale ventures. Hustling serves as a critical analytical lens through which we can elucidate the differential impacts of governmental policies and societal attitudes towards the pandemic. It is perhaps one of the enduring legacies of the COVID-19 pandemic in East Africa, and an analysis of creativity by college-level students in Kenya and Tanzania shows that it continues to aid them in navigating the compounded precarities brought on by the COVID-19 pandemic. What, then, is "hustling"?

2.1 Definition

The term "hustling" refers to a form of informal, entrepreneurial activity that individuals engage in as a means of livelihood, often in response to economic instability, lack of formal employment opportunities, and other socio-economic challenges. Hustling encompasses a wide range of activities, from street vending and informal trading to small-scale, self-employed work, including using online platforms and social media to market goods and services. It is often characterised by its informal nature, lack of regulation, and reliance on personal networks. Hustling is a prevalent practice for navigating, coping with, and managing compounded precarities. As a concept of getting-by through acquiring practices in conditions of enduring and chronic crises, hustling has become a new way of conceptualising work in creative methods, by youths in precarious conditions in sub-Saharan Africa. In hustling, youths are reimagining and reinvigorating work, bringing hopefulness, resourcefulness, and inventive actions in precarious contexts to create meaningful lives in spite of daunting economic hardships and health emergencies (Thieme 2017; Amankwaa et al. 2020; Chułek 2020).

[4] For studies related to 2022 election strategy in Kenya see (Pike 2021; The Continent 2022; Lockwood 2023).

2.2 Scholarship on Hustling

Many forms of work in neoliberal market conditions have become insecure, promoting a prevalence of freelance, temporary, short-term, casual, and undocumented employment (Hesmondhalgh and Baker 2010; McRobbie 2016). Precarious work conditions in neoliberal markets often render a large proportion of people ineligible for the state's safety net programmes (Khlystova et al. 2022). With this deficit, scholars suggest that hustling shows how marginalised people creatively and entrepreneurially work with the resources they have available to them to build lives that they personally find meaningful, such as semi-legal dealings and small-time crime in urban "ghettos" (Hall et al. 1978) and gig work in the platform economy (Carter 2016; van Doorn and Velthuis 2018). The character of these types of work is the savvy resourcefulness and hopeful future-orientation displayed by the actors, who navigate their precarious present both to create a life worth living in the present and to build a better future, finding ways to be beneficial (Alacovska et al. 2021). Furthermore, hustling encourages improvisation, that may include "the ingenuity and flexibility to maintain and enhance self-respect through economic activity" (Chułek 2020, p. 343).

The concept of hustling challenges traditional economic theories that focus on formal employment and regulated markets within a statist framework. Hustling often depicts precariousness associated with work in neoliberal market conditions (Hesmondhalgh and Baker 2010; McRobbie 2016; Joffe 2021; Flore et al. 2021). Hustling is therefore a crucial survival skill in precarious environments, such as those entrenched in the lived experiences of marginalised communities in Kenya and Tanzania. It reflects the ways individuals and small groups creatively and entrepreneurially utilise available resources to forge meaningful lives, navigating through both semi-formal endeavours and legitimate gig economy opportunities. The pandemic compounded, complicated, intensified and exacerbated an already existing high levels of precarity (Comunian and England 2020; Eikhof 2020; Flore et al. 2021). Moreover, the pandemic, rather than instigating precarity, "helped amplify some long-instituted feelings of precariousness" (Banks 2020, p. 650). The pandemic "did more than bring regular income streams to a complete standstill; it made visible the fragility of cultural work and project-based income generation in Africa" (Joffe 2021, p. 30).

The practice of hustling unites various survival strategies through a display of savvy resourcefulness and an optimistic outlook towards future possibilities, allowing individuals to construct a worthwhile present and aspire for a sustainable future. Alacovska et al. (2021) asserts that the ability to improvise including "the ingenuity and flexibility to maintain and enhance self respect through economic activity" is crit ical to hustling (Chułek 2020, p. 343). Thus, hustling is "more than mere opportunism rooted in social and economic survival" (Thieme et al. 2021, p. 10). A cornerstone of the hustling approach is to recognise both the precarious conditions through which workers hustle and their agency to build meaningful lives and careers through their practices of hustling. It thus avoids either victimising or romanticising marginalised workers (Chułek 2020; Thieme et al. 2021). Hustling is, therefore, a conclusively creative strategy to deal with the failure of both the state and global economy to address the social and economic needs of marginalised communities.

3 Living Through Disruptions

At a general level, the disruptions had a negative effect on participants' lives and livelihoods. They also had a unique character, which is that they laid bare, or revealed, the pre-existing vulnerabilities of those at the bottom of the pyramid. For example, when the schools closed, months before the establishment of online classes, students wanted to continue with studies individually. In this respect, students sought to utilise the public libraries, as they followed the protocols laid down by the authorities. However, in their testimony, they assert "I had never thought of a library before, but now I needed one because I had to prepare for my final exams. I could not find any near me, the closest needed me to pay too much for transport."[5] This kind of response from the students showed that such public amenities were inaccessible. The tendency of the state to ignore making public amenities available for the public good, jeopardised the students' zeal to pursue individual studies out of their classrooms, and homes. By this time, homes were said to be not conducive for studies since everybody was at home, therefore presenting students with further difficulties in addition to the access and reliability of online classes.[6]

The COVID-19 preventive measures not only exposed the shortcomings of the past in the state's provision of public facilities, but also the infrastructural deficits in implementing the proposed protocols. The changes in class delivery modes from face to face to online were without a doubt abrupt. This was despite earlier efforts to implement online learning. Under Kenya's Vision 2030, online learning has been a critical component of the state's vision and policy framework with the establishment of facilities such as Open Distance and e-Learning (ODeL) at the University of Nairobi since 2015. The University of Dar es Salaam's progression towards enhanced utilisation of technology in its teaching and learning processes was previously delineated in the university's Vision 2061 and the Five Years Strategic Rolling Plan (FYSRP) 2020/2021–2024/2025. Vision 2061 specifically articulates the imperative to harness the full potential of ICT to transform University of Dar es Salaam into an e-University in terms of IT infrastructure and services. These institutions had to solicit new means to install digital systems to enable learning as the existing infrastructures were insufficient to accommodate the new demands for online learning. Furthermore, despite the existence of online learning frameworks, when the universities introduced new learning methods to enable continuity of education during the pandemic, students were required to fully adopt these methods by applying new skills beyond what they had been familiarised with on online learning platforms. Examples of these methods

---

[5] Interview with Brian, February 2022.

[6] Interview with Makau, Baraka, and Fundi, February 2023.

include Zoom for classes and examination delivery, google meet, and WhatsApp for classes (basically for disseminating learning materials). Students were largely unfamiliar with these new learning methods, although they pointed out that they were quick to adopt them.[7] The difficulty of adopting new technologies was also compounded with the accessibility of online education's amenities.

The adoption of new modes of learning exposed students to various risks primarily emanating from digital access to classrooms but also spilling over to broader issues. One student expressed frustrations with digital classes, criticising the manner in which online classes were conducted:

> Imagine using your small phone to attend a class on Zoom? First off, I had to think about the cost for data bundles. Before Corona, I only used 20 bob per day. Now I have to use more. Zoom was difficult. It was hard to load, especially for lecturers, omg, they kept hanging and asking what should I do here, they could not even mute the noises in the background. We then moved to google classroom. This was much better. It was easy to use on many phones. But still when I attended classes I felt like lecturers were really not serious about online classes. It did not feel like a class, and they made it so. Many of them are used to just speaking in the normal classroom. They don't use anything like PowerPoint or give reading materials. They just come and dictate the notes, and we write them down. Imagine doing that online? It was draining. Should I mention that sometimes the power would go off and everything freezes? Let me not.[8]

The sentiments out of this participant's frustrations points out key themes tabulated from the questionnaires. These included unfamiliarity with technology, difficulties with technology, accessibility of internet and digital gadgets, unstable or fluctuating internet, and class delivery modes. The impact of these disruptions in class delivery not only limited students' access to quality education, but strained families and relationships that students relied upon for fiscal support. They also sparked compromises to standards of education, given the unfamiliarity of faculty with the new modes of class delivery.[9]

Our data reveals changes sparked by the shifts to digital spaces to administer education touching on friendships, familial, and institutional relationships. This change was critical to embracing "hustles" in at least two ways: first mental shift, in terms of the meaning of education, what education can attain, and second the realization that students needed to look outwards to boost and build new safety nets outside of familial support networks. As the universities and colleges shifted to digital spaces, students came face to face with the complexities of what education means. Migration to online learning exposed the institutional shortcomings to the students, creating levels of mistrust about institutional capacity to meet students' needs.[10] The mistrust made it easier for students to dismiss the primacy of institution as the sole provider of education, as seen in words like "we now have class in our fingertips," referring to various modes to access class materials beyond what the university

---

[7] Interview with Mutua, Makau, and Dickie, August 2023; Focused Group Discussion in Kangaru and Machakos.

[8] Interview with Mwema, February, 2023.

[9] Interview with Katana, August, 2023.

[10] Interview with Bodana, February, 2022.

provided. Mistrust in the institutions was also closely related to the deteriorating student-teacher relations. To a large extent, students conflated teachers with institutions, and its failures were also teachers' failures. One of the pandemic's impacts on student-teacher relationships was significant loss of opportunities for consultation with teachers. Although some students described similarities with pre-pandemic days, the majority of the students' expressed feelings of anxiety caused by limited student-teacher contact.

The students-teachers-institutional strains occurred because of the limited interactions.[11] This strain exerted pressure on family and friends who had to take care of students as they took classes online. Our respondents show alteration of the students-parents/guardian bonds described in words such as "worsening" or "improving." Through the students' narratives, we learn that the alteration of the student-parent/guardian relationships occurred as digital expenses required students to demand more than usual from their financial supporters. During this time, parents had also lost their sources of income, which resulted in students no longer receiving the usual assistance from their parents in forms such as buying internet data bundles. The increased expenses on digital devices to enable online learning was therefore met with the strain of lower income from guardians. In addition, the absence of safe spaces such as recreational activities, which our informants claimed were crucial for "keeping them out of trouble," students had to struggle with the realities of spending more time with their parents, most of whom at this point were unable to fiscally support them.[12]

4 Layers of Hustles

Ethnographic field data in Kenya and Tanzania reveals diverse and complex dynamics of students' savviness, improvisation, resourcefulness, and future-orientation through hustling as they navigated the precarity of the pandemic and pre-pandemic state failures stated above. Specifically, disruptions in education reveal the faultiness of the COVID-19 preventive measures. Nevertheless, these faults provided students with savviness and improvisation necessary to see them through the hard times.

Students' uptake of hustling was determined by the fiscal support they received. In this regard, students were asked about their primary source of income in order to

[11] Students are here describing interactions in the confinement of their homes.

[12] This scenario can be studied in COVID-19 pandemic as underscoring the mental health crises in African societies. Although these issues featured prominently in students' responses, such as "…people showed their true colours," we have not explored these issues in this chapter. However, we take note that students associated these vices with how they came to "rethink what they wanted in life". A key strategy of this "want" was "being fiscally independent" to avoid conflict with their fiscally overburdened guardians. This is then underscored as the main motivator for the students to scheme strategies out of the crisis of the pandemic by engaging in small scale entrepreneurial activities to expand their livelihoods.

measure how their streams of income were affected by pandemic preventive measures and establish other means of self-support besides parents and guardians. A significant proportion of the participants reported accessing education and personal support through state-funded programmes. This data character provides insights into the students' dependability and the impact of government-sponsored education as much as they relied on parental or relative support to maintain their daily upkeep. Our survey established that students leveraged state support to establish hustles with an aim to expand their fortunes. For example, a respondent from Nairobi said in an interview, *"nilitumia HELB kijipanga bro. Vile hii serikali haiaminiki unaweza kuta hakuna pesa itaingia tena. Nilitaka tu nikuwe safe"* "I used up my earning from the Higher Education Loans Board (HELB) to organise myself. Our government is not to be trusted, we cannot be assured that there will be another payment. So, I just wanted to be safe."[13]

A relatively smaller portion of the target students relied on manual jobs for income. Since finding a job is generally scarce for the young people, it is even more difficult to find part time jobs. Therefore, many students did not mention part time jobs as an alternative for extra income.

The data also covered students at different stages of their studies. This included a subset of participants (10%) who were awaiting graduation, providing insights into the experiences and challenges faced by students transitioning from higher education to the workforce. The subset of students awaiting graduation presented an opportunity to explore perceptions and concerns about entering the job market during the pandemic's disruptions, characterised by an urge to hustles as opposed to entering into formal jobs as one informant asserted, "the pandemic led to a surge in home-made soap production. Since I was due to graduate, I ventured into soap making and created its visibility online. It continues to date."[14] These data shed light on the preparedness and expectations of graduating students in precarious economic situations, also revealing a shift in the mindset regarding what constitutes work. Students seemed to agree that work, that is hustling, is "more than mere opportunism rooted in social and economic survival" (Thieme et al. 2021, p. 10). They recognised the precarious conditions, using their agency to build meaningful lives and careers through their practices of hustling.[15] The pursuit of hustles also exhibits students as young people navigating uncertainty in African urban and rural environments (Amankwaa et al. 2020; Munive 2010; Muthoni Mwaura 2017; Thieme 2013, 2015). Our data shows how students "seize[d] opportunities to navigate uncertainty, earn an income, and follow-up desired aspirations or occupational choices" (Amankwaa et al. 2020, p. 364) by claiming a space to work on their own terms (Thieme 2013; Muthoni Mwaura 2017).[16]

[13] Interview with Matayo, February 2022.

[14] Interview with Juma, February 2023.

[15] Interview with Baraka in February 2023 who said, "I was honestly fixated on getting a formal job with Teachers Service Commission (TSC). But here I am selling all manner of things on the streets. I do not think much about TSC now, I am learning to enjoy my hustle, day by day."

[16] This view is also backed by an informant in an interview in August 2022 who said, *"Mimi sipendi kupangwa. Vijana siku hizi tuko tu sawa. Unaamka asubuhi masaa unataka. Saa ingine niko online*

The students' responses reflect a range of attempts to reflect on the strategies to cope with the challenges posed by the pandemic. As we stated earlier, the majority of respondents turned to entrepreneurial activities primarily driven by the need to find alternative income streams. These kinds of activities are also labelled "hustling" and came in many forms, characterised by income generation. Examples of categories that were mentioned included hawking of the snacks, selling tea and coffee, hawking boiled eggs and sausages, selling face masks etc. Although some young people were uncomfortable associating with these activities, largely because they looked forward to a better working scenario in the future, they were positive about engaging with "something meaningful" for their lives as they waited. Hustling, however, is also seen in a negative light as referring to semi-legal dealings or small crime in urban ghettos (Hall et al. 1978). These aspects of hustling featured prominently in our surveys. Students expounded on how they work online to write assignments for a fee for overseas students primarily targeting students outside Africa who needed assistance with projects, theses, and other academic tasks.[17]

4.1 Digitally Inspired Storytelling

The researchers' use of online surveys to explore popular narratives about the pandemic on various social media platforms, particularly YouTube channels and WhatsApp groups, provided insights into the public discourse and sentiment surrounding the pandemic and its impact on students. Digital spaces became a safe alternative to many ordinary people to access education, share their stories, and make fiscal returns. Besides online classes, students attested to using various digital platforms for schoolwork (see Fig. 6.1). Inspired by media personalities in Kenya and Tanzania affected by COVID-19, and manifestations of the effects of retrenchments that cut across many job segments, young people adopted digital platforms for storytelling. After their retrenchments, the media personalities actively used the digital spaces to re/design themselves. Storytelling appeared as a convenience for many of them, and thus an increase in the launch of YouTube channels that focused on giving ordinary people platforms to narrate their stories. Storytelling was chosen in part since the tellers were optimistic about returning to formal employment as broadcasters. As the pandemic persisted, however, it became more and more unclear what lay ahead. A common strategy then became to extend the stay in the digital storytelling platforms, focusing on expanding the storytelling pools and digitising the content aired. Examples of such personalities are Lynn Ngugi and Millard Ayo.[18]

kuhustle, nafanya trading. So unaeza nipata saa saba usiku niko macho na hakuna ile." (As for me, I do not want anyone to dictate to me how to live. We the youths are not like that these days. You can get up in the morning whatever time you want. Sometimes I stay up all night doing trading, so I do not care much what time I get to sleep, as long as I am hustling).

[17] Interview with Matayo, February 2022.

[18] Lynn Ngugi, now with a channel called Lynn Ngugi Network, is a former journalist known for her storytelling skills on YouTube after leaving her position at Tuko.co.ke. She launched her

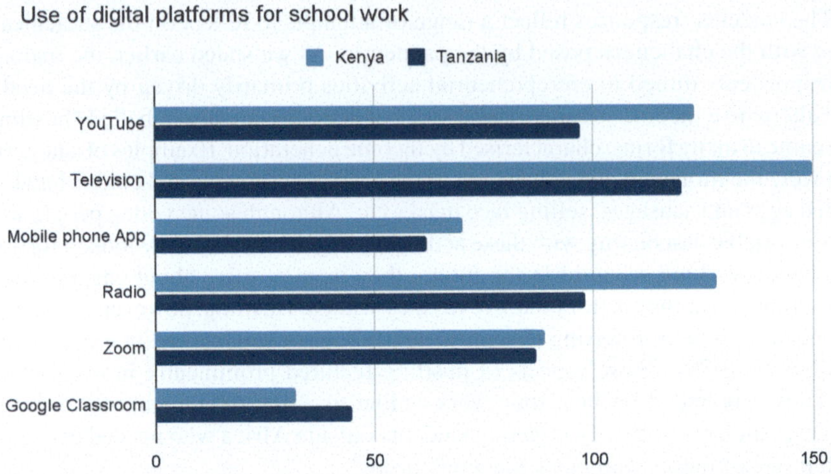

Fig. 6.1 Use of digital platforms for schoolwork in Kenya and Tanzania. *Source* Created by author (2024) based on Questionnaire in 2023

When they were forced to leave their jobs, both Lynn Ngugi and Millard Ayo started their own channels. These channels are dominated by stories of ordinary people during the pandemic. They provide narrations of how people faced and overcame the wide-ranging risks in the pandemic.

The stories inspired students to turn to digital spaces in order to secure new streams of livelihood through content creation. This path was dominated by students who feared going to the streets, where most hustles were taking place. Making digital content looked attractive to many students, who foresaw a better future in it. However, it was also an extremely difficult path to chart as it required specific skill sets and the hosts' gift to connect with the story givers, as an informant asserted, "I did not personally try that, my friend did. But he failed really terribly [...] you needed some special skills in that line."[19] These streams were hustles that aided more stable livelihoods among the students, with some succeeding and others failing.[20]

own channel where she highlights human interest stories, giving ordinary Kenyans a platform to share their experiences. The channel became a popular destination for real-life stories, including those affected by the pandemic, as Ngugi expanded her reach into digital storytelling. Millard Ayo, a Tanzanian journalist and media personality, adapted quickly to the digital space by growing his YouTube channel, Millard Ayo TV. During the pandemic, the channel became a space for Tanzanians to narrate their personal experiences and the impact of COVID-19 on their livelihoods. Initially, many contributors were hopeful about returning to traditional media, but as the uncertainty persisted, the platform continued to grow, digitizing content and expanding its storytelling pool.

[19] Interview with Millie, February 2023.

[20] Interview with Millie, Wadera, and Juma February 2023.

4.2 Lessons from Loss

Pandemic-related layoffs also exposed students to direct risks. Our informants asserted that they relied on parents or guardians for fiscal support. In various instances, it is this category of students, who were often at the risk of low or no fiscal support from parents and guardians, who sought ways to mitigate the fiscal downturn through hustling. However, hustling was not exclusive to students. The wider population laid off due to COVID-19 related downsizing often looked to small-scale entrepreneurship as new means of earning a livelihood. "At times, people starting a small venture were better positioned in the social structure: for example they accessed the market place and the streets with their personal cars, and used their car boots to display the products they wanted to sell, often sparking a fierce competition with the *mama mbogas* (women vegetable vendors), who can be to some extent called 'rightful owners' of the market spaces."[21] Just like students were inspired by media personalities to pursue digital based hustles, others were mentored by those laid off from their work, internal competition notwithstanding as one of our informant asserted, "I decided to start my street food hustle when I talked to my pastor. I heard his story of how his income had gone low. He encouraged me that he was now focused on selling eggs to the community besides preaching."[22]

Such actions show that the conglomeration of hustles was gathering momentum and became a visible existential reality. This visibility caught the attention of the political class, who would often seek to support individuals who were struggling to make ends meet but engaged in somewhat unique ventures.[23] Politician would then engage the digital spaces to popularise their generosity and philanthropic actions, eventually transforming these activities into election mobilisation clarion calls. In 2022, Ruto was seeking to win the support of the Agikuyu in Kenya's central region, which due to their high numbers is critical to being elected. As a non-Gikuyu candidate, Ruto needed a rhetoric beyond "our man."[24] Aligning with the struggles of the ordinary Gikuyu people, the majority of whom are in small scale business, resonated with the community since they saw an opportunity to improve their social status. Our findings found no strong correlation between political discourse and hustling, but since the political class capitalised on the hustler narrative for vote mobilisation, the political climate informed students' choice and participation in hustling, more so with an expectation of a reward from the political class as one of our key informants stated, "We organised a student group to start a hustle. You know, many politicians are supporting hustles. I know we will get something."[25] Furthermore, that even

[21] Interview with Mueni Mwema, August 2022.

[22] Interview with Gitonga, February 2022,

[23] It became a common place for small scale traders to be hosted by the political class, and rewarded for their own hustles. See (Kenya Digital News 2020).

[24] This term often refers to tribal based political mobilisaton in Kenya by appealing to the fellow tribesmen/women that there are benefits attached to voting their own member, which include "their own time to eat" see Wrong (2010).

[25] Interview with 23 year old student leader, Mwawasi in February 2022.

leading politicians embraced the "hustler" narrative in their campaigns demonstrates how marginalised communities can shape political discourse, even though not all of them might benefit politically from it.

4.3 *Hustling as a Communal Entanglement*

Hustling emerged as a dynamic and communal response to the pandemic, closely tied to spirituality and resilience. Religious leaders utilised online platforms to provide spiritual mentorship and emotional support to their followers during an uncertain time. However, the role of spirituality extended beyond the religious sphere, intertwining with other forms of hustling. The expressions of spirituality, intertwining to the digital spaces helped to play a significant role in coping with the pandemic. Religious leaders utilised online platforms to provide support and mentorship to their followers. However, mentorship was not limited to the spiritual realm, as parents and other individuals also offered guidance to those in need.[26]

At the same time, hustling took on innovative forms among students, with content creation becoming a notable venture. Youths recorded vibrant spiritual gatherings and community events, posting them on digital platforms, where the communal characteristic of these activities blurred the boundaries of individual financial gain. For instance, some members used these platforms to build independent channels, capitalising on the visibility created by collective efforts. Students also took this up as a venture, terming it as part of "content" creation. This content creation extended to vibrant support groups organised via WhatsApp. Within religious communities, youths gathered and sang together, and since they recorded these events, they posted them on digital platforms. It was at times unclear who benefited financially since most of these groups had a communal characteristic, but following up we found that some individuals in the groups had built up their own channels.

Similar to organising within spiritual communities and harnessing fiscal opportunities therein, students often engaged in charitable activities within their communities, providing essential supplies to those who were vulnerable. Organised as community self-help groups, students appealed to their common ties to embark on rescue missions as conglomerations of former high school students, colleges, universities, or common characteristics, such as the Embu County Comrades Association (ECCA) that comprises students from all universities residing in Embu County. They gathered resources via WhatsApp groups and virtually sent these resources to the needy. These groups mobilised resources virtually and provided essential supplies to vulnerable

[26] Our informants shared that some of their parents were struggling with loan repayments, which are not a common form of financing for housing in Kenya and Tanzania but have recently gained popularity. The ability to repay these loans came into question, with some students expressing disillusionment with the concept of urban living and contemplating alternative lifestyles in more rural settings. One student narrated his parent's decision to relocate to rural Kiambu and commute to work in Nairobi, inspired by this new way of life, but strongly stating that this decision could not have succeeded without moral support from his group mates.

families. While these activities lacked immediate financial rewards, youths proudly referred to them as "hustles," reflecting a broader understanding of hustling as a survival-driven endeavor rooted in solidarity.

5 Conclusion: Youths in the Wait

Respondents highlighted significant challenges in adapting to new modes of learning during the pandemic. The abrupt transition to online education revealed gaps in institutional preparedness, infrastructure, and support systems. While some students appreciated the flexibility of online classes, others lamented the lack of practical engagement, which diminished the effectiveness of learning. This dichotomy underscores the need for a balanced approach that integrates practical and theoretical education, particularly in resource-constrained settings. Ratings on the impact of pre-existing vulnerabilities and complexities of everyday life during the pandemic further emphasised the fragility of higher education systems in the face of crises.

Amidst the turmoil, entrepreneurial activities emerged as a critical coping mechanism for many individuals. Students and workers engaged in diverse ventures, including online trading, selling face masks, and farm produce. Lockdowns and restrictions provided the impetus for these initiatives, demonstrating resilience and adaptability in the face of adversity. Moreover, some respondents noted that the disruptions encouraged innovative practices, such as delivery services and digital marketplaces, which continue to reshape local economies. These entrepreneurial efforts often took place within the context of "waithood," (Honwana 2012) a period marked by deferred life milestones and structural barriers. Youth in waithood exhibited remarkable creativity and resourcefulness, engaging in both active hustling and strategic waiting to navigate uncertainties and forge a path towards stability.

The central theme of coping strategies in Kenya was the concept of "hustling." This idea was sometimes referred to as "side hustling," implying that individuals engage in additional activities to earn extra income or gratification. At its most basic level, hustling required very little capital to start, often just 15 US dollars. It is worth noting that hustling played a significant role in the daily lives of many Kenyans and Tanzanians, to the extent that during the 2022 political campaigns, one faction employed the "hustler" label as part of their strategy. Hustling presented a variety of challenges. For instance, in some cases it pitted one class against the other. In Nairobi, the middle class who had been laid off due to the pandemic utilised cars to engage in trade of minor commodities such as vegetables, resulting in competition with ordinary women who held significant influence in this domain. This may have led to the emergence of new battlefields between the poor and middle class and shaped the political and economic landscape in 2022.

During our data collection process, we discovered that university students, who were part of the affected population, were perceived as having a greater ability to avert risks, but nonetheless suffered consequences. Some respondents were indifferent to the risks associated with COVID-19 due to the belief that the pandemic had subsided. However, our research has shown that the risks were not isolated, but rather exacerbated by pre-existing vulnerabilities. It is crucial to acknowledge that coping mechanisms were influenced by the prevailing social, political, religious, and cultural environments.

To advance our understanding, it is essential to focus on the "realities" of everyday life and use tools that can uncover intricate and complex narratives. The resilience strategies adopted by Tanzanian communities during the COVID-19 pandemic were deeply intertwined with political leadership, cultural beliefs, and public health measures. The transition from a denialist regime to a more conventional public health approach highlighted the critical role of political and cultural factors in shaping societal resilience.

The comparative analysis of Kenya and Tanzania responses to the COVID-19 pandemic reveals the critical role of young people in facing complexities and shaping resilience strategies out of a disrupted period of education. Both countries faced unique challenges that were influenced by their respective political landscapes and cultural contexts. Despite these challenges, local students demonstrated remarkable resilience, adopting various strategies to navigate the crisis. The findings of this study underscore the importance of understanding the multifaceted interplay between politics, culture, religion, and public health in managing future crises. By learning from the experiences of Kenya and Tanzania, policymakers can develop more effective and context-specific strategies for enhancing societal resilience in the face of global health emergencies.

The emergence of hustling as both a theoretical framework and social-economic practice both in Kenya and Tanzania, is something to celebrate and study even more carefully and rigorously. The coping strategies through hustling, which standard economic theorists have not paid much attention to, might in fact hold the key to Africa's political economic transformation. Policymakers and international development agencies, without trying to paternalise or even hijack the hustling economy, can build on its strengths while designing a development agenda. Measures should be taken to enhance and safeguard the entrepreneurial spirit ingrained in the hustling economy that this research has explored.

Moreover, the college-level students targeted by this study employed hustling as a strategic practice to cope with and manage the compounded precarity exacerbated by the COVID-19 pandemic. Therefore, hustling, especially characterised by digitalization, diversification, and social engagement, was not just a survival tactic but an agentic effort that turned precarious circumstances into opportunities for both individual and communal advantage. Exploring hustling as embedded with communalities is yet another promising area of scholarship that may lead to better understanding of the agency of young Africans, as well as new perceptions of work and the avenues that these are creating for social change and personal growth, especially during the precarious situations precipitated by pandemics.

References

Alacovska, A., Langevang, T., & Steedman, R. (2021). The work of hope: Spiritualizing, hustling and waiting in the creative industries in Ghana. *Environment and Planning A: Economy and Space, 53*(4), 619–637. https://doi.org/10.1177/0308518X20962810

Amankwaa, E. F., Esson, J., & Gough, K. V. (2020). Geographies of youth, mobile phones, and the urban hustle. *Geographical Journal, 186*(4), 362–374. https://doi.org/10.1111/geoj.12354

Banks, M. (2020). The work of culture and C-19. *European Journal of Cultural Studies, 23*(4), 648–654. https://doi.org/10.1177/1367549420924687

Bol, D., Giani, M., Blais, A., & Loewen, P. J. (2020). The effect of COVID-19 lockdowns on political support: Some good news for democracy? *European Journal of Political Research, 60*(2), 497–505. https://doi.org/10.1111/1475-6765.12401

Carter, D. (2016). Hustle and brand: The sociotechnical shaping of influence. *Social Media + Society, 2*(3), 1–12. https://doi.org/10.1177/2056305116666305

Chułek, M. (2020). Hustling the *mtaa* way: The brain work of the garbage business in Nairobi's slums. *African Studies Review, 63*(2), 331–352. https://doi.org/10.1017/asr.2019.46

Comunian, R., & England, L. (2020). Creative and cultural work without filters: Covid-19 and exposed precarity in the creative economy. *Cultural Trends, 29*(2), 112–128. https://doi.org/10.1080/09548963.2020.1770577

Digitala. (2023, December 22). *Digital 2023 – Kenya - Digital 4 Africa*. Digital 4 Africa. https://digital4africa.com/digital-2023/

Eikhof, D.R. (2020). COVID-19, inclusion and workforce diversity in the cultural economy: What now, what next? *Cultural Trends, 29*(3), 234–250.

Flore, J., Hendry, N.A., & Gaylor, A. (2021). Creative arts workers during the Covid-19 pandemic: Social imaginaries in lockdown. *Journal of Sociology, 59*(1),197–214. https://doi.org/10.1177/14407833211036757

Hall, S., Critcher, C., Jefferson, T., Clarke, J., & Roberts, B. (1978). *Policing the Crisis: Mugging, the State, and Law and Order*. Macmillan.

Hesmondhalgh, D., & Baker, S. (2010). 'A very complicated version of freedom': Conditions and experiences of creative labour in three cultural industries. *Poetics, 38*(1), 4–20. https://doi.org/10.1016/j.poetic.2009.10.001

Honwana, A. (2012). The Time of Youth: Work, Social Change, and Politics in Africa. Boulder, USA: Lynne Rienner Publishers. https://doi.org/10.1515/9781565494732

Janssens, W., Pradhan, M., De Groot, R., Sidze, E., Donfouet, H. P. P., & Abajobir, A. (2020). The short-term economic effects of COVID-19 on low-income households in rural Kenya: An analysis using weekly financial household data. *World Development, 138*, 105280. https://doi.org/10.1016/j.worlddev.2020.105280

Joffe, A. (2021). Covid-19 and the African cultural economy: An opportunity to reimagine and reinvigorate? *Cultural Trends, 30*(1), 28–39. https://doi.org/10.1080/09548963.2020.1857211

Kenya Digital News. (2020, September 29). *SEE RUTO HAVING FUN WITH HUSTLERS AT HIS KAREN RESIDENCE!!* [Video]. YouTube. https://www.youtube.com/watch?v=flkmxC63O8U

Khlystova, O., Kalyuzhnova, Y., Belitski, M. (2022). The impact of the COVID-19 pandemic on the creative industries: A literature review and future research agenda. *Journal of Business Research, 139*, 1192–1210. https://doi.org/10.1016/j.jbusres.2021.09.062

Lockwood, P. (2023). Hustler populism, anti-Jubilee backlash and economic injustice in Kenya's 2022 elections. *African Affairs, 122*(487), 205–224. https://doi.org/10.1093/afraf/adad011

Macdonald, R., & Molony, T. (2023). Future pandemics and elections: Lessons from the COVID-19 pandemic in the Central African Republic, Ghana, Kenya and Tanzania. *Journal of African Elections, 22*(2), 46–67. https://doi.org/10.20940/jae/2023/v22i2a3

Macdonald, R., Molony, T., & Lihiru, V. (2023). The reception of Covid-19 denialist propaganda in Tanzania. *Journal of Southern African Studies, 49*(4), 697–716. https://doi.org/10.1080/03057070.2023.2298152

McRobbie, A. (2016). *Be Creative: Making a Living in the New Culture Industries*. Polity Press.

Munene, G. (2021, August 20). Embu brothers died the day they started a butchery business. *Nation*. https://nation.africa/kenya/counties/embu/embu-brothers-died-the-day-they-started-a-butchery-business--3518578
Munive, J. (2010). The army of 'unemployed' young people. *Young, 18*(3), 321–338. https://doi.org/10.1177/110330881001800305
Muthoni Mwaura, G. (2017). The side-hustle: Diversified livelihoods of Kenyan educated young farmers. *IDS Bulletin, 48*(3), 51–66. https://doi.org/10.19088/1968-2017.126
Mwananziche, J., Myovella, G., Karacuka, M., Haucap, J., & Moshi, G. (2023). Is digitalization a booster for economic growth in Africa? Short run and long run evidence from Tanzania. *Telecommunications Policy, 47*(10), 102679. https://doi.org/10.1016/j.telpol.2023.102679
Opalo, K. O. (2022). Hustlers versus dynasties? The elusive quest for issue-based politics in Kenya. *SSRN Electronic Journal*. https://doi.org/10.2139/ssrn.4232325
Oyoo, S., Mwaura, P., Kinai, T., & Mutua, J. (2020). Academic burnout and academic achievement among secondary school students in Kenya. *Education Research International*, 2020, 1–6. https://doi.org/10.1155/2020/5347828
Pike, I. (2021, March 26). "Hustlers versus dynasty": Kenya's new class politics, *Global Challenges, No.9*. Geneva Graduate Institute. https://globalchallenges.ch/issue/9/hustlers-versus-dynasty-kenyas-new-class-politics/
The Continent. (2022, August 6). The Continent: Kenyan Election Special. *The Continent, Issue 94*, 2–5. https://mg.co.za/wp-content/uploads/2022/08/dd8debd7-thecontinentissue94.pdf
Thieme, T., Ference, M.E., & van Stapele, N. (2021). Harnessing the 'hustle': Struggle, solidarities and narratives of work in Nairobi and beyond Introduction. *Africa*, 91(1), 1–15. https://doi.org/10.1017/S0001972020000819
Thieme, T. (2013). The "hustle" amongst youth entrepreneurs in Mathare's informal waste economy. *Journal of Eastern African Studies, 7*(3), 389–412. https://doi.org/10.1080/17531055.2013.770678
Thieme, T. (2015). Turning hustlers into entrepreneurs, and social needs into market demands: Corporate-community encounters in Nairobi, Kenya. *Geoforum, 59*, 228–239.
Thieme, T. A. (2017). The hustle economy: Informality, uncertainty and the geographies of getting by. *Progress in Human Geography, 42*(4), 529–548. https://doi.org/10.1177/0309132517690039
van Doorn, N., & Velthuis, O.(2018). A good hustle: The moral economy of market competition in adult webcam modeling. *Journal of Cultural Economy,* 11(3), 177–192. https://doi.org/10.1080/17530350.2018.1446183
Warah, R. (2021, August 16). A brutal pandemic: Kenya police under fire for the death of two brothers. ONE.org Africa. https://www.one.org/africa/stories/ndwiga-brothers-death-police-brutality-kenya/
Were, M. (2020). *COVID-19 and socioeconomic impact in Africa: The case of Kenya* [Background Note]. UNU Wider. https://doi.org/10.35188/unu-wider/wbn/2020-3
Wrong, M. (2010). *It's Our Turn to Eat: The Story of a Kenyan Whistle-Blower*. Harper Perennial.

Laban Kithinji Kinyua Research Fellow at the African Studies Center, Tokyo University of Foreign Studies, Tokyo, Japan. Dr. Kinyua holds a Ph.D. in Global Studies, with a research focus on decentralization, rural livelihoods, and African youth engagement with digital platforms. His recent work investigates how digital spaces facilitate political participation and resource mobilization among rural communities. Recent publications include "Digital Spaces and Democratization in Rural Africa: Participation, Mobilization, and Laying Claim to Resources" in the *Journal of African Studies* (2023) and "Decoding Political Discourse on Digital Platforms in Africa: Rumor Networks Among Rural Populace in Kenya's 2022 Elections" in *ASC-TUFS Working Papers* (2023).

Odomaro Mubangizi Deputy Director Academic and Student Affairs for the Proposed Hekima University (Kenya) and visiting professor at Sophia University (Japan). He was Dean of the Philosophy Department at the Institute of Philosophy and Theology (Ethiopia) and taught social and political philosophy at Arrupe Jesuit University (Zimbabwe). He holds a doctorate and Licentiate in social ethics (Boston College, USA); an MA in Social and Political Philosophy (University of Zimbabwe); a BA in Theology from the Catholic University of Eastern Africa (CUEA), Kenya; and a BA in Philosophy from Urbaniana University, Rome. His areas of research include globalization and Africa, political ethics, ethics and global public health, and African philosophy and theology.

Maureen Akinyi Obare Development communication professional with an MA in Communication Studies from the University of Nairobi and a BSc in Communication and Journalism from Moi University. With over a decade of experience in communication and research, she specializes in research, data analysis, report writing, and presentation design. She works as Communications and Assistant Researcher at the Proposed Hekima University (Kenya). Maureen coordinates data collection, analyzes findings, and contributes to publications. She is skilled at producing impactful reports and presentations that support decision-making and foster collaboration.

Chapter 7
Establishing Misinformation as a Key Downside Risk in COVID-19 Vaccination: Evidence from Ethiopia

Christian Samen Otchia

Abstract The containment measures implemented during the early stages of the COVID-19 pandemic were primarily designed to mitigate the spread of the virus, with vaccination quickly emerging as the most effective public health strategy to curb its impact. However, vaccine uptake remained low in Africa, particularly in sub-Saharan regions, where various challenges have hindered effective vaccination campaigns. This chapter establishes misinformation as a key downside risk factor affecting COVID-19 vaccination uptake in Ethiopia. Our findings reveal that general misinformation has a profound and detrimental impact on both the initial acceptance of vaccines and the subsequent number of doses received, while conspiracy theories play a comparatively non-significant role in influencing vaccine hesitancy. This evidence challenges the prevailing narrative that conspiracy theories are the predominant drivers of vaccine reluctance, highlighting the pervasive and damaging effects of broader misinformation beliefs. The results underscore the urgent need for targeted communication strategies that effectively leverage trusted institutions and influential community figures to address and counter misinformation.

1 Introduction

The worldwide and local repercussions of COVID-19 in terms of mortality, economic collapse, and social upheaval have been profound. As of July 2024, the pandemic has led to over 775 million reported cases and more than 7 million deaths globally (World Health Organization, 2024a). Beyond its toll on physical health, COVID-19 has significantly impacted mental health and social interactions (Fancourt et al., 2021; Toffolutti et al., 2022). The pandemic has also exacerbated inequalities both within and between countries. Emerging economies and socioeconomically disadvantaged groups are expected to face prolonged recovery periods from the income and livelihood losses inflicted by the pandemic (World Bank, 2022).

C. S. Otchia (✉)
Graduate School of International Development, Nagoya University, Nagoya, Aichi, Japan
e-mail: otchia@gsid.nagoya-u.ac.jp

K. Hanai et al. (eds.), *Practical Wisdom and Resilience Overcoming Downside Risk*,
https://doi.org/10.1007/978-981-96-4455-1_7

Early containment measures, such as lockdowns, stay-at-home orders, hand washing, social distancing, and the closure of educational institutions and public spaces, were implemented to curb the spread of the virus (Aragie et al., 2020; Ayele et al., 2021; Hategeka et al., 2021; Jacobs et al., 2021). Vaccination emerged as the most crucial tool for ending the pandemic and protecting lives and livelihoods. Ensuring equitable access to safe and effective vaccines was vital, particularly in Africa, where the principle that "no one is safe until everyone is safe" underscored the importance of widespread vaccination (World Health Organization, 2024c).

Despite the availability of vaccines, low vaccination rates in certain regions can be attributed to logistical challenges related to vaccine distribution, such as difficulties in transporting vaccines to remote areas and the constraints posed by seasonal weather conditions. These factors have significantly hindered access, particularly in rural and underserved populations, thereby exacerbating the pandemic's impact (Hassen et al., 2022). Furthermore, vaccine hesitancy has emerged as a significant barrier to achieving higher vaccination coverage, thereby exacerbating the pandemic's impact (Hassen et al., 2022). High levels of vaccine hesitancy can increase mortality rates by up to eight times compared to scenarios with optimal vaccine uptake (Olivera Mesa et al., 2022). Countries with large populations and low vaccination rates are at higher risk of increased death rates. Studies indicate that a substantial proportion of adults in Africa exhibit hesitancy toward COVID-19 vaccines (Cooper et al., 2018; Dinga et al., 2021).

In developing countries, limited vaccine availability is a critical issue, but misinformation has also significantly influenced vaccine uptake. The WHO Director-General's statement, "We're not only fighting an epidemic; we're fighting an infodemic," highlights the challenge posed by the global spread of misinformation through social media and other channels, which presents a severe public health threat (Jember et al., 2024; World Health Organization, 2021). For instance, some people believe that the Chinese government deliberately manufactured COVID-19 to wage war on the USA (or vice versa) (Douglas, 2021). Therefore, to improve our understanding of low vaccine uptake in Africa, especially in Ethiopia, we assess the impact of misinformation on COVID-19 vaccination.

Ethiopia serves as an important case study for understanding the multifaceted barriers to vaccine uptake, particularly in developing contexts during the COVID-19 pandemic. As one of Africa's most populous nations, Ethiopia is characterized by a rich tapestry of ethnic diversity and cultural traditions, which can complicate public health initiatives, including vaccination campaigns. The country has a complex sociopolitical landscape marked by historical conflicts and ongoing tensions that can influence public trust in government health interventions and exacerbate misinformation surrounding vaccines. Furthermore, Ethiopia faces significant logistical challenges in healthcare delivery, particularly in rural areas where infrastructural deficits hinder access to essential services. These unique characteristics make Ethiopia emblematic of the broader challenges faced by many countries in sub-Saharan Africa, where vaccine distribution and acceptance are critical to public health outcomes.

Ethiopia, although not as stringent as some other African countries like Rwanda or Nigeria, implemented a range of response measures starting on March 16, 2020.

These included the closure of schools, a ban on public gatherings, and restrictions on sports, bars, entertainment outlets, hotels, and restaurant services. Ethiopian Airlines, the national carrier, suspended many of its scheduled flights to limit cross-border transmission of the virus. Additionally, all passengers entering the country were required to undergo a 14-day mandatory quarantine. The Ethiopian government also closed all land borders and imposed restrictions on inter-city transport, requiring public transport providers to operate at less than half capacity (Aragie et al., 2020). These measures were essential in attempting to limit the spread of the virus, yet they also revealed the underlying vulnerabilities in the healthcare system. Furthermore, while the Ethiopian government sought to enhance vaccine availability through partnerships with international organizations, the overall public trust in these initiatives has been challenged by the historical context of health governance in the country.

The remainder of this chapter is structured as follows. The next section reviews the theoretical and empirical literature, laying the groundwork for understanding vaccination uptake during the COVID-19 pandemic. Section 3 examines the context of Ethiopia during the pandemic, highlighting the country's unique challenges and responses. Section 4 outlines the research methods used in this study, followed by a description of the data. Section 5 presents the findings and Sect. 6 concludes.

2 Literature Review and Framework

2.1 Covid-19 Vaccine Hesitancy and Uptake

Prior to the work of the SAGE Working group on vaccine hesitancy, there was no established definition in previous literature due to the multifaceted nature of vaccine hesitancy and its variation across context, population, and vaccine type. Vaccine hesitancy is "the delay in acceptance or refusal of vaccination despite the availability of vaccination services" (MacDonald, 2015). Other studies have extended this definition to include people who accept or receive some vaccines but remain concerned about their safety, effectiveness, or importance (Salmon et al., 2015). Other studies have used the term vaccine support instead of vaccine hesitancy. Farhart et al. (2022) defined vaccine support as the inverse of hesitancy. The vaccine uptake in this study measures whether the respondent has received the vaccine or not. This approach is unlike other studies where hesitancy assesses respondents' likelihood of getting the vaccine should the vaccine be available.

2.2 Understanding Misinformation

The concept of misinformation is defined in many ways. According to (Scheufele & Krause, 2019), misinformation is incorrect information, the probable outcome of an accident. On the other hand, Wardle and Derakhshan (2017) defined misinformation as false information that is being shared unconsciously (not knowing that the information is correct or not) and without any purpose to harm anyone. On the other hand, disinformation is false information that is shared consciously to cause harm intentionally (Wardle & Derakhshan, 2017). Additionally, mal-information is defined as authentic private information shared with the public to cause harm by creating hate speech and harassment.

Health misinformation is defined as a "health-related claim of fact that is currently false due to a lack of scientific evidence." Building on the previous studies, the following definition of misinformation is adopted as "mother-term" of both (mis and dis): (i) inaccurate information shared unconsciously by believing that the information is true, and (ii) inaccurate information shared consciously. According to Krause et al. (2020), misinformation refers to false information that can be challenged with the best available evidence pertaining to COVID-19. Additionally, Barua et al. (2020) define misinformation as an umbrella term for general misinformation belief, conspiracy belief, and religious misinformation belief.

2.3 Relation to the Literature

Conspiracy theories have been extensively studied in the psychological literature to enhance our understanding of their development and impact. According to Douglas (2021), conspiracy theories emerge when significant psychological needs are unmet. These needs include the desire to satisfy curiosity, avoid uncertainty, restore a threatened sense of security and control (Kruglanski et al., 2021), and maintain a positive self-image.

During the COVID-19 pandemic, people's psychological needs were particularly frustrated. The high levels of uncertainty, coupled with widespread fear for the future and the well-being of loved ones, led individuals to seek information to answer pressing questions about the pandemic's trajectory (Douglas, 2021). The complex information landscape, filled with contradictory messages, further exacerbated the situation. Research indicates that conspiracy theories thrive in times of crisis as people look for ways to manage difficult and uncertain circumstances (van Prooijen & Douglas, 2017). Consequently, the pandemic created a fertile ground for conspiracy theories to flourish. Notable COVID-19 conspiracy theories included claims that 5G phone masts spread the virus (Jolley & Paterson, 2020) and that hydroxychloroquine, garlic, and colloidal silver were effective treatments (Bertin et al., 2020; Teovanović et al., 2021).

Conspiracy theories have significant consequences, and those related to COVID-19 were no exception. Recent research highlights their negative impact on people's intentions to comply with government recommendations. For instance, Jember et al. (2024) investigated the extent of misinformation about the COVID-19 vaccine and associated factors among residents in Gondar, Ethiopia, in a 2022 survey. The study found that about 48% of respondents were misinformed about the vaccine despite most being vaccinated. Social media was identified as the primary source of misinformation for about half of the respondents, followed by family and friends (41.1%). Similarly, Dereje et al. (2022) examined the level of COVID-19 vaccine hesitancy and its associated factors in Addis Ababa, Ethiopia. The study revealed that mass media was most respondents' main information source. However, about 78% were unwilling to get vaccinated. Among these, 43.6% cited fear of side effects, and 41% believed the vaccine might be a biological weapon. Additionally, some respondents suggested that developed nations could use vaccines to cause infertility and control the population size of poorer countries.

Other studies on vaccine uptake further highlight the pervasive impact of misinformation and conspiracy theories on vaccination intentions. In Jordan, a study found that about 47% of respondents believed COVID-19 was part of a global conspiracy (Sallam et al., 2020). In Korea, research revealed that 49.76% of respondents encountered misinformation about the COVID-19 vaccine, and those endorsing at least one misinformation item were significantly less likely to be vaccinated (Perlis et al., 2022). In Australia, a study showed that 22% of participants believed the myth that heat kills the virus (Pickles et al., 2021). A cross-country study in the USA, UK, Ireland, Spain, and Mexico examined predictors of belief in common misinformation about the virus and its impact on health behaviors. The findings suggested that increased susceptibility to misinformation negatively affects self-reported compliance with public health guidance and willingness to vaccinate or recommend the vaccine to vulnerable individuals (Roozenbeek et al., 2020).

Similarly, a study using two survey samples from before and after the U.S. 2020 presidential election found that greater consistency in COVID-19 conspiracy beliefs predicted vaccine hesitancy and a decline in support for vaccination (Farhart et al., 2022). Romer and Jamieson (2020) investigated the effect of conspiracy theories disseminated by mainstream media on the uptake of preventive behaviors and vaccination intentions in the U.S. Their study, conducted in March and July 2020, found that COVID-19-related conspiracy beliefs were inversely related to both reporting of preventive actions and intentions to vaccinate. Additionally, Pivetti et al. (2021) explored the role of antecedents, such as political ideology and moral purity values, in shaping COVID-19 conspiracy beliefs. The study suggested that conspiracy beliefs negatively predicted general attitudes toward vaccines.

This chapter makes important contributions to this literature. First, this chapter extends the existing literature by focusing specifically on the unique socio-cultural and psychological landscape of Ethiopia during the COVID-19 pandemic. While previous studies have explored conspiracy theories and misinformation in various global contexts, our findings highlight the distinct mechanisms through which these beliefs manifest and influence vaccine uptake in a developing country setting. Notably, the chapter identifies the interplay between general misinformation, conspiracy beliefs, and religious trust—an aspect that has not been sufficiently addressed in prior research. Second, by examining the psychological underpinnings of conspiracy theories, this chapter contributes to the understanding of why such beliefs proliferate in times of crisis. As Douglas (2021) notes, unmet psychological needs drive individuals to seek alternative narratives to make sense of uncertainty. This chapter contextualizes this assertion within the Ethiopian experience, illustrating how high levels of fear and misinformation during the pandemic led to increased conspiracy beliefs, as supported by findings from Jember et al. (2024) and Dereje et al. (2022). Thus, our study adds empirical evidence to the theoretical frameworks proposed in the literature. Finally, this chapter provides critical insights into the role of information sources in shaping beliefs and vaccine uptake. Previous literature has shown that social media is a significant source of misinformation (Jolley & Paterson, 2020; Bertin et al., 2020). However, our findings reveal that trust in traditional and religious leaders plays a more crucial role in Ethiopia, suggesting that interventions must be tailored to leverage these trusted figures to counter misinformation effectively. This dimension contributes to the literature by emphasizing the need for culturally relevant communication strategies in combating misinformation and enhancing vaccine confidence.

3 Context: Ethiopia During the COVID-19 Pandemic

For several compelling reasons, Ethiopia provides a fruitful context for investigating vaccination uptake during the COVID-19 pandemic. Firstly, as Africa's second most populous country (World Bank, 2024), Ethiopia faced a high risk of significant contamination if proper measures were not taken. Today, Ethiopia is one of the countries most affected by coronavirus cases on the African continent, with cumulative cases reported to the WHO in 2024 being twice as high as those in Nigeria (STATISTA, 2024).

The Ethiopian government acted quickly to counter the pandemic's negative effects. Although not reaching the response levels of some African countries like Rwanda and Nigeria, Ethiopia introduced a series of measures to contain the spread of COVID-19. The first confirmed case in Ethiopia was reported on March 13, 2020 (Aragie et al., 2020). By March 16, 2020, the Office of the Prime Minister had implemented school closures, a ban on public gatherings, and various service restrictions. Additionally, Ethiopia suspended many flights of its national carrier, enforced mandatory quarantine for incoming passengers, closed land borders, and restricted inter-city transport (Aragie et al., 2020).

However, despite these efforts, Ethiopia remains one of the most affected countries in Africa, with relatively low vaccine uptake compared to the rest of the world (World Health Organization, 2024b). The first COVID-19 vaccine was introduced on March 13, 2021, but by December 31, 2023, only 38% of the population had completed the primary vaccination series, and just 5% had received at least one booster dose. This aligns with the wider African context, where 33% of the population had completed the primary series, and 6% had received a booster by the same date. In comparison, the global context shows a more favorable uptake, where 56% of the population had completed the primary series (World Health Organization, 2024b).

Furthermore, Ethiopia has a long tradition of vaccine uptake and immunization programs, which makes the current low COVID-19 vaccination rate even more intriguing. The country introduced the Extended Program on Immunization (EPI) in the early 1980s to reduce childhood morbidity and mortality from vaccine-preventable diseases such as measles, polio, and diphtheria-tetanus-pertussis. According to the 2019 Ethiopia Mini Demographic and Health Survey (EMDHS 2019), 73% of children aged 13–23 months received the BCG vaccine, 78% received the polio vaccine, and 59% received the measles vaccine (EPHI and ICF, 2019). However, only 43% received all basic vaccines, and 19% received none. The report also highlighted regional disparities, with the Somali region having the highest proportion of unimmunized children at 49%, compared to just 3% in Dire Dawa. To address these issues, Ethiopia introduced immunization catch-up vaccination guidelines in 2022 to improve the overall health of its population (Ministry of Health-Ethiopia, 2022).[1]

4 Methods

4.1 Study Design and Implementation

The initial data collection phase involved a comprehensive survey designed to gather information on various dimensions relevant to COVID-19 vaccination. This included respondents' beliefs about the virus, levels of trust in information sources, and critical sociodemographic characteristics. The survey was administered using Qualtrics, an online survey platform, which allowed for a structured and systematic approach to data collection. To ensure accessibility for participants with limited internet access, the survey was supplemented by phone interviews. This combination of data collection methods aimed to minimize selection bias and enhance the representativeness of the sample, allowing for a more inclusive understanding of public sentiments regarding vaccination.

Following the initial phase, a follow-up and extension survey was conducted from November 2023 to December 2023. This phase was crucial for capturing any changes in attitudes toward vaccine uptake and misinformation exposure over time. The longitudinal nature of this data collection enabled us to track shifts in public perceptions related to COVID-19 vaccination in Ethiopia, offering insights into how misinformation may evolve and affect community health behaviors.

In addition to the quantitative surveys, focus group discussions were facilitated through WhatsApp groups in January 2023. These discussions provided qualitative insights that enriched the quantitative findings, enabling participants to share their experiences and perspectives regarding COVID-19 vaccination and the influence of misinformation. The use of WhatsApp, a widely used communication platform in

[1] For details related to the objective of the guidelines, see the following link (https://publications.jsi.com/JSIInternet/Inc/Common/_download_pub.cfm?id=25790&lid=3).

Ethiopia, facilitated engagement with a diverse participant pool, thereby enhancing the depth and richness of the qualitative data collected.

4.2 Measurement

The constructs "Conspiracy Theories" and "General Misinformation" were measured using reflective latent variable models, which allow us to capture the complexity of public beliefs and attitudes toward COVID-19. This methodological approach leverages individual item responses as observed variables, thereby facilitating a nuanced understanding of how each item contributes to the overall construct. By employing this framework, the study not only assesses the prevalence of conspiracy beliefs and misinformation but also the interrelationship among these constructs, which is critical for understanding their impact on vaccine uptake in Ethiopia (Table 1).

Conspiracy Theories

The measurement of conspiracy theories was operationalized through five specific items that reflect common beliefs about secrecy and manipulation in the context of public health. Each item was crafted to resonate with prevalent sentiments among the Ethiopian population regarding transparency and information dissemination during the pandemic. The items included:

- The government keeps many important secrets from the public.
- The rapid spread of COVID-19 is the result of the deliberate, concealed efforts of some organizations.
- Government-funded scientists manipulate evidence to support existing government policy.
- A lot of information about diseases and treatments is withheld from the public.
- The government fakes evidence relating to significant world events to deceive citizens.

The factor loadings for these items ranged from 0.811 to 0.858, indicating a strong correlation between the items and the underlying construct of conspiracy theories. This robust correlation supports the validity of these items in capturing this dimension of misinformation, demonstrating that respondents' beliefs are significantly in line with the conceptual framework of conspiracy theories. Qualitative data from focus group discussions further illuminated these findings, as many participants conveyed a sense of distrust toward various narratives surrounding COVID-19. For instance, one participant remarked, "There are many important secrets that may not be disclosed to the public," reflecting a broader skepticism echoed by others in the discussions. This sentiment underscores the importance of conspiracy theories in shaping public perceptions and behaviors regarding vaccination, indicating that such beliefs may

Table 1 Measurements of misinformation and conspiracy beliefs

Constructs	Code	Reflective latent measures	Factors loading
Conspiracy theories	CB1	The government keeps many important secrets from the public	0.811
	CB2	The rapid spread of COVID-19 is the result of the deliberate, concealed efforts of some organizations	0.827
	CB3	Government funded scientists manipulate evidence in order to support existing government policy	0.858
	CB4	A lot of information about disease and treatments is withheld from the public	0.848
	CB5	The government fakes evidence relating to significant world events to deceive citizens	0.846
Religious misinformation	RMB1	The information provided by our religious leaders about COVID-19 are correct	0.754
	RMB2	The information provided by our religious leaders about COVID-19 are not harmful	0.878
	RMB3	The information provided by our religious leaders is more accurate than the information of scientists/doctors about COVID-19	0.872
General misinformation	GMB1	The Corona virus is not heat-resistant and will be killed by a temperature of just 26/27 degrees	0.784
	GMB2	Eating garlic, drinking ginger tea, sipping mild-hot water could safe me from corona virus	0.843
	GMB3	Bats are to blame for the spread of the corona virus in China	0.853

Source Author's computation
Note Factor loadings obtained from the Principal Component Analysis

play a critical role in influencing individuals' willingness to engage with health interventions.

General Misinformation

Similarly, the construct of general misinformation was assessed using three items that reflect prevalent misconceptions about COVID-19:

- The Coronavirus is not heat-resistant and will be killed by a temperature of just 26/27 degrees.
- Eating garlic, drinking ginger tea, sipping mild-hot water could save me from the Coronavirus.
- Bats are to blame for the spread of the Coronavirus in China.

The factor loadings for these items ranged from 0.784 to 0.853, demonstrating a robust relationship with the general misinformation construct. This indicates that the selected items effectively capture the essence of misinformation beliefs that may hinder vaccination efforts.

Qualitative responses collected during focus group discussions further illuminate how these misconceptions manifest, particularly in the Ethiopian context, where traditional beliefs and practices play a significant role in health-related decisions. Participants frequently mentioned their reliance on local remedies, reflecting a deep-rooted cultural belief in the efficacy of traditional foods and herbal treatments. For instance, one participant noted, "My neighbor told me that drinking ginger tea will protect me from the virus," which highlights the persistence of misinformation tied to local practices. Another participant expressed confidence in the immune-boosting properties of garlic: "I always add garlic to my food because it is said to help fight off infections." This reliance on garlic and other local remedies, such as various herbal concoctions, underscores a widespread belief that traditional foods can serve as effective preventative measures against COVID-19. Furthermore, the focus groups revealed that many individuals felt a disconnect between scientific information and their traditional practices. One participant remarked, "We trust our elders and their knowledge about natural remedies more than what we hear from the government or health officials." This sentiment indicates that misinformation is not just about incorrect facts; it also encompasses a complex interplay of trust in local knowledge systems versus official health communications.

Empirical Estimation

The main goal of the empirical analysis was to investigate misinformation's effect on COVID-19 vaccine uptake in Ethiopia. Following existing literature our empirical model is as follows:

$$Y_{ic} = \beta_0 + \beta_1 D1_{ic} + \beta_2 D2_{ic} + X_{ic}\delta + \varepsilon_{ic} \tag{1}$$

In this equation, *i* denotes a respondent, *and c* denotes a county. Where Y_{ic} is our dependent variable, namely the vaccine uptake, which is a dummy variable taking the value of 1 if the respondent took a vaccine and 0 otherwise. The second dependent variable is the number of vaccine doses measured continuously. Our independent variables include $D1_{ic}$ and $D2_{ic}$, which capture general misinformation and conspiracy beliefs. Our general misinformation beliefs are an index composed of three different subcomponents. For example, the index is composed of factor loading above 0.7.

These measures include statements such as: "The coronavirus is not heat-resistant and will be killed by a temperature of just 26/27 degrees," "eating garlic, drinking ginger tea, sipping mild-hot water could save me from coronavirus," and finally, "Bats are to blame for the spread of the Coronavirus in China." Our conspiracy theory beliefs are composed of five different subfactors. These factors include "the government keeps many important secrets from the public," "the rapid spread of COVID-19 is the result of the deliberate, concealed efforts of some organizations," and "government-funded scientists manipulate the evidence in order to support existing government policy," "a lot of information about the diseases and treatments is withheld from the public," finally "the government fakes evidence relating to significant world events to deceive citizens." X_{ic} is a vector of control variables, including sociodemographic, economic, health, and attitude factors. ε_{ic} represents a random idiosyncratic error term.

5 Findings

5.1 *Predictors of General Misinformation and Conspiracy Beliefs*

Figures 1a, b present a comparative analysis of the most important predictors of "general misinformation beliefs" and "conspiracy beliefs." The results highlight distinct differences in the factors influencing these two types of beliefs. For general misinformation beliefs, trust in religious leaders emerges as the most important predictor, followed closely by trust in scientists and scientific knowledge. Trust in traditional and ancestral leaders also plays a crucial role in shaping beliefs. This is consistent with the findings of Jember et al. (2024), which emphasize the influence of local and religious authorities in the dissemination of health-related information. In contrast, trust in medical doctors and nurses and trust in politicians are less important predictors (Fig. 1a).

Conversely, conspiracy beliefs are predominantly predicted by trust in medical doctors and nurses. This suggests that when individuals have confidence in healthcare professionals, they may be less likely to endorse conspiracy theories related to health interventions. Following trust in medical professionals, trust in journalists, traditional and ancestral leaders, and religious leaders also significantly influences conspiracy beliefs. However, the least important predictors for conspiracy beliefs include trust in politicians, traditional and ancestral knowledge, and trust in people in general (Fig. 1b).

This comparative analysis reveals a crucial distinction: while trust in medical professionals is a key factor in shaping conspiracy beliefs, trust in religious and scientific authorities is more influential in determining general misinformation beliefs. These dynamics reflect the complex interplay of trust in various social and institutional contexts, underscoring how different sources of information resonate with individuals based on their beliefs and experiences. The varying importance of trust in

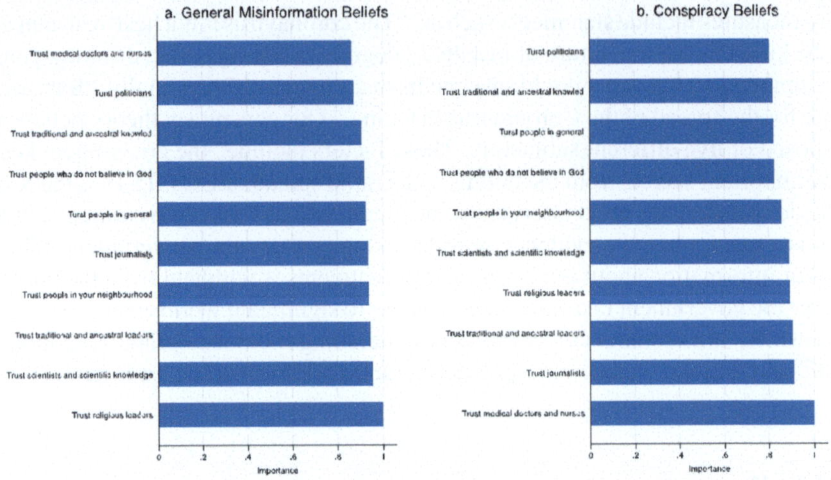

Fig. 1 Predictors of general misinformation and conspiracy beliefs. *Source* Author's computation

traditional and ancestral leaders across both contexts further highlights the nuanced ways in which cultural factors influence belief systems.

To further illustrate these dynamics, qualitative data from our focus group discussions provide valuable insights into the complex interplay of trust in various authority figures and how it shapes public perceptions of COVID-19 vaccination. Respondent 1, a 35-year-old community health worker, noted, "I often hear people say they trust their religious leaders more than anyone else when it comes to health advice. If a pastor says the vaccine is dangerous, many will believe it, even if a doctor says otherwise." This sentiment aligns with the quantitative findings, emphasizing the pivotal role of religious authority in shaping public perceptions. The weight of religious beliefs in Ethiopia cannot be underestimated, as they often dictate not only moral and ethical frameworks but also influence health-related decisions in a deeply interconnected social fabric.

Similarly, Respondent 2, a university student, remarked, "I trust doctors, but sometimes I feel they are not telling us the full truth. When I see a video on social media that says vaccines are a scam, I get confused. It's hard to know who to believe." This highlights the tension between medical trust and the pervasive influence of misinformation, reflecting the broader challenges in public health communication. The student's perspective exemplifies how the digital landscape complicates trust in medical authority; misinformation proliferates rapidly through social media, undermining the efficacy of public health messaging and often leading individuals to question the integrity of medical professionals. Additionally, Respondent 3, an elderly community member, stated, "Our traditional leaders are respected in our villages. If they speak against vaccines, it resonates with people. They are seen as guardians of our culture and health." This indicates the significant role that traditional leaders play in the discourse surrounding vaccination, further complicating the landscape of belief and trust. The reliance on traditional knowledge and the authority of local leaders is particularly pronounced in rural areas, where access to formal medical education and resources may be limited. Traditional leaders often serve as intermediaries between formal health systems and local communities, which can either facilitate or hinder vaccine acceptance based on their stance toward vaccination. Furthermore, Respondent 4, a 28-year-old teacher, added, "We often rely on what our community leaders say. They are the ones who understand our culture and values. If they support the vaccine, many will follow. If not, it creates fear." This underscores the critical influence of community dynamics in shaping health behaviors, suggesting that interventions aimed at increasing vaccine uptake must engage these leaders as allies in public health efforts. By harnessing their influence, public health campaigns can potentially mitigate misinformation and enhance trust in vaccination programs.

5.2 *Impacts of General Misinformation and Conspiracy Beliefs on Vaccine Uptake*

Having explored the predictors of general misinformation and conspiracy beliefs, we now analyze how misinformation and conspiracy beliefs affect vaccine uptake among the Ethiopian population. To gauge the impact of these factors, we conducted an Ordinary Least Squares (OLS) regression analysis to estimate their influence on individuals' likelihood of getting vaccinated. The results are presented in Table 2, which details the regression results of general misinformation and conspiracy beliefs' effect on vaccine uptake in Ethiopia. Specifically, columns 1 to 5 report the results when the dependent variable is vaccine uptake, defined as a dummy variable taking the value of 1 if the respondent received the vaccine and 0 otherwise.

In column 1, we regressed vaccine uptake on general misinformation and conspiracy beliefs while controlling for county and demographic characteristics. Our findings reveal that both general misinformation and conspiracy beliefs are associated with decreased vaccine uptake. Notably, the results indicate that the impact of general misinformation is both significant and more pronounced than that of conspiracy beliefs. This suggests that general misinformation acts as a more substantial barrier to vaccination efforts. In columns 2 through 5, we added additional controls such as economic, health, and attitudes variables. The results regarding general misinformation beliefs remained robust even with these additional controls, underscoring the detrimental impact of misinformation on vaccine uptake in Ethiopia. Interestingly, the results on conspiracy beliefs remain statistically non-significant.

The qualitative narratives derived from our survey respondents provide critical context and substantiate the quantitative findings regarding the detrimental effects of misinformation on vaccine uptake. For instance, Respondent 5, a 40-year-old farmer, expressed, "I hear many people say the vaccine is a way for the government to control us. If my neighbor says they won't take it, I feel scared to take it too. I trust

Table 2 The effect of misinformation and conspiracy beliefs on vaccines uptake

	(1)	(2)	(3)	(4)	(5)
Variables	Vaccine	Vaccine	Vaccine	Vaccine	Vaccine
General misinformation beliefs	−0.042***	−0.042***	−0.039**	−0.039**	−0.039**
	(0.016)	(0.015)	(0.016)	(0.016)	(0.016)
Conspiracy beliefs	−0.026	0.012	0.011	0.011	0.011
	(0.016)	(0.021)	(0.021)	(0.021)	(0.021)
Constant	0.335**	0.210	0.211	0.164	0.164
	(0.134)	(0.147)	(0.147)	(0.149)	(0.149)
Observations	548	548	548	548	548
R-squared	0.207	0.226	0.229	0.242	0.242
County dummy	Yes	Yes	Yes	Yes	
Demographic controls	Yes	Yes	Yes	Yes	
Economic controls		Yes	Yes	Yes	
Healthy controls			Yes	Yes	
Attitudes controls				Yes	

Source Author's computation

what they say." This sentiment illustrates how misinformation can permeate community networks, leading to increased vaccine hesitancy. It highlights the importance of social influence and the role that personal relationships play in shaping health behaviors. Similarly, Respondent 6, a community health worker, noted, "Even when I tell people about the benefits of the vaccine, they still refer to what they read on social media. They say vaccines cause infertility, which makes them fearful." This observation underscores the significant influence of social media as a primary source of misinformation, which aligns with our regression results indicating a strong association between general misinformation beliefs and decreased vaccine uptake. The pervasive nature of misinformation on social media platforms can undermine public health messaging and create an environment of distrust.

Moreover, Respondent 7, a university student, shared, "I was hesitant at first because I read online that there might be severe side effects. Then, I talked to my doctor, who reassured me. But many people don't have that access to a doctor, and they just believe what they hear from other people." This response points to a critical gap in access to reliable information, suggesting that the lack of trust in medical professionals can exacerbate the effects of misinformation. It highlights the need for accessible health education and the importance of fostering trust between healthcare providers and the community.

The convergence of findings from the regression analyses and qualitative narratives indicates that general misinformation beliefs have a more substantial negative impact on COVID-19 vaccine uptake than conspiracy beliefs. This suggests that while conspiracy theories may capture public attention and generate discussion, the more pervasive and insidious spread of general misinformation poses a greater threat to public health efforts. The implications of this are profound, signifying a need for targeted interventions that specifically address the misinformation landscape.

In Table 3, we further investigated the effect of general misinformation and conspiracy beliefs on the number of vaccine doses received. Following a similar analytical approach to that of vaccine uptake, we began by regressing vaccine doses on general misinformation and conspiracy beliefs while controlling for county and demographic characteristics. Consistent with our findings regarding vaccine uptake, we discovered that higher levels of general misinformation correlate with a decrease in the number of vaccine doses received (columns 1–5).

The qualitative insights from our respondents reinforce these findings. For instance, Respondent 8, a 55-year-old teacher, remarked, "After hearing so many stories about the vaccine being harmful, I decided to wait. Now, I've only gotten one dose when I could have had all three." This statement reflects how misinformation not only affects initial vaccine uptake but also the willingness to receive subsequent doses, emphasizing the need for targeted interventions to address such fears and encourage full vaccination series. Furthermore, Respondent 9, a local leader, stated, "I always tell my community that we need to listen to the health experts. But when misinformation spreads, it often drowns out the voices of reason."

Table 3 The effect of misinformation and conspiracy beliefs on vaccine doses

	(1)	(2)	(3)	(4)	(5)
Variables	How many doses of vaccines have you received?				
General misinformation beliefs	−0.047**	−0.048*	−0.049*	−0.049*	−0.061**
	(0.020)	(0.027)	(0.028)	(0.028)	(0.028)
Conspiracy beliefs	−0.038	0.020	0.021	0.024	0.022
	(0.039)	(0.037)	(0.037)	(0.037)	(0.038)
Constant	0.246	0.023	0.012	−0.072	0.966***
	(0.387)	(0.259)	(0.259)	(0.265)	(0.270)
Observations	548	548	548	548	548
R-squared					0.300
County dummy	Yes	Yes	Yes	Yes	Yes
Demographic controls	Yes	Yes	Yes	Yes	Yes
Economic controls		Yes	Yes	Yes	Yes
Healthy controls			Yes	Yes	Yes
Attitudes controls				Yes	Yes

Source Author's computation

5.3 Discussion

The findings of this study provide critical insights into the complex dynamics of trust, misinformation, and their impacts on public health behaviors, particularly vaccine uptake. By examining the predictors of general misinformation and conspiracy beliefs, the determinants of trust across various domains, and the effects of these beliefs on COVID-19 vaccine uptake, several key themes emerge that have significant implications for policy, education, and public health communication strategies. Our analysis reveals that trust in religious leaders is the strongest predictor of general misinformation beliefs, surpassing trust in scientists and scientific knowledge and in traditional and ancestral knowledge. This finding underscores religious leaders' profound influence within communities, particularly in shaping beliefs that can either support or undermine public health efforts. Given the central role of religious leaders in many societies, especially in settings where religious institutions are deeply integrated into daily life, this finding suggests that misinformation can be amplified when it aligns with or is endorsed by these trusted figures.

Moreover, religiosity emerges as a consistently significant positive determinant of trust across various domains, including trust in medical professionals, scientists, journalists, and traditional leaders. This consistency highlights the pervasive role that religious beliefs play in shaping trust and, by extension, the reception of information. The fact that religiosity influences trust across such a broad spectrum suggests that any public health communication strategy must consider the religious context of the target population. This finding is consistent with the assumption that people use religion as one of their coping mechanisms during crisis and adversity (Bentzen, 2021).

Perhaps most critically, our findings indicate that general misinformation beliefs have a more substantial negative effect on COVID-19 vaccine uptake and the number of vaccine doses received than conspiracy beliefs. This suggests that while conspiracy theories are often sensationalized and receive considerable attention, the more pervasive and insidious spread of general misinformation poses a greater threat to public health efforts. The implication for policy and education is clear: there is a pressing need to develop targeted interventions that address and counter general misinformation. This is consistent with the previous studies. For instance, Dereje et al. (2022) found in the case of Addis Ababa, in Ethiopia, that vaccine hesitancy was due to the lack of proper information, the misconception about the effectiveness of the COVID-19 vaccine, and the possible side effects. This finding is supported by similar studies elsewhere in Africa (Dereje et al., 2022; Jember et al., 2024).

6 Conclusion

The findings of this study underline the critical role that general misinformation plays as a significant downside risk to COVID-19 vaccination uptake in Ethiopia. Our analysis reveals that while conspiracy theories do exist within the public discourse, it is the broader spectrum of misinformation beliefs that has a more pronounced negative impact on both the initial acceptance of vaccines and the willingness to receive subsequent doses. This insight challenges the common perception that conspiracy theories are the primary drivers of vaccine hesitancy, suggesting instead that a more comprehensive approach is necessary to address the range of misinformation that undermines public health efforts.

The qualitative data collected during our study further substantiates these findings, illustrating how deeply ingrained cultural beliefs and local practices influence perceptions of vaccination. Many participants expressed reliance on traditional remedies and local knowledge, often prioritizing these over scientifically backed health information. This highlights the necessity for public health initiatives to engage with local contexts and address the specific misconceptions that pervade communities, as failing to do so may exacerbate the downside risks associated with misinformation and hinder vaccination efforts.

Given the urgent need to counter misinformation, we advocate for targeted communication strategies that leverage trusted institutions and key individuals within Ethiopian society. Religious leaders, community health workers, and local influencers can play pivotal roles in disseminating accurate information and dispelling myths surrounding COVID-19 vaccines. By aligning health messaging with the values and beliefs of the community, these trusted figures can effectively combat misinformation and foster a more favorable environment for vaccination. Such grassroots engagement is essential to mitigate the adverse effects of misinformation and encourage vaccine uptake.

Acknowledgements The authors would like to express their sincere gratitude to Fekadu Deresse for his support with data collection and research. Special thanks to Habtom Tesfaye and Mikael Yohannes for their invaluable field support. We also extend our thanks to Jean-Fidele SIE, Rehema Karata, and Adefolake Adeniyi for their excellent research assistance.

References

Aragie, E., Taffesse, A. S., & Thurlow, J. (2020). *Assessing the short-term impacts of COVID-19 on Ethiopia's economy: External and domestic shocks and pace of recovery* (0 ed.) [ESSP, Working Paper 153]. International Food Policy Research Institute (IFPRI). https://doi.org/10.2499/p15738coll2.134181

Ayele, Z. A., Fessha, Y. T., Dessalegn, B., & Gebeye, B. A. (2021). Ethiopia: Legal Response to Covid-19. In J. King & O. L. Ferraz (Eds.), *The Oxford Compendium of National Legal Responses to COVID-19 (OUP, 2021)*. Oxford University Press. https://doi.org/10.1093/law-occ19/e18.013.20

Barua, Z., Barua, S., Aktar, S., Kabir, N., & Li, M. (2020). Effects of misinformation on COVID-19 individual responses and recommendations for resilience of disastrous consequences of misinformation. *Progress in Disaster Science*, *8*, 100119. https://doi.org/10.1016/j.pdisas.2020.100119

Bentzen, J. S. (2021). In crisis, we pray: Religiosity and the COVID-19 pandemic. *Journal of Economic Behavior & Organization*, *192*, 541–583. https://doi.org/10.1016/j.jebo.2021.10.014

Bertin, P., Nera, K., & Delouvée, S. (2020). Conspiracy Beliefs, Rejection of Vaccination, and Support for Hydroxychloroquine: A Conceptual Replication-Extension in the COVID-19 Pandemic Context. *Frontiers in Psychology*, *11*, 565128. https://doi.org/10.3389/fpsyg.2020.565128

Cooper, S., Betsch, C., Sambala, E. Z., Mchiza, N., & Wiysonge, C. S. (2018). Vaccine hesitancy—A potential threat to the achievements of vaccination programmes in Africa. *Human Vaccines & Immunotherapeutics*, *14*(10), 2355–2357. https://doi.org/10.1080/21645515.2018.1460987

Dereje, N., Tesfaye, A., Tamene, B., Alemeshet, D., Abe, H., Tesfa, N., Gideon, S., Biruk, T., & Lakew, Y. (2022). COVID-19 vaccine hesitancy in Addis Ababa, Ethiopia: A mixed-method study. *BMJ Open*, *12*(5), e052432. https://doi.org/10.1136/bmjopen-2021-052432

Dinga, J. N., Sinda, L. K., & Titanji, V. P. K. (2021). Assessment of Vaccine Hesitancy to a COVID-19 Vaccine in Cameroonian Adults and Its Global Implication. *Vaccines*, *9*(2), 175. https://doi.org/10.3390/vaccines9020175

Douglas, K. M. (2021). COVID-19 conspiracy theories. *Group Processes & Intergroup Relations*, *24*(2), 270–275. https://doi.org/10.1177/1368430220982068

Ethiopian Public Health Institute (EPHI) and ICF. (2019). *Ethiopia mini demographic and health survey 2019: Key indicators*. Rockville, MD: EPHI and ICF.

Fancourt, D., Steptoe, A., & Bu, F. (2021). Trajectories of anxiety and depressive symptoms during enforced isolation due to COVID-19 in England: A longitudinal observational study. *The Lancet. Psychiatry*, *8*(2), 141–149. https://doi.org/10.1016/S2215-0366(20)30482-X

Farhart, C. E., Douglas-Durham, E., Lunz Trujillo, K., & Vitriol, J. A. (2022). Chapter Seven - Vax attacks: How Conspiracy Theory Belief Undermines Vaccine Support. In T. Bolsen, & R. Palm (Eds.), *Progress in Molecular Biology and Translational Science, 188*(1): Molecular Biology and Clinical Medicine in the Age of Politicization, 135–169. Academic Press. https://doi.org/10.1016/bs.pmbts.2021.11.001

Hassen, H. D., Welde, M., & Menebo, M. M. (2022). Understanding determinants of COVID-19 vaccine hesitancy: an emphasis on the role of religious affiliation and the individual's reliance on traditional remedy. *BMC Public Health*, *22*(1), 1142. https://doi.org/10.1186/s12889-022-13485-2

Hategeka, C., Carter, S. E., Chenge, F. M., Katanga, E. N., Lurton, G., Mayaka, S. M.-N., Mwamba, D. K., Kleef, E. van, Vanlerberghe, V., & Grépin, K. A. (2021). Impact of the COVID-19 pandemic and response on the utilization of health services in public facilities during the first wave in Kinshasa, the Democratic Republic of the Congo. *BMJ Global Health*, *6*(7), e005955. https://doi.org/10.1136/bmjgh-2021-005955

Jacobs, C., Kyamusugulwa, P. M., Katembera, R. S., & Kintuntu, H. (2021). Containing COVID-19 in the Democratic Republic of the Congo: Government Measures and Women's Compliance. *Journal of African Law*, *65*(S2), 287–310. https://doi.org/10.1017/S0021855321000371

Jember, M. Z., Jemere, A. T., Gashu, K. D., & Shibabaw, A. A. (2024). Misinformation on COVID-19 Vaccine and Its Associated Factors among Residents in Gondar, Ethiopia, 2022. *BioMed Research International*, *2024*(1), 9947720. https://doi.org/10.1155/2024/9947720

Jolley, D., & Paterson, J. L. (2020). Pylons ablaze: Examining the role of 5G COVID-19 conspiracy beliefs and Support for violence. *British Journal of Social Psychology*, *59*(3), 628–640. https://doi.org/10.1111/bjso.12394

Krause, N. M., Freiling, I., Beets, B., & Brossard, D. (2020). Fact-checking as risk communication: The multi-layered risk of misinformation in times of COVID-19. *Journal of Risk Research*, *23*(7–8), 1052–1059. https://doi.org/10.1080/13669877.2020.1756385

Kruglanski, A. W., Molinario, E., & Lemay, E. P. (2021). Coping with COVID-19-induced threats to self. *Group Processes & Intergroup Relations*, *24*(2), 284–289. https://doi.org/10.1177/1368430220982074

MacDonald, N. E. (2015). Vaccine hesitancy: Definition, scope and determinants. *Vaccine*, *33*(34), 4161–4164. https://doi.org/10.1016/j.vaccine.2015.04.036

Ministry of Health-Ethiopia. (2022). *Routine Immunization: Catch-Up Vaccination Guidelines*. Ministry of Health - Ethiopia. https://publications.jsi.com/JSIInternet/Inc/Common/_download_pub.cfm?id=25790&lid=3

Olivera Mesa, D., Hogan, A. B., Watson, O. J., Charles, G. D., Hauck, K., Ghani, A. C., & Winskill, P. (2022). Modelling the impact of vaccine hesitancy in prolonging the need for Non-Pharmaceutical Interventions to control the COVID-19 pandemic. *Communications Medicine*, *2*(1), 1–8. https://doi.org/10.1038/s43856-022-00075-x

Perlis, R. H., Ognyanova, K., Santillana, M., Lin, J., Druckman, J., Lazer, D., Green, J., Simonson, M., Baum, M. A., & Della Volpe, J. (2022). Association of Major Depressive Symptoms With Endorsement of COVID-19 Vaccine Misinformation Among U.S. Adults. *JAMA Network Open*, *5*(1), e2145697. https://doi.org/10.1001/jamanetworkopen.2021.45697

Pickles, K., Cvejic, E., Nickel, B., Copp, T., Bonner, C., Leask, J., Ayre, J., Batcup, C., Cornell, S., Dakin, T., Dodd, R. H., Isautier, J. M. J., & McCaffery, K. J. (2021). COVID-19 Misinformation Trends in Australia: Prospective Longitudinal National Survey. *Journal of Medical Internet Research*, *23*(1), e23805. https://doi.org/10.2196/23805

Pivetti, M., Melotti, G., Bonomo, M., & Hakokängäs, E. (2021). Conspiracy Beliefs and Acceptance of COVID-Vaccine: An Exploratory Study in Italy. *Social Sciences*, *10*(3), 108. https://doi.org/10.3390/socsci10030108

Romer, D., & Jamieson, K. H. (2020). Conspiracy theories as barriers to controlling the spread of COVID-19 in the U.S. *Social Science & Medicine*, *263*, 113356. https://doi.org/10.1016/j.socscimed.2020.113356

Roozenbeek, J., Schneider, C. R., Dryhurst, S., Kerr, J., Freeman, A. L. J., Recchia, G., Van Der Bles, A. M., & Van Der Linden, S. (2020). Susceptibility to misinformation about COVID-19 around the world. *Royal Society Open Science*, *7*(10), 201199. https://doi.org/10.1098/rsos.201199

Sallam, M., Dababseh, D., Yaseen, A., Al-Haidar, A., Taim, D., Eid, H., Ababneh, N. A., Bakri, F. G., & Mahafzah, A. (2020). COVID-19 misinformation: Mere harmless delusions or much more? A knowledge and attitude cross-sectional study among the general public residing in Jordan. *PLOS ONE*, *15*(12), e0243264. https://doi.org/10.1371/journal.pone.0243264

Salmon, D. A., Dudley, M. Z., Glanz, J. M., & Omer, S. B. (2015). Vaccine hesitancy: Causes, consequences, and a call to action. *Vaccine*, *33*(4), D66–D71. https://doi.org/10.1016/j.vaccine.2015.09.035

Scheufele, D. A., & Krause, N. M. (2019). Science audiences, misinformation, and fake news. *Proceedings of the National Academy of Sciences*, *116*(16), 7662–7669. https://doi.org/10.1073/pnas.1805871115

STATISTA. (2024). *Coronavirus cases by country in Africa 2022*. Statista. https://www.statista.com/statistics/1170463/coronavirus-cases-in-africa/

Teovanović, P., Lukić, P., Zupan, Z., Lazić, A., Ninković, M., & Žeželj, I. (2021). Irrational beliefs differentially predict adherence to guidelines and pseudoscientific practices during the COVID-19 pandemic. *Applied Cognitive Psychology*, *35*(2), 486–496. https://doi.org/10.1002/acp.3770

Toffolutti, V., Plach, S., Maksimovic, T., Piccitto, G., Mascherini, M., Mencarini, L., & Aassve, A. (2022). The association between COVID-19 policy responses and mental well-being: Evidence from 28 European countries. *Social Science & Medicine*, *301*, 114906. https://doi.org/10.1016/j.socscimed.2022.114906

van Prooijen, J.-W., & Douglas, K. M. (2017). Conspiracy theories as part of history: The role of societal crisis situations. *Memory Studies*, *10*(3), 323–333. https://doi.org/10.1177/1750698017701615

Wardle, C., & Derakhshan, H. (2017). *INFORMATION DISORDER: Toward an interdisciplinary framework for research and policy-making* (DGI(2017)09). Council of Europe. https://firstdraftnews.org/wp-content/uploads/2017/11/PREMS-162317-GBR-2018-Report-de%CC%81sinformation-1.pdf?x21167

World Bank. (2022). *World Development Report 2022: Finance for an Equitable Recovery*. Washington, DC: World Bank. https://doi.org/10.1596/978-1-4648-1730-4

World Bank. (2024). *The World Bank in Ethiopia: Overview* [Text/HTML]. World Bank. https://www.worldbank.org/en/country/ethiopia/overview

World Health Organization. (2021). *WHO publishes public health research agenda for managing infodemics.* https://www.who.int/news/item/02-02-2021-who-public-health-research-agenda-for-managing-infodemics

World Health Organization. (2024a). *COVID-19 cases.* (WHO COVID-19 dashboard). https://data.who.int/dashboards/covid19/cases

World Health Organization. (2024b). *COVID-19 vaccination.*(WHO COVID-19 dashboard.). https://data.who.int/dashboards/covid19/vaccines

World Health Organization. (2024c). *COVID-19 vaccines.* WHO African Region. https://www.afro.who.int/health-topics/coronavirus-covid-19/vaccines

Christian Samen Otchia Associate Professor of Development Economics at the Graduate School of International Development, Nagoya University, Japan, where he teaches Development Microeconomics and Industrial Development. He is an affiliate member of the African Growth and Development Policy modeling consortium and has extensive experience in industrial policy design and implementation, collaborating with local governments and organizations like FAO and UNECA. His research focuses on the impact of special economic zones on local development through skills and technology transfer. Dr. Otchia holds a Ph.D. in International Development (Nagoya University) and has published in several academic journals.

Chapter 8
Resilience Under Pressure: The Impact of COVID-19 on Self-Esteem Among Vulnerable Women in Eastern Democratic Republic of Congo

Christian Samen Otchia, Kazuyo Hanai, Jean-Claude Maswana, and Akemi Ishikawa

Abstract This paper examines how the COVID-19 pandemic affected self-esteem among vulnerable women in conflict-affected Eastern Democratic Republic of Congo. Using unique survey data, we analyze the psychological impacts on internally displaced persons (IDPs), survivors of sexual and gender-based violence, and host community members. Our findings indicate that economic disruptions, particularly food insecurity and job loss, were the strongest predictors of reduced self-esteem across all groups. Limited healthcare access significantly increased mental health challenges and reduced community participation. While the pandemic intensified pre-existing vulnerabilities in this fragile setting characterized by weak institutions and armed conflict, we find no evidence of community resilience through local support networks. The results highlight the need for integrated interventions addressing both economic and psychological needs in conflict zones.

1 Introduction

In the discourse surrounding the impacts of global health crises, a significant gap exists in understanding how these crises disproportionately affect vulnerable women in resource-constrained settings. Existing research has established that vulnerable

C. S. Otchia (✉)
Graduate School of International Development, Nagoya University, Nagoya, Aichi, Japan
e-mail: otchia@gsid.nagoya-u.ac.jp

K. Hanai
Institute for Future Initiatives, The University of Tokyo, Bunkyo, Tokyo, Japan

J.-C. Maswana
Graduate School of Economics, Ritsumeikan University, Kyoto, Japan

A. Ishikawa
Division of Agri-Business, UNIDO HQs in Vienna, Vienna, Austria

K. Hanai et al. (eds.), *Practical Wisdom and Resilience Overcoming Downside Risk*,
https://doi.org/10.1007/978-981-96-4455-1_8

women, particularly in resource-constrained environments, face pre-existing socio-economic challenges and systemic inequalities that are further exacerbated during global health emergencies like the COVID-19 pandemic. These women often experience compounded negative impacts on their mental health and overall well-being, as the pandemic intensifies issues such as income loss, limited access to healthcare, and restricted educational opportunities (WHO, 2020). The erosion of financial stability and social support networks can lead to heightened feelings of anxiety, stress, and hopelessness among vulnerable women, further undermining their self-confidence and self-worth. However, the literature also suggests that while the pandemic has deepened these socio-economic hardships, it has simultaneously fostered collective resilience and solidarity in some communities. Women in these settings have been found to band together, forming support networks, sharing resources, and innovating solutions to navigate the crisis. This duality, where the same crisis both exacerbates vulnerabilities and catalyzes community-driven resilience, highlights the complex and multifaceted nature of the situation. The interplay between economic instability and psychological stress significantly shapes the self-perception and social dynamics among vulnerable women in resource-constrained environments (UN Women, 2022). This chapter leverages a unique dataset from women's empowerment program in Eastern Democratic Republic of Congo (DRC) to better understand these dynamics and inform effective interventions.[1]

The eastern DRC offers a compelling context for analyzing the psychological impact of the COVID-19 pandemic on vulnerable women. This region has been plagued by recurring conflicts for over two decades, resulting in immense human suffering and displacement. According to the International Rescue Committee, the period from 1998 to 2008 alone saw more than 5 million deaths (IRC, 2007) and around 1.7 million internally displaced people in the DRC (Internal Displacement Monitoring Centre, 2011). These protracted conflicts have severely compromised the region's development and exacerbated existing gender disparities country (Vlassenroot and Raeymaekers, 2004; Pellillo, 2012; Dagnelie et al., 2018). Since the 1990s, the area has been characterized by fragmented governance, with numerous armed groups exercising control over local populations (Vogel, 2018). This fragmentation, coupled with the region's ethnic diversity and varying degrees of social cohesion, provides a unique opportunity to examine how community dynamics shape individual resilience and self-esteem during crises. This distinctive setting allows for a granular analysis of the pandemic's socio-economic and psychosocial impacts on vulnerable women, informing gender-responsive crisis interventions in conflict-affected areas.

The historical roots of conflict in the eastern DRC can be traced back to the colonial era, as Belgian rule exacerbated ethnic divisions and prioritized resource extraction, setting the stage for future exploitation and violence. The First and Second Congo Wars (1996–2003) represented critical junctures, involving numerous regional and international actors and resulting in millions of deaths and displacements. Although

[1] The data used in this chapter comes from the socio-economic survey conducted under the UINDO project, funded by the Japanese government. The project information URL is as follows: https://open.unido.org/projects/CD/projects/210142.

the Second Congo War officially ended in 2003, conflict has persisted in Eastern DRC, with an estimated 70 to 120 armed groups vying for territorial control, perpetuating violence and humanitarian crises. These groups, which fluctuate over time as they disband, splinter, or form alliances, can be broadly categorized into local militias (Mai-Mai), foreign armed groups like the Allied Democratic Forces (ADF) and the Democratic Forces for the Liberation of Rwanda (FDLR), and splinter factions such as the March 23 Movement (M23). Major actors include the ADF, known for its brutal violence, the FDLR, a Rwandan Hutu rebel group, and CODECO, a militia composed of Lendu ethnic group members. These groups operate primarily in conflict-ridden provinces such as North Kivu, South Kivu, Ituri, Tanganyika, and Maniema, further complicating efforts to establish peace. The ongoing instability, compounded by fragmented governance, has severe implications for the psychological well-being and self-esteem of vulnerable women, particularly as they face additional challenges from the COVID-19 pandemic.

The social and political landscape of eastern DRC is marked by intricate divisions and fragile dynamics. The region's ethnic diversity, weak state institutions, rampant corruption, and the influential role of armed groups severely undermine efforts to establish effective governance. However, grassroots activism and a vibrant civil society provide a crucial counterbalance, with local organizations working towards peace, justice, and human rights. Economically, eastern DRC is rich in natural resources, which, paradoxically, have fueled conflict rather than fostering development. Armed groups and informal networks often control extraction activities, profiting from conflict financing and exploitative practices that perpetuate violence. Decades of instability have worsened the region's dire economic conditions, leaving many communities entrenched in poverty and vulnerable to manipulation by armed factions. The conflict in eastern DRC is also intricately linked to a complex web of international actors with diverse interests. Regional dynamics, peacekeeping missions, international aid agencies, NGOs, and the private sector all play significant roles in both the perpetuation of the conflict and potential pathways to its resolution. Recent data indicate that the number of internally displaced persons (IDPs) has reached an estimated 7.1 million, with over 1 million returnee IDPs, approximately 200,000 returnee refugees, and countless survivors of sexual and gender-based violence (SGBV), underscoring the profound human cost of the ongoing conflict.

Our most striking findings emerge from the comparative analysis of IDPs and survivors of sexual and SGBV, two distinctly vulnerable populations in Eastern DRC. While the host community exhibits the highest and most concentrated peak in self-esteem measures, SGBV survivors display significantly broader distributions with pronounced left-tail skewness, indicating a substantially higher prevalence of very low self-esteem cases. The divergence in self-esteem distributions is particularly pronounced in the negative range, where SGBV survivors are disproportionately represented. However, the convergence of distributions in the positive self-esteem domain suggests that certain resilience-building mechanisms may operate similarly across groups, regardless of their vulnerability status.

Our analysis reveals differentiated impact pathways of the pandemic across these vulnerable groups. For IDPs, the primary determinants of declining self-esteem were disruptions in access to basic necessities and healthcare services. SGBV survivors faced these same challenges compounded by severe economic shocks through job and income loss, reflecting the layered nature of their vulnerability. The pre-existing vulnerabilities of these women, such as their exposure to conflict-related trauma, displacement, and gender-based violence, have significantly diminished their capacity for resilience. These compounded challenges have left them with few mechanisms to absorb the socio-economic shocks caused by COVID-19. For SGBV survivors in particular, the pandemic has exacerbated these pre-existing conditions to such an extent that traditional coping mechanisms—whether through community support or individual resilience—proved insufficient. As a result, their ability to maintain self-esteem and psychological well-being during the crisis was severely compromised. Our findings highlight the importance of considering both immediate and long-term impacts of crises on psychological well-being, particularly in conflict-affected regions where institutional support may be limited.

The rest of this chapter is organized as follows: In Sect. 2, we present a detailed review of the existing literature on the impact of the COVID-19 pandemic on vulnerable populations, with a focus on women in conflict-affected regions. Section 3 outlines the methodology and data collection process, including the respondent-driven sampling approach used to gather data from hard-to-reach populations. In Sect. 4, we provide a comprehensive analysis of the socio-economic and psychological impacts of the pandemic on self-esteem among vulnerable women, and Sect. 5 concludes.

2 Related Literature

The existing literature on the impact of the COVID-19 pandemic on women's self-esteem offers valuable insights, but also highlights important gaps that the proposed research aims to address. Several studies have examined the rise in gender-based violence during the pandemic and its implications for women's mental health. Akel et al. (2022) and Sánchez et al. (2020) report significant increases in intimate partner violence (IPV) during lockdowns, though they do not directly link this to self-esteem. However, the established relationship between IPV and low self-esteem is well-documented in the literature. Sabri et al. (2020) found that the pandemic has led to an increase in IPV, particularly affecting immigrant women, and that the heightened isolation and stressors during the pandemic created an environment where IPV could thrive, directly impacting the self-esteem of these women. Legrand et al. (2022) further demonstrated that engaging in regular physical activity significantly improved self-esteem and perceptions of body image among women facing domestic violence during lockdown, suggesting that promoting physical health could be an essential strategy for mitigating the psychological impacts of IPV during the pandemic. The role of social media during the pandemic has also emerged as a critical factor influencing self-esteem among women. Vall-Roqué et al. (2021) found that the lockdowns intensified social comparisons among young women, leading to feelings of inadequacy regarding their body image, which negatively impacted their self-esteem.

The literature also explores the protective role that self-esteem can play in mitigating the adverse effects of the pandemic. Rossi et al. (2020) found that women with higher self-esteem reported lower levels of anxiety and depressive symptoms, suggesting that interventions aimed at boosting self-esteem could be crucial in promoting mental well-being during crises. Matheson et al. (2015) argue that rebuilding self-esteem is a critical component of recovery from IPV, highlighting the importance of addressing self-esteem in psychological interventions for women affected by both IPV and the pandemic.

Beyond the direct impact of the pandemic on self-esteem, several studies highlight its broader mental health implications, which are closely intertwined with self-esteem. Ramírez Vera et al. (2022), in their systematic review of the pandemic's mental health effects on women, noted increased rates of depression, anxiety, and post-traumatic stress, all of which are interrelated with self-esteem. While the review does not specifically focus on self-esteem, the well-established correlation between mental health challenges and self-esteem suggests that the decline in mental health during the pandemic likely contributed to diminished self-esteem among women. These compounded challenges underscore the urgent need for targeted psychological interventions that promote resilience, positive adaptation, and support for women's mental health during and after the pandemic.

A study by Nyashanu et al. (2020) on self-employed women in Zambia provides critical insights into the economic dimensions of the pandemic's impact. The authors found that the lockdown caused significant economic challenges, including food insecurity and business closures, which led to psychological trauma among women. Although the study does not directly address self-esteem, the economic hardships experienced by women in conflict-affected regions like Eastern DRC, many of whom rely on informal economies and subsistence farming, likely had a similar or more severe impact. Economic instability, compounded by pre-existing poverty, has been shown to severely diminish women's self-esteem, as financial independence and agency are critical components of self-worth.

Despite the wealth of research on the pandemic's impact on women's mental health and self-esteem, there is a notable gap in studies specifically focused on conflict-affected regions. Much of the existing literature draws on data from Western or more stable contexts, limiting its applicability to regions where women face compounded vulnerabilities due to conflict, displacement, and poverty. Moreover, while studies such as Rossi et al. (2020) emphasize the protective role of self-esteem, there is a lack of research on how pre-existing traumas, such as those experienced by women in Eastern DRC, may compromise this protective effect during times of crisis like the pandemic. Furthermore, there is limited research on the effectiveness of interventions aimed at improving self-esteem among women in conflict-affected regions. Existing studies often recommend psychosocial support, trauma-informed care, and economic empowerment initiatives, but few have empirically tested these interventions in the context of the COVID-19 pandemic. Understanding the unique needs of women in Eastern DRC, particularly in relation to their self-esteem and mental health, is critical for developing effective support programs.

This chapter makes three main contributions to the literature on COVID-19 impacts and self-esteem. First, we provide novel evidence on the heterogeneous effects of COVID-19 on self-esteem across different vulnerable populations in a conflict-affected region, documenting distinct patterns between internally IDPs, SGBV, and host communities. Second, we identify specific mechanisms through which the pandemic affected self-esteem, showing that while IDPs primarily suffered from disrupted access to basic services, SGBV survivors experienced compounded effects through both service disruption and severe economic shocks. This finding extends previous work by authors like Rossi et al. (2020) and Sabri et al. (2020) who examined pandemic impacts on women's mental health but did not explore these differential vulnerability channels. Third, we demonstrate that pre-existing trauma from conflict exposure significantly moderates women's psychological resilience during subsequent crises, contributing to the broader literature on compounded vulnerabilities in fragile settings. Our unique context from Eastern DRC allows us to document these effects in a way that previous studies of pandemic impacts on vulnerable populations have not been able to achieve.

3 Methods and Data

3.1 Data

We employed a mixed-methods approach to analyze the socio-economic and psychological impacts of COVID-19 on vulnerable women in the DRC. Our field data collection spanned from October 24 to November 8, 2022. Our sample comprised IDPs, returnee IDPs, returnee refugees, survivors of SGBV, and host community members, with targeted minimums of 10% IDPs and 30% SGBV survivors. In the absence of a comprehensive sampling frame, we implemented respondent-driven sampling (RDS), a chain-referral method effective for studying hard-to-reach populations (Heckathorn 1997; Gile and Handcock 2010). This sampling method facilitated unbiased population estimates from non-random samples of hidden populations (Volz and Heckathorn 2008). We aimed for a sample of 330 vulnerable women, accounting for potential non-responses and data quality issues. The RDS process was initiated with six non-randomly chosen "seeds" per study area, representing diverse, vulnerable women categories. Each seed received four recruitment coupons, triggering a chain-referral process until reaching the target sample size.

Data collection consisted of face-to-face interviews using structured questionnaires conducted in private settings to ensure confidentiality and adhere to ethical guidelines for research with vulnerable populations (World Health Organization 2007).

Table 1 presents descriptive statistics for our sample, revealing significant differences across vulnerability groups. The SGBV group has the highest proportion of younger women (54.8% aged 15–35), while the host community has the highest proportion of older women (26.3% aged 55+). These differences are statistically significant ($p = 0.007$) and may reflect varying vulnerabilities and life experiences across age groups. Host community women have the lowest education levels, with 84.8% reporting no schooling. IDPs and SGBV survivors have similar education levels, with about 31–33% having some schooling. Most women across all groups live in households of 6 or more people (55–64%), with no significant differences between groups. Approximately half of the women in each group are married, and employment levels are similar across groups. These similarities suggest that marital status and employment may not be key differentiating factors in our analysis. Regarding mental health and social impacts, SGBV survivors report significantly higher rates of mental breakdown (34%), limited community events (35%), and limited social activities (34%) compared to the other two groups. These differences are highly statistically significant ($p < 0.001$) and indicate that SGBV survivors may be particularly vulnerable to the psychosocial impacts of the pandemic. Taken together, these descriptive statistics highlight the importance of considering group-specific characteristics when analyzing the impacts of COVID-19 on vulnerable populations.

3.2 Measuring Self-Esteem for Vulnerable Women

Self-esteem has been widely regarded in the realm of social sciences as a crucial framework for understanding a wide array of psychological and behavioral processes. In the field of psychology, a substantial and expanding body of literature, starting with seminal works like Rosenberg (1965), utilizes measures of self-esteem both as an outcome and as an explanatory variable for various aspects of mental health and social functioning. This body of work includes significant contributions from scholars such as Baumeister et al. (2003), who explored the effects of self-esteem on aggression and interpersonal relationships, and Orth and Robins (2014), who examined its long-term stability and impact on life outcomes. Similarly, disciplines such as sociology, education, and public health have generated extensive research into the causes and effects of self-esteem, highlighting its critical importance. The sheer volume of scholarly work across these fields attests to self-esteem's pivotal role in shaping individual behavior, social interactions, and overall well-being.

We measure global self-esteem using the Rosenberg Self-Esteem Scale (RSES), a validated 10-item instrument with a 4-point Likert scale. The RSES was selected for its reliability and validity across diverse populations. We conducted translation, back-translation, and pilot testing with local women to ensure cultural appropriateness, resulting in minor adaptations to reflect local idioms and self-worth concepts. To operationalize our analysis, we project all items onto their respective components using principal component analysis. We then construct z-score indices for

Table 1 Descriptive statistics

	Host community	Internally displaced	Sexual and gender-based violence	Test
	(N = 99)	(N = 116)	(N = 115)	
Self-esteem	−0.05 (0.86)	−0.17 (1.07)	0.21 (1.00)	0.013
Age				
15–35	46 (46.5%)	45 (38.8%)	63 (54.8%)	0.007
36–44	17 (17.2%)	32 (27.6%)	29 (25.2%)	
45–54	10 (10.1%)	18 (15.5%)	14 (12.2%)	
55 +	26 (26.3%)	21 (18.1%)	9 (7.8%)	
Education				
No schooling	84 (84.8%)	78 (67.2%)	79 (68.7%)	0.006
Some schooling	15 (15.2%)	38 (32.8%)	36 (31.3%)	
Household size				
1–2	7 (7.1%)	9 (7.8%)	4 (3.5%)	0.564
3–5	35 (35.4%)	43 (37.1%)	38 (33.0%)	
6 +	57 (57.6%)	64 (55.2%)	73 (63.5%)	
Married	0.54 (0.50)	0.48 (0.50)	0.49 (0.50)	0.703
Employment	1.91 (0.77)	1.91 (0.82)	1.94 (0.78)	0.939
Household head	0.53 (0.50)	0.58 (0.50)	0.62 (0.49)	0.399
Mental breakdown	0.02 (0.14)	0.05 (0.22)	0.34 (0.48)	<0.001
Limited community events	0.05 (0.22)	0.18 (0.39)	0.35 (0.48)	<0.001
Limited social activities	0.01 (0.10)	0.09 (0.29)	0.34 (0.48)	<0.001

positive self-esteem and negative self-esteem components, allowing interpretation of regression results as standard deviation increases in the normalized score.

Figure 1 illustrates the density distributions of self-esteem indices across three distinct populations: the host community, internally displaced persons, and survivors of sexual and gender-based violence. All groups exhibit approximately normal distributions with slight negative skewness, centered near a standardized mean of zero. The host community shows the highest, most concentrated peak, while sexual and gender-based violence survivors display the broadest distribution with the heaviest left tail, indicating a higher proportion of individuals with very low self-esteem in this group. Internally displaced persons fall between these extremes. Notably, while the distributions diverge more in the negative range, they converge in the positive self-esteem domain, suggesting that factors contributing to high self-esteem may be more uniform across groups. These nuanced differences in distribution shapes provide insights into how varied life circumstances, such as the COVID-19 pandemic, might differentially impact self-esteem levels.

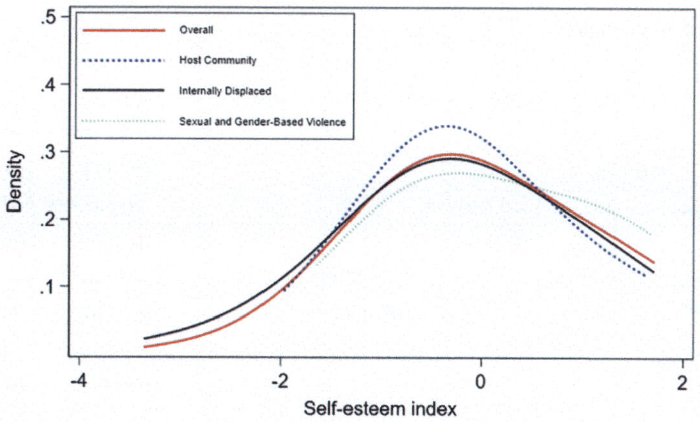

Fig. 1 Self-esteem index

4 Findings

4.1 COVID-19 and Self-Esteem

Table 2 presents the results of our Ordinary Least Squares (OLS) regression analysis investigating the impact of COVID-19-related challenges on self-esteem among vulnerable women in Eastern DRC. The dependent variable, self-esteem, is measured using z-scores from the RSES. Interestingly, we find that the loss of jobs and income during the COVID-19 pandemic is consistently associated with a significant negative impact on self-esteem across all model specifications. The effect ranges from −0.236 to −0.297 standard deviations, depending on the model. Specifically, in models (1), (5), and (6), the coefficients are significant at the 5% and 1% levels, indicating that job/income loss significantly erodes emotional well-being in the form of lower self-esteem. This result aligns with existing literature, which suggests that economic shocks disproportionately affect vulnerable groups, leading to psychological distress and diminished self-worth. Food insecurity, measured as harder access to food due to COVID-19 disruptions, emerges as the most significant predictor of reduced self-esteem. The estimated coefficients range from −0.530 to −0.648 standard deviations, with p-values < 0.01 across all models where this variable is included (columns (2), (5), and (6)). This strong negative relationship suggests that food scarcity directly undermines women's psychological resilience, likely because access to basic necessities like food is a fundamental component of security and well-being. These results support theories in behavioral economics that highlight the role of basic needs in psychological health.

Limited access to healthcare during the pandemic also has a significant negative impact on self-esteem, with coefficients ranging from −0.279 to −0.348 standard deviations (p-values < 0.05 or 0.01). This finding, reported in columns (3), (5), and

Table 2 OLS Main impact

	Self-esteem	Self-esteem	Self-esteem	Self-esteem	Self-esteem	Self-esteem
	(1)	(2)	(3)	(4)	(5)	(6)
Job/income loss	−0.236**				−0.258**	−0.297***
	(0.118)				(0.111)	(0.109)
Harder access to food		−0.530***			−0.585***	−0.648***
		(0.166)			(0.185)	(0.191)
Harder access to healthcare			−0.279**		−0.348***	−0.337***
			(0.108)		(0.110)	(0.113)
Increased family conflicts				−0.028	−0.102	−0.074
				(0.132)	(0.144)	(0.143)
Constant	−0.515*	−0.217	−0.364	−0.628**	0.288	0.887***
	(0.309)	(0.320)	(0.323)	(0.309)	(0.353)	(0.210)
Observations	330	330	330	330	330	330
R-squared	0.141	0.151	0.149	0.132	0.183	0.061
Controls	Yes	Yes	Yes	Yes	Yes	No

Note This table presents the results from OLS regressions where the dependent variable is self-esteem, measured using the Rosenberg Self-Esteem Scale, with z-scores as the outcome variable. Columns (1) through (6) report the estimated coefficients for various explanatory variables related to the socio-economic impacts of the COVID-19 pandemic. Each column progressively introduces different covariates. Robust standard errors, reported in parentheses, account for heteroscedasticity and sampling design biases inherent in the respondent-driven sampling (RDS) method. Coefficients marked with ***, **, and * correspond to statistical significance at the 1%, 5%, and 10% levels, respectively. Control variables (age, education, marital status, household size, and employment status) are included in all specifications except column (6), which serves as a baseline model without controls

(6), emphasizes the psychological toll of reduced access to medical services, which likely heightened feelings of vulnerability and insecurity among these women. In economic terms, this underscores the importance of healthcare as a public good that contributes to both physical and mental well-being. Although we observe a negative coefficient for increased family conflicts, the effect is not statistically significant in any of the models. For example, in column (4), the coefficient is −0.028 (p-value = 0.868), suggesting that, while family conflicts may contribute to stress, they do not have a strong direct effect on self-esteem in this context. This could imply that external, structural factors like food and healthcare access play a more dominant role in shaping self-esteem during crises, compared to intrafamily dynamics.

These results contribute to the understanding of how economic shocks, such as those induced by the COVID-19 pandemic, can affect psychological well-being, particularly among vulnerable populations. The significant impact of job/income loss and food insecurity on self-esteem aligns with human capital theory (Becker, 1964), which posits that shocks to economic resources (e.g., income) can undermine individual productivity by affecting mental health and self-perception. Similarly, the strong effect of food insecurity supports basic needs theory (Maslow, 1943), which holds that psychological well-being is contingent on the fulfillment of fundamental needs like food and shelter.

4.2 *Heterogeneity in the Impacts of COVID-19: Vulnerability Group-Specific Analysis*

To explore how the impacts of COVID-19-related challenges vary across different groups of vulnerable women, we conducted separate regression analyses for three key subgroups: host community women, IDPs, and survivors of SGBV. The results, displayed in Table 3, highlight important differences in the factors that affect self-esteem across these populations.

Table 3 Main impact by vulnerability group

	Self-esteem	Self-esteem	Self-esteem
	(1)	(2)	(3)
Job/income loss	−0.373**	0.188	−0.607***
	(0.165)	(0.238)	(0.196)
Harder access to food	0.303	−0.947***	−0.565*
	(0.238)	(0.280)	(0.302)
Harder access to healthcare	−0.096	−0.505***	−0.418**
	(0.177)	(0.190)	(0.207)
Increased family conflicts	−0.416*	0.064	0.265
	(0.234)	(0.224)	(0.258)
Constant	−1.550***	0.745	1.118*
	(0.523)	(0.575)	(0.615)
Observations	99	116	115
R-squared	0.379	0.240	0.256
Vulnerability status	Host community	Internally displaced	Sexual and gender-based violence
Controls	Yes	Yes	Yes

Note This table presents the results of separate OLS regressions examining the impact of COVID-19-related challenges on self-esteem across three distinct vulnerability groups: host community women (column 1), internally displaced women (column 2), and survivors of sexual and gender-based violence (SGBV) (column 3). The dependent variable in each regression is self-esteem, measured using z-scores from the Rosenberg Self-Esteem Scale. Robust standard errors are reported in parentheses

Host Community Women

For women in the host community, the two most significant predictors of reduced self-esteem are job/income loss and increased family conflicts. Job/income loss has a substantial negative impact on self-esteem, with a coefficient of −0.373 ($p < 0.05$). This suggests that economic stability plays a critical role in maintaining self-esteem for women who, while vulnerable, may have more stable living conditions than IDPs or SGBV survivors. The loss of income or employment likely represents a significant blow to their perceived self-worth and security. Increased family conflicts also significantly reduce self-esteem, with a coefficient of −0.416 ($p < 0.1$). This finding suggests that interpersonal dynamics within the family unit are particularly important for the psychological well-being of host community women, potentially because these women are more embedded within family structures compared to displaced or marginalized groups.

Taken together, our results suggest that for host community women, economic stability and family dynamics are critical for sustaining self-esteem, aligning with economic theories that emphasize the role of social capital and intra-household dynamics in shaping well-being (Becker, 1981).

Internally Displaced Women

For IDPs, the analysis reveals that harder access to food and harder access to healthcare are the primary drivers of reduced self-esteem. Harder access to food has the most significant and largest negative impact, with a coefficient of −0.947 ($p < 0.01$). This is the largest effect observed in any group, indicating that food insecurity is a critical issue for internally displaced women, likely exacerbated by their already precarious living conditions and limited access to social safety nets. Harder access to healthcare also significantly reduces self-esteem, with a coefficient of −0.505 ($p < 0.01$). This reflects the heightened vulnerability of IDPs to health-related issues, as reduced access to healthcare can exacerbate both physical and mental health problems, further eroding self-esteem. The overwhelming importance of food and healthcare access highlights the relevance of basic needs theory (Maslow, 1943), as access to these fundamental resources appears to be the primary determinant of self-esteem. This suggests that in resource-constrained environments, addressing basic survival needs is paramount for improving psychological well-being.

SGBV Survivors

For survivors of sexual and gender-based violence, a broad range of factors significantly contributes to reduced self-esteem, reflecting the complex vulnerabilities of this group. Job/income loss has a large negative impact on self-esteem, with a coefficient of −0.607 ($p < 0.01$). This suggests that economic security is crucial for SGBV survivors, who may already face significant social stigma and psychological trauma. Harder access to food also significantly reduces self-esteem, with a coefficient of −0.565 ($p < 0.1$), indicating that food insecurity exacerbates the vulnerabilities of this already marginalized group. Harder access to healthcare has a similarly negative effect on self-esteem, with a coefficient of −0.418 ($p < 0.05$). The broad range of factors affecting self-esteem reflects the multidimensional nature of vulnerability, consistent with the theoretical framework of capability deprivation (Sen, 1999). Economic, social, and health-related factors all contribute to the deprivation of SGBV survivors, requiring multi-pronged interventions to restore their sense of autonomy and self-worth.

4.3 Factor of Resilience: Mechanisms Linking COVID-19 Challenges to Well-Being

To deepen our understanding of the pathways through which COVID-19-related challenges affect women's self-esteem, we explore the extent to which vulnerable women have demonstrated resilience in the face of COVID-19 challenges, specifically in terms of three key dimensions: mental breakdown, limited participation in community events, and limited social activities. These outcomes reflect critical aspects of well-being, including mental health and social support, both of which are essential for resilience. Our analysis examines how economic difficulties, healthcare access, and family dynamics influence these outcomes, and whether women in vulnerable groups can maintain resilience despite these challenges (Table 4).

Resilience to Job/income Loss

Job and income loss has been one of the most significant challenges faced by women during the pandemic, and it strongly predicts negative outcomes in terms of mental health and social engagement. However, the question remains: how resilient are women in overcoming the mental and social consequences of job/income loss? Our regression analysis shows that job/income loss is significantly associated with an increased likelihood of mental breakdown (−0.112, $p < 0.01$), indicating that the economic shock of losing a job or income severely undermines mental health. This suggests that many women struggle to maintain emotional resilience in the face of financial insecurity, as the stress and anxiety associated with job loss often led to mental health breakdowns. Resilience, in this case, may be compromised by insufficient safety nets or support systems that would otherwise help women cope with the psychological toll of economic hardship.

In terms of community engagement, job/income loss is significantly linked to limited participation in community events (−0.111, $p < 0.05$). This finding highlights that financial constraints and emotional stress prevent women from engaging in social

Table 4 Mechanisms

	Mental breakdown	Limited community events	Limited social activities
	(1)	(2)	(3)
Job/income loss	−0.112***	−0.111**	−0.129***
	(0.036)	(0.044)	(0.038)
Harder access to food	0.037	0.010	−0.084
	(0.075)	(0.075)	(0.091)
Harder access to healthcare	−0.072*	−0.112**	−0.069*
	(0.040)	(0.046)	(0.041)
Increased family conflicts	−0.090*	−0.084	−0.045
	(0.048)	(0.054)	(0.051)
Constant	−0.160	−0.123	−0.129
	(0.122)	(0.147)	(0.133)
Observations	330	330	330
R-squared	0.246	0.194	0.228
Controls	Yes	Yes	Yes

Note This table presents the results of OLS regressions exploring the mechanisms through which COVID-19-related challenges impact women's well-being, focusing on three outcomes: mental breakdown (column 1), limited community events (column 2), and limited social activities (column 3). The independent variables include job/income loss, harder access to food, harder access to healthcare, and increased family conflicts. Robust standard errors are reported in parentheses

or community activities, which are often key sources of support during crises. The decrease in community participation suggests a reduction in social capital, which is essential for resilience. Without the ability to engage in community events, vulnerable women may find it more difficult to access the social support networks needed to recover from economic setbacks.

Similarly, job/income loss is associated with reduced social activities (−0.129, $p < 0.01$), further indicating that the social resilience of vulnerable women is challenged by economic difficulties. The social isolation resulting from reduced participation in social activities can exacerbate feelings of loneliness and helplessness, which in turn may weaken their mental health and overall resilience. To foster resilience, it is crucial to address the factors that hinder social engagement, such as financial barriers and emotional distress.

Resilience to Healthcare Access Challenges

Limited access to healthcare during the pandemic also plays a critical role in shaping resilience, particularly in terms of mental health and social participation. The ability to access healthcare is essential not only for physical well-being but also for maintaining emotional and social resilience. The analysis shows that harder access to healthcare is linked to a higher likelihood of mental breakdown (−0.072, $p < 0.1$). This suggests that difficulties in accessing healthcare contribute to psychological distress, making it harder for women to demonstrate resilience in the face of mental health challenges. The inability to receive timely medical care, including mental health services, may leave women feeling unsupported and vulnerable, thus reducing their ability to cope with the pressures of the pandemic.

Healthcare access challenges are also significantly associated with limited participation in community events (−0.112, $p < 0.05$). This finding suggests that women who face barriers to healthcare may withdraw from community life, either due to health concerns or the emotional toll of managing unmet healthcare needs. Community engagement is a key aspect of resilience, as it provides social support, fosters a sense of belonging, and helps individuals recover from adversity. The reduced participation in community activities indicates that healthcare barriers weaken social resilience by isolating women from their support networks.

Furthermore, women with harder access to healthcare are more likely to experience reduced social activities (−0.069, $p < 0.1$). The social isolation resulting from healthcare access difficulties further highlights the challenges to resilience. Without regular social interactions, women may lose the emotional and practical support that is essential for withstanding and recovering from crises. Ensuring that healthcare is accessible and inclusive during pandemics is thus crucial for bolstering both mental and social resilience.

Increased Family Conflicts

Family dynamics are another important factor influencing resilience. Conflicts within the family can escalate during crises, leading to increased emotional distress and a higher risk of mental health challenges. However, the extent to which these conflicts affect women's ability to maintain resilience in other dimensions, such as community engagement and social activities, is less clear. The analysis reveals that increased family conflicts are significantly associated with a higher likelihood of mental breakdown (−0.090, $p < 0.1$). This indicates that strained family relationships contribute to psychological stress, making it harder for women to maintain mental resilience during the pandemic. Family conflicts can create an emotionally charged environment where women are more vulnerable to mental health breakdowns. It is critical to provide support systems, such as counseling and conflict resolution programs, to help women navigate these challenges and maintain their mental well-being.

Interestingly, the results show that increased family conflicts are not significantly associated with reduced participation in community events or social activities. This suggests that while family conflicts deeply affect mental health, they do not necessarily prevent women from maintaining their social networks or participating in community life. In this sense, women may exhibit social resilience by continuing to engage with their communities despite internal family tensions. This ability to maintain social connections, even in the face of family conflicts, may serve as a protective factor that helps to buffer against the negative effects on mental health.

5 Conclusion

This study offers an in-depth analysis of the impact of COVID-19 on the self-esteem of vulnerable women in the Eastern DRC, a region already burdened by ongoing conflict, displacement, and gender-based violence. In this chapter, we examined how the pandemic exacerbated existing socio-economic challenges and affected the psychological well-being of IDPs, survivors of SGBV, and women from host communities. The key findings indicate that the economic disruptions caused by the pandemic—particularly job loss and food insecurity—had the most significant negative impact on self-esteem across all groups. Food insecurity emerged as the strongest predictor of reduced self-esteem, with IDPs being the most severely affected. Limited access to healthcare also contributed to diminished self-esteem, especially among IDPs and SGBV survivors, whose pre-existing traumas and precarious living conditions heightened their vulnerability. Interestingly, while family conflicts were initially hypothesized to play a substantial role, they did not emerge as a significant determinant of self-esteem in this context. This suggests that structural challenges, such as access to food and healthcare, are more critical in shaping women's psychological resilience during crises.

These findings carry important implications for policymakers and international organizations working in conflict-affected settings such as the eastern DRC. They highlight the urgent need for gender-responsive interventions that address both the material and psychological needs of vulnerable women. Ensuring food security and access to healthcare should be prioritized, as these are fundamental to sustaining women's self-esteem and overall mental well-being. Additionally, economic empowerment programs, such as those promoting income-generating activities, could help mitigate the adverse effects of job loss on women's self-worth. Moreover, the findings suggest that psychosocial support services should be integrated into humanitarian aid efforts, especially for SGBV survivors, who experience compounded vulnerabilities.

Future research should investigate the long-term effects of the pandemic on women's self-esteem and mental health in conflict-affected regions, particularly as the socio-economic recovery process unfolds. There is also a pressing need for more rigorous evaluations of interventions aimed at improving self-esteem and psychological resilience among conflict-affected women. Furthermore, studies should explore the intersection of self-esteem, gender-based violence, and economic insecurity in other resource-constrained environments to enhance the generalizability of these findings.

Acknowledgements The authors express their sincere gratitude to the United Nations Industrial Development Organization (UNIDO) for providing the opportunity to conduct this research using the results of the socio-economic profile survey from the UNIDO project, which was funded by the Government of Japan (see footnote 1). We also extend our heartfelt thanks to the Institute for Future Initiatives (IFI) at the University of Tokyo, Professor Satoshi Ohara, and the NPO RITA-Congo for their invaluable contributions and collaboration throughout this project. Special thanks to Jean-Fidele SIE, Rehema Karata, and Adefolake Adeniyi for their excellent research assistance. The views expressed here are those of the authors and do not reflect the views of the UNIDO.

References

Akel, M., Berro, J., Rahme, C., Haddad, C., Obeid, S., & Hallit, S. (2022). Violence against women during COVID-19 pandemic. *Journal of Interpersonal Violence, 37*(13–14), NP12284-NP12309. https://doi.org/10.1177/0886260521997953

Baumeister, R. F., Campbell, J. D., Krueger, J. I., & Vohs, K. D. (2003). Does high self-esteem cause better performance, interpersonal success, happiness, or healthier lifestyles? *Psychological Science in the Public Interest, 4*(1), 1-44. https://doi.org/10.1111/1529-1006.01431

Becker, G. S. (1964). *Human capital: A theoretical and empirical analysis, with special reference to education*. University of Chicago Press.

Becker, G. S. (1981). *A treatise on the family*. Harvard University Press.

Dagnelie, O., De Luca, G., & Maystadt, J.-F. (2018). Violence, selection and infant mortality in Congo. *Journal of Health Economics, 59*, 153–177. https://doi.org/10.1016/j.jhealeco.2018.02.004

Heckathorn, D. D. (1997). Respondent-driven sampling: A new approach to the study of hidden populations. *Social Problems, 44*(2), 174–199. https://doi.org/10.2307/3096941

Internal Displacement Monitoring Centre. (2011, Sep 14). *Democratic Republic of Congo: IDPs need further assistance in context of continued attacks and insecurity.* Norwegian Refugee Council .

International Rescue Committee (IRC). (2007). *Mortality in the Democratic Republic of Congo: An ongoing crisis*. International Rescue Committee.

Gile, K. J., & Handcock, M. S. (2010). Respondent-driven sampling: An assessment of current methodology. *Sociological Methodology, 40*(1), 285–327. https://doi.org/10.1111/j.1467-9531.2010.01223.x

Legrand, F. D., & Crombez-Bequet, N. (2022). Physical exercise and self-esteem in women facing lockdown-related domestic violence. *Journal of Family Violence, 37*, 1005–1011. https://doi.org/10.1007/s10896-021-00308-y

Matheson, F. I., Daoud, N., Hamilton-Wright, S., Borenstein, H., Pedersen, C., & O'Campo, P. (2015). Where did she go? The transformation of self-esteem, self-identity, and mental well-being among women who have experienced intimate partner violence. *Women's Health Issues, 25*(5), 561–569. https://doi.org/10.1016/j.whi.2015.04.006

Mathew, N., Deborah, I., Karonga, T., & Rumbidzai, C. (2020). The impact of COVID-19 lockdown in a developing country: Narratives of self-employed women in Ndola, Zambia. *Health Care for Women International, 41*(11–12), 1370–1383. https://doi.org/10.1080/07399332.2020.1823983

Maslow, A. H. (1943). A theory of human motivation. *Psychological Review, 50*(4), 370–396. https://doi.org/10.1037/h0054346

Nyashanu, M., Ikhile, D., Karonga, T., & Chireshe, R. (2020). The impact of COVID-19 lockdown in a developing country: Narratives of self-employed women in Ndola, Zambia. *Health Care for Women International*. https://doi.org/10.1080/07399332.2020.1823983

Orth, U., & Robins, R. W. (2014). The development of self-esteem. *Current Directions in Psychological Science, 23*(5), 381–387. https://doi.org/10.1177/0963721414547414

Pellillo, A. (2012). Conflict and development: Evidence from the Democratic Republic of the Congo. *Unpublished manuscript*. Available at https://www.upces.cerge-ei.cz/pdf/events/papers/120402_t.pdf (accessed 2024, December 10).

Ramírez Vera, Y. E., Navarro Chaya, H. Y., & Ortiz Cáceres, D. C. (2022). Effects of COVID-19 on women's mental health: A systematic review. *Gaceta Médica De Caracas, 130*(3S). https://doi.org/10.47307/GMC.2022.130.s3.21

Rosenberg, M. (1965). *Society and the adolescent self-image*. Princeton University Press.

Rossi, A., Panzeri, A., Pietrabissa, G., Manzoni, G. M., Castelnuovo, G., & Mannarini, S. (2020). The anxiety-buffer hypothesis in the time of COVID-19: When self-esteem protects from the impact of loneliness and fear on anxiety and depression. *Frontiers in Psychology, 11*, 2177. https://doi.org/10.3389/fpsyg.2020.02177

Sabri, B., Hartley, M., Saha, J., Murray, S., Glass, N., & Campbell, J. C. (2020). Effect of COVID-19 pandemic on women's health and safety: A study of immigrant survivors of intimate partner violence. *Health Care for Women International, 41*(11–12), 1294–1312. https://doi.org/10.1080/07399332.2020.1833012

Sánchez, O. R., Vale, D. B., Rodrigues, L., & Surita, F. G. (2020). Violence against women during the COVID-19 pandemic: An integrative review. *International Journal of Gynecology & Obstetrics, 151*(2), 180–187. https://doi.org/10.1002/ijgo.13365

Sen, A. (1999). Development as freedom. New York: Alfred A. Knopf.

UN Women. (2022). *The impacts of COVID-19 on women and girls in East and Southern Africa.* https://africa.unwomen.org/sites/default/files/2022-04/ImpactsCovid19-Africa-Fin%20-%20REPORT.pdf

Vall-Roqué, H., Andrés, A., & Saldaña, C. (2021). The impact of COVID-19 lockdown on social network sites use, body image disturbances, and self-esteem among adolescent and young women. *Progress in Neuro-Psychopharmacology and Biological Psychiatry, 110*, 110293. https://doi.org/10.1016/j.pnpbp.2021.110293

Vlassenroot, K., & Raeymaekers, T. (2004). *Conflict and social transformation in Eastern DR Congo.* Academia Press.

Vogel, C. (2018). Between tags & guns: Fragmentations of public authority around eastern Congo's artisanal 3T mines. *Political Geography, 63*, 94–103.

Volz, E., & Heckathorn, D. D. (2008). Probability based estimation theory for respondent driven sampling. *Journal of Official Statistics, 24*(1), 79–97.

World Health Organization. (2007). *Ethical and safety recommendations for researching, documenting and monitoring sexual violence in emergencies.* https://apps.who.int/iris/handle/10665/43709

World Health Organization. (2020). COVID-19 disrupting mental health services in most countries, WHO survey. *World Health Organization.* https://www.who.int/news-room/detail/05-10-2020-covid-19-disrupting-mental-health-services-in-most-countries-who-survey (accessed 2024, December 15).

Christian Samen Otchia Associate Professor of Development Economics at the Graduate School of International Development, Nagoya University, Japan, where he teaches Development Microeconomics and Industrial Development. He is an affiliate member of the African Growth and Development Policy modeling consortium and has extensive experience in industrial policy design and implementation, collaborating with local governments and organizations like FAO and UNECA. His research focuses on the impact of special economic zones on local development through skills and technology transfer. Dr. Otchia holds a Ph.D. in International Development (Nagoya University) and has published in several academic journals.

Kazuyo Hanai Project Assistant Professor at the Institute for Future Initiatives, The University of Tokyo, Japan and Representative Director of NPO RITA-Congo. She holds a PhD in International Cooperation Studies from The University of Tokyo. She researches the role of resources in the conflicts in Africa and the responsibility of global society. In particular, her research focuses on the relations between the conflict minerals issue in the Democratic Republic of Congo and the responsibility of Japanese consumer society. Her main publication is *Justice of Resource Issue: Responsibility of Consumers on Conflict Minerals Issue in DR Congo* (Toshindo, 2016, in Japanese). She has served as president of JSAS since 2023 and the principal investigator for the JSAS Hitachi project.

Jean-Claude Maswana Professor at Graduate School of Economics, Ritsumeikan University, Japan. He is recognized for his influential research on economic growth theories, financial development, and international trade theories. He holds a PhD from Nagoya University and brings a wealth of international expertise to his roles as a former President of the African Finance and Economic Association (AFEA) and Allied Board Member of the Allied Social Sciences Association (ASSA) under the American Economic Association (AEA). Additionally, he chairs the Congo Economic Circle (CEC), has lectured at top-tier institutions, including Kyoto University, the University of Tokyo, and Tsukuba University, and has previously been a Macroeconomist Research Fellow with the Japan International Cooperation Agency (JICA).

Akemi Ishikawa Industrial Development Expert at the Division of Agri-business, UNIDO HQs in Vienna, Austria. She holds a PhD in Human Security Studies from the University of Tokyo. She is a development practitioner with over 21 years of experience in Programme/Project Management. She specializes in agricultural and rural development, livelihoods support, and Women's Economic Empowerment in Africa, Middle-East and Asia including fragility, conflict, and violence affected countries such as Afghanistan, DRC, South Sudan, and Yemen mainly targeting at refugees, IDPs and their host communities. She is passionate about serving the most vulnerable groups of the population and people in need.

Chapter 9
Conclusion

Kazuyo Hanai

In our three-year project, we collected grassroots voices in sub-Saharan Africa and explored how local people perceived and coped with the impact of COVID-19. In this project, we defined risk as the likelihood that something negative will happen to harm a valuable aspect of human life. We hypothesized that COVID-19 and government prevention policies would cause a risk trade-off that exacerbates other risks, which would act as a downside risk that exacerbates various risks in people's lives, including economic and social activities. We used a variety of formats for data collection, including web-based questionnaires, online and in-person interviews, and focus group discussions, to gather the voices of more than 2600 people living in seven African countries. In this chapter, we summarize the conclusions we have reached through this research.

1 Risk Perception Regarding COVID-19 and Its Function as a Downside Risk

Through our research, it became clear that COVID-19 was not necessarily perceived as a severe risk by African citizens. The general analysis of an online survey conducted in the seven countries (Chapter 2) revealed that people in the target areas perceived economic distress and governance issues as more severe risks than COVID-19 infection. As seen in the interviews in Zimbabwe, in rural areas where COVID-19 was not widespread, it was sometimes perceived that one would only be infected if one went to the cities. Moreover, even in countries with high rates of infection, such as South Africa, the perception of COVID-19 as a risk was low.

K. Hanai (✉)
Institute for Future Initiatives, The University of Tokyo, Bunkyo, Tokyo, Japan
e-mail: hanai@g.ecc.u-tokyo.ac.jp

K. Hanai et al. (eds.), *Practical Wisdom and Resilience Overcoming Downside Risk*,
https://doi.org/10.1007/978-981-96-4455-1_9

However, it would be inappropriate to infer from these findings that the impact of the COVID-19 pandemic was minimal. As the results in each country revealed, behavioral restrictions such as lockdowns and curfews exacerbated the economic distress that people were most concerned about. It is now clear that our assumption that COVID-19 functions as a downside risk that snowballs into other risks was correct. COVID-19 itself was not perceived as an outstandingly serious risk in African countries where other infectious diseases such as malaria, Ebola, and HIV/AIDS are frequent. Nevertheless, the field survey highlighted how infectious disease prevention measures, as well as the infectious disease itself, have led to a number of increased risks that threaten people's lives through economic distress, educational disruptions, and increased violence. As of 2024, mpox is endemic in some areas, including the Democratic Republic of the Congo (DRC), and because of this successive outbreak of infectious diseases throughout Africa, there may have been less awareness of COVID-19 than in developed countries, where it was a special concern. In streamlining the implementation of infectious disease control measures and the promotion of vaccination, it is necessary to consider policies based on people's perceptions.

2 Potential Politicization of COVID-19 Policies

This research also highlights the potential for politicization of COVID-19 prevention measures in African countries with political problems such as autocracy and electoral fraud. As illustrated in the chapters on Uganda and Kenya, in countries where elections were held during the pandemic, COVID-19 prevention measures were used to the advantage of the ruling party's electoral campaign. While there have been previous instances noted such as aid to victims of floods and earthquakes being used to garner votes for politicians in disaster areas, the COVID-19 prevention measures were used politically in a way that was even more likely to gain the support of the international community. The social consequences of this political use will continue even after the pandemic has subsided, and the centralization that has been reinforced through the use of pandemic prevention measures may affect the future of democracy in Africa. COVID-19 prevention measures could strengthen the authority of the government and pave the way for authoritarian politics. We discuss this issue below.

3 People's Evaluation of Their Governments' COVID-19 Policies

A third and unexpected finding of our study concerns people's evaluation of their governments' COVID-19 policies. Despite the severe impacts on livelihoods caused by policies such as lockdowns, curfews, and school closures, over time in all countries surveyed, people moved toward a tendency to evaluate government policies as appropriate. As the saying goes, "If the heat goes away, you will forget the heat": once a crisis is overcome, the memory of the difficulties of the time may fade. At the same time, however, the fact that the pandemic in African countries did not become as severe as initially feared likely contributed to the perception that the policies were effective.

We need to be careful about this assessment. In the spring of 2020, when the pandemic spread around the world, historian Yuval Noah Harari noted that the COVID-19 pandemic was bringing about a critical phase not only in the medical field, but also in the political one (Asahi Shimbun, April 15, 2020). In the long term, Harari notes, democracies are better able to deal with crises. This is because people who are informed and able to act spontaneously are better able to cope with crises than obedient people who act under police crackdowns, and because a free press and citizen pressure can correct a government's misguided policies when they have been implemented (ibid). Still, examples of enhanced government authority for rapid policy implementation could be seen in Europe as well. In Hungary, for example, a law giving the government the power to order extensive emergency measures during the COVID-19 pandemic was applied from March to June 2020. In our research in Uganda, we found that years of concentration of political power prevented local governments from implementing effective COVID-19 prevention measures, making them a target of public complaints. Continued attention will be required to ensure that each of these actions does not lead to the strengthening of the central government's authority, favoritism by the ruling party, or restrictions on people's rights through authoritarian politics.

4 Basis for Coping Strategies to Overcome Crisis

This study also highlights the importance of people's networks and informal businesses as the basis for coping strategies to overcome livelihood crises associated with pandemics. The importance of networks of relatives and friends as a safety net in African countries where public services are inaccessible has been noted in many regions, but stay-home policies and behavioral restrictions have constrained contact between these persons. Not being able to see relatives and friends affects people's mental health, as evidenced in the voices of those featured in this book. Despite these constraints, people's networks played an important role in overcoming hardships, as exemplified by the black tax and white guilt noted in the South African case in Chapter 3. While previous studies have portrayed black tax and white guilt negatively, this research is unique in that it is portrayed as the basis for collective resilience that supports others. As noted in the Kenya chapter (Chapter 6), there were also examples of people who were able to overcome difficulties through ingenuity in the field of informal business. These are the roots of the resilience of people who overcome hardships. This is why promoting informal businesses and helping people strengthen their connections during peacetime can improve their capacity to recover from a pandemic.

Overall, although COVID-19 functioned as a downside risk in Africa and COVID-19 prevention measures resulted in trade-offs that increased other risks, people were able to overcome their hardships through their coping strategies, which were based on networks and informal business. On the other hand, the political impact of the COVID-19 prevention measures must continue to be closely monitored. While the resilience of the people is observed, there are also signs of the politicization of COVID-19 policies by the government, and the strengthening of authoritarianism, which threatens democracy.

5 Implications and Contributions from Our Research

At the time of writing in 2024, the international community has begun negotiations to create a Pandemic Treaty and is in the process of drawing lessons from COVID-19 in preparation for the next pandemic. It is worth recalling the Siracusa Principles (formally known as "The Siracusa Principles on the Limitation and Derogation Provisions in the International Covenant on Civil and Political Rights"). As the name implies, the Siracusa Principles set forth the conditions that may justify derogations from the obligations set forth in the International Covenant on Civil and Political Rights, and limitations on human rights. After being adopted by the United Nations in 1985, the WHO adopted these principles in 2007, stating that limitations on civil and political rights can be justified if they serve a public purpose, such as the prevention of infectious diseases. The main points are summarized in the following five criteria (WHO 2012).

- The restriction is provided for and carried out in accordance with the law;
- The restriction is in the interest of a legitimate objective of general interest;
- The restriction is strictly necessary in a democratic society to achieve the objective;
- There are no less intrusive and restrictive means available to achieve the same objective;
- The restriction is based on scientific evidence and not drafted or imposed arbitrarily, i.e., in an unreasonable or otherwise discriminatory manner.

Were the COVID-19 prevention policies in line with these principles? Was it appropriate to close borders without complementary measures to ensure the livelihoods of local populations, were there less intrusive and less restrictive measures, and were the policies based on scientific evidence? In light of these criteria, it is necessary to examine whether the policies of African governments were appropriate. Donors are expected to play a certain role in such evaluations, because if humanitarian assistance ends up strengthening authoritarian regimes (even if implicitly), it will not be supported by the taxpaying public. Ultimately, while policy improvements are important, measures to address complex crises such as pandemics are also elaborated by people themselves, based on their initiatives, and implemented from the bottom up regardless of what the government does. The significance of African citizens learning from the experiences of those in other African countries cannot be overemphasized. In this sense, this research, which was conducted by teams of African and Japanese researchers based on the principle of African ownership, will serve as a model for future research.

We are proud that this research has succeeded in capturing some of the effects that the COVID-19 pandemic and government measures in Africa have had on people and their reactions to the crises. We would like to emphasize the academic and practical importance of our work, which involved three years of field research to understand people's perceptions and behaviors at the grassroots level. It is our sincere hope that the results of this research will be useful for future countermeasures in the event of a pandemic or other situation that threatens human security.

References

Asahi Shimbun. (2020, April 15). *This is the political crossroads: The COVID-19, Yuval Noah Harari, professor and historian at Hebrew University.*

World Health Organization (WHO). (2012). *WHO Guidance on human rights and involuntary detention for xdr-tb control.* https://www.who.int/news/item/11-12-2012-who-guidance-on-human-rights-and-involuntary-detention-for-xdr-tb-control

Kazuyo Hanai Project Assistant Professor at the Institute for Future Initiatives, The University of Tokyo, Japan and Representative Director of NPO RITA-Congo. She holds a PhD in International Cooperation Studies from The University of Tokyo. She researches the role of resources in the conflicts in Africa and the responsibility of global society. In particular, her research focuses on the relations between the conflict minerals issue in the Democratic Republic of Congo and the responsibility of Japanese consumer society. Her main publication is *Justice of Resource Issue: Responsibility of Consumers on Conflict Minerals Issue in DR Congo* (Toshindo, 2016, in Japanese). She has served as president of JSAS since 2023 and the principal investigator for the JSAS Hitachi project.

The manufacturer's authorised representative in the EU is Springer Nature Customer Service Centre GmbH, Europaplatz 3, 69115 Heidelberg, Germany. If you have any concerns regarding our products, please contact ProductSafety@springernature.com

Printed and bound by CPI Group (UK) Ltd, Croydon, CR0 4YY
01/10/2026
02225930-0020